Books by Ian St. James

THE BALFOUR CONSPIRACY   1981
THE MONEY STONES   1980

The Balfour Conspiracy

The Balfour Conspiracy

IAN ST. JAMES

Atheneum   New York   1981

LIBRARY OF CONGRESS CATALOGING IN PUBLICATION DATA

St. James, Ian.
  The Balfour conspiracy.

  I. Title.
PR6069.A423B3   1981   823'.914   80-69378
ISBN 0-689-11140-1   AACR2

For Patsy and my family –
for their never-failing help and patience

"There is a danger that, to some degree, fissile products may fall into the hands of the irresponsible and even criminal groups. The need for national and international actions to safeguard against this must be emphasized."

The Pugwash Conference on
World Affairs meeting at Oxford

"Experience suggests that the first rule of politics is never to say never. The ingenious human capacity for manoeuvre and compromise may make acceptable tomorrow what seems outrageous or impossible today."

William V. Shannon,
'Vietnam: America's Dreyfus Case'.
The New York Times March 3rd, 1968

Prologue

Most of it was pieced together afterwards. Those who died carried most of their secrets to the grave. But enough had been gleaned along the way to make the file look respectable. Reputations were retained intact, at least those of the living, and nobody cared about the dead. It was Ross who labelled the file *The Balfour Conspiracy*. Naturally Twomey objected. He pointed out that Balfour was long since dead, and anyway Balfour could hardly be blamed for what happened years later. But Ross argued otherwise. He even quoted the Balfour Declaration: "His Majesty's Government view with favour the establishment in Palestine of a national home for the Jews." That had nothing to do with it according to Twomey, but Ross disagreed. Without Balfour, he claimed, there would not have been a Suzy Katoul. And without Suzy, who knows what would have happened? Twomey pulled rank in the end and had the file re-christened with the usual numerals, followed by the security code, so that it became simply *857509-AQT*. But Ross's name stuck and thereafter everyone referred to it as *The Balfour Conspiracy*. Which pleased Ross no end because it gave the impression that the whole thing was a British cock-up and that the Americans were in no way involved. But that was Ross all over. He was as American as apple pie. Just as Twomey was old tweeds English and Orlov as Russian as the Bolshoi. It was the others who were hard to place.

The Balfour Conspiracy

"Patriotism is a kind of religion;
it is the egg from which wars are hatched."
Guy De Maupassant,
My Uncle Sosthenes

"We're making enquiries about Suzy Katoul," the English police-man said.

Even without the quick glimpse of his warrant card, I would have known he was Special Branch. His eyes had already quartered the room, catalogued its contents, priced the chesterfields and the silver cigarette box next to the Zola first editions. Probably he overvalued the ormolu clock on the mantelpiece and underpriced the Kashan rug he was standing on – but even the insurance boys did that.

"Has anything happened to Suzy?" I asked, anxious but not yet alarmed. Officials had made enquiries about Suzy before.

No doubt because their lives are spent asking questions, senior policemen lose the habit of answering them. It must be true because he said: "When did you last see her?"

"Three or four months ago."

"Here?" he gestured at the room.

I shook my head. "No. At her apartment in Paris."

"That would be the one at 14 Avenue de Friedland, near the Étoile?" He said it without even looking at his notebook. His accent wasn't bad either.

"Very good," I said.

"And since then? Have you heard from her? A letter? A phone call perhaps?"

"No." For Suzy and I to go months without communicating wasn't unusual – especially after our last meeting. Anyway, I had only just returned from Brussels. Not that I volunteered the infor-mation. If they didn't know that already, they would get around to asking within the next few minutes.

Special Branch didn't wait that long. "You've been away recently, I believe?"

"Do you?" I served his question back at him, which upset him enough to flush his face pink.

"Don't waste time, Mr Brand. This is desperately urgent and I'd appreciate your co-operation."

"And I'd appreciate yours," I said flatly. "Has anything happened to Suzy?"

That really nettled him and it sounded in his voice. "Most people work with us quite readily – but perhaps you don't like policemen?"

"Not political ones. Or those who won't answer a simple question."

The American interrupted. "Will you buy *don't know* for an answer?"

"Don't know?" I echoed, looking at him. He was short and squat, barrel-chested and powerfully built, like a fair-haired gorilla in a well-cut suit. Earlier the English policeman had introduced him as Major Ross, an American colleague. "But you *think* something's happened to her?"

He shrugged, watching me closely. "She's missing."

"And she's not in Paris," LeClerc ventured. "We *do* know that."

"So you all turn up here?" I stared at them. "An Inspector from Special Branch, another from the Sûreté Nationale, and –" I paused for another look at the American. "And *Major* Ross."

Ross smiled. "Well, you do have a rather special relationship with the lady."

"It's of a non-political nature," I pointed out.

"She hasn't got a *non-political* nature," he said emphatically.

I was more than half inclined to agree with that, so I said nothing and waited. The ormolu clock showed 6.15 pm and I was ready for a drink, but choosy with whom I shared my Chivas Regal. Deep down I wished they would go away and spoil someone else's evening.

"Of course you know she's been involved with the Palestinian Liberation Movement for years," Ross said.

"Everyone knows that."

He smiled bleakly. "Until some months ago, when she joined an even more fanatical bunch of terrorists."

"One man's terrorist is another man's freedom fighter," I pointed out.

"You're defending them?"

"Not exactly. But I've been reporting the world's wars and its politics for thirty years now. It's a dirty game – whoever plays it."

2

He disagreed. "International politics are quite different from individual acts of terrorism."

"I doubt the poor bastards fried by napalm in Nam would agree with you."

His look sharpened. "You're anti-American?"

"Some of my best friends are Americans."

We were getting on like a house on fire until Special Branch ruined it. "We really were hoping for a better reception," he complained. "In fact we are relying on your help." Which sounded almost plaintive until he added, "One way or the other." And that sounded ominous.

"We need to find Suzy Katoul," Ross said.

"And quickly," LeClerc chimed in.

"I'm sorry, but I can't help you," I answered truthfully. "I've no idea where she is."

"You're going to help," Ross said grimly. "And *we're* going to find her. There's just a chance she'll listen to you – if we reach her in time."

Something in his voice held my attention long enough for me to notice things missed earlier. Like fatigue, which showed as dark smudges beneath his eyes, and anxiety, which turned his voice to a dry croak at times. Major Ross didn't strike me as the kind who frightens easily, but at that moment I guessed him to be as nervous as a kitten. And when I looked at them as people, instead of depressing symbols of state authority, Special Branch and LeClerc seemed drained and edgy as well.

"Hadn't you better tell me what this is all about?" I asked quietly. The Chivas Regal beckoned like an old friend and I joined it at the sideboard.

Special Branch opened his briefcase. "You'll have to sign the Official Secrets Act first. I take it you've not signed it before."

"Bloody right I haven't! I write the news – *you* suppress it."

"Well, you'll have to make an exception this time, won't you?" he said spitefully, the inevitable buff folder already half open on his knees.

"Wrong! This time *you'll* have to make an exception." I glared at him, the whisky bottle in my hand still poised over the open mouth of the glass. "I'm not signing anything until I know what this is all about. Not even then, if I forfeit my rights."

The long silence was eventually broken by the sound of whisky splashing into the glass. Glancing up I caught their hungry eyes on the bottle and reluctantly I poured three more. "Weren't you warned about drinking on duty?" I asked Ross, as I handed him a glass.

"No," he shook his head. "Only about falling over."

"The Official Secrets Act," Special Branch reminded.

"Could be written in Hebrew for all I care."

"Why Hebrew?" Ross queried. "You anti-semitic too?"

It was all a bit much when the three of them were sitting there drinking my twelve-year-old Scotch. I didn't even bother to answer.

Ross rubbed the side of his jaw and looked speculatively at Special Branch. "You know, I wonder if your Official Secrets Act applies? After all, it's not necessarily a matter of British security."

My ears pricked up. Help from an unexpected quarter? I wondered if they would go away to debate the issue, fail to agree and never return.

"We're going to have to tell him," Ross pointed out. "Whether he signs or not." Which stumped them all for a moment, until Ross turned traitor and had a brain-wave. "How many times a year do you visit the States?" he asked.

I shrugged. "It varies. Six or seven I suppose. Sometimes more."

"And if you were unable to go? Would it impair your livelihood?"

I write about politics for the British Press and syndicate a column through Europe. Mobility of movement is essential. And Ross knew it. In a voice sweeter than syrup he asked, "Ever had any trouble getting an entry visa?"

I shook my head.

"You will," he smiled. "I guarantee it. Unless you co-operate."

LeClerc cleared his throat. "And I speak for the Minister of the Interior. You could have a lot of problems at the Rue des Saussaies. Access to France could become impossible for you."

Special Branch smirked and sipped my whisky. "You could even have trouble renewing your British passport."

"It's just been renewed."

"Really?" he seemed genuinely interested. "Genuine or forged?"

"Are you kidding?"

He sighed and scratched the side of his nose. "Forgeries are getting so good these days, it's sometimes impossible to tell them from the real thing. I know a chap who had his declared false and was unable to leave the country for eight months." He tut-tutted to show how concerned he was. "Turned out to be genuine in the end, but you'll never believe the trouble he had."

I groaned. "You three prove my point about politics. It's a game for dirty players. You're all eminently qualified."

4

Ross accepted it as a compliment and smiled like a benign uncle. "We're just working for the tax-payers." He hitched his belt in a notch, as if to show he wasn't getting fat on it. "Let's kick a few ideas around. I'm sure we'll sink our differences," his smile broadened. "Isn't that what you British do? *Sink* your differences?"

I sank half my whisky instead and carried the rest back to my chair. Special Branch fumbled with his papers, until an encouraging nod from the American loosened his tongue. "We're concerned about an incident which happened yesterday," he said. "In the afternoon. A half-sized container was loaded aboard a freighter at Felixstowe, nothing special about it, just one amongst fifty or sixty the vessel was carrying. The ship, the *Marisa*, put to sea at just after seven on a routine, once-a-month scheduled trip to Marseilles. About seven hours later they were fifty miles or so south of the Scilly Isles when they sighted a distress flare. A minute later another flare pinpointed a yellow life-raft with four people in it – a girl and three men. The freighter picked them up and the girl went up to the bridge to say thank you to the Captain. Meanwhile one of the men, speaking mostly French but with a smattering of English, asked to be taken to the radio cabin to send an urgent message. Then all hell broke loose. All four of the castaways produced pistols, Mausers probably from what we can make out, and they wrecked the radio equipment. The girl on the bridge warned the Captain to stand by to receive a boarding party and a minute later a launch loomed out of the darkness, possibly an ex-M.T.B. or something of the sort, big Merlin engines, easily capable of outrunning the freighter."

He paused to sip his whisky and accept a cigarette from an open packet held out to him by LeClerc. When he finished blowing smoke rings, he continued. "One of the officers fancied himself a hero or something, because he tried to grab the gun from the girl. There was a scuffle and the officer was shot." He shook his head. "We're not even sure if he was killed by the girl or one of her boyfriends. Anyway, while all that was going on, half a dozen men boarded the freighter, opened the hatches and lifted *our* container out with a winch and lifting tackle transferred from the launch. The whole thing was over inside half an hour. The castaways and the rest of them got back to their patrol boat and vanished into the night – taking our container with them. And with its radio and flares and other equipment smashed up, all the freighter could do was to divert course and steam full speed to Cherbourg – where they reported the incident."

"Some incident," I said, thinking that the whole story had been hushed up. Not a word of it had reached the wire services.

LeClerc took over. "The local police contacted my department and I reached Cherbourg three hours later." He scratched a balding spot on the crown of his head, the gesture a man might make when he's puzzled. "Identification's always difficult. In this case the boarding party was all hooded anyway, so the only possible descriptions were of the four castaways. And most attention focused on the girl – because she was the leader." He gave Ross a wry grin of apology. "If nothing else, all witnesses are agreed on that."

Ross stared at me. "And we're quite sure who the girl was."

My stomach muscles knotted in panic. Silly really, because once I knew that a girl was involved I guessed where they were leading.

"She was your goddaughter," Ross said, "Suzy Katoul."

Despite the whisky, my mouth went dry. I sensed a nightmare about to come true. Confused, and more in an effort to make sense of the story than anything else, I asked: "And what was in the container?"

"In non-scientific language?" Ross was reaching for another cigarette. "Plutonium, Mr Brand – enough plutonium to make an atomic bomb five times bigger than the one dropped on Hiroshima."

There was no moon and the light from the stars was diffused and patchy through the overcast. Low clouds scudded across the night sky, driven by a bitter north-westerly which snagged the waves in passing and laced black water with an edge of white foam. Not that it was a rough sea. Once he had crossed this ocean in a force ten gale. He had worried himself sick about that. Bad weather would make their task impossible. Months of work would be wasted. A chance of a lifetime missed when time was against them in any case. But tonight the forecasts were right for once, the sea *was* relatively calm and conditions could hardly be better.

Next to him one of the Irishmen lit a cigarette and the acrid smell of cheap tobacco soured the air-conditioned atmosphere of the bridge so that one of the officers stiffened, twitching his nostrils with disapproval as he stood poised over the radar scanner. But nobody said a word.

The huge tanker barely moved through the water, its speed reduced to less than five knots. They were as good as in position now. He glanced at his watch. Four minutes past three. It should be all over. Suzy should be on her way. He stared out through the glass, his gaze drawn south where ten miles away lay some of the busiest shipping lanes in British waters. Not long now. He steeled himself to wait out the last few minutes, his face impassive beneath his *kaffiyeh*. Alongside him the four dark-haired crew members were clad in navy-blue uniforms and the two Irishmen wore heavy-knit pullovers above rough trousers pushed into sea boots. But he had chosen to wear the traditional dress of the Palestinian, a *kaffiyeh* head-dress above a long black-striped *djellaba*, stretching down to goat-skin sandals. Later, if all went well, he would change into the Western work clothes of an Irish fisherman, but it was important to greet Suzy as he was now – the *symbolism* was important – for her, for him, and above all for the success of the mission. He grunted. Symbolism – wasn't that what they taught at the Psychological Studies Centre? Brainwash your subject well enough and after that control was easy. Just say the right words, paint the right pictures and the response was guaranteed – just like Pavlov's dogs.

A sudden burst of chatter drew him back from the darkness and two quick steps took him to the radar scanner, source of the excitement. His knuckles whitened on the brass rail surrounding the instrument panel as his gaze fastened on the fast-moving blip dancing across the green background. Only the *one* tiny blip raced in their direction. Nothing followed, nothing gave chase. The larger, more shadowy dots at the edge of the screen adhered to routes miles apart, oblivious of what had happened. He sighed with relief and returned to the window, to where the others peered into the night, watching and waiting for the boat from the south.

In flagrant breach of maritime regulations, the tanker lay in almost total darkness. No red and green navigation lights, no white spot atop the mast-head, even on the bridge the lighting was dimmed and muted. An entry in the ship's log falsely described how a massive electrical failure had caused almost complete loss of light and rendered the ship's radio inoperable. As a result, the Captain had steamed north to a position well clear of normal shipping lanes until the fault could be traced and repaired. Utter nonsense of course, but it would serve if there was an enquiry later. With luck that would be avoided. With luck an hour should see everything completed and an hour after that the tanker would be back on her registered route, lights and radio fully "operational" again, with only that one small entry in her log to mar an otherwise uneventful voyage.

It was comfortably warm on the bridge, but on the ship's rails thirty feet below it would be cold. Bitterly cold, with an air tempera-

7

ture of two centigrade and the sea near freezing. The hoar of frost would have made the decks slippery and any seaman whose bare flesh brushed freezing metal risked the agony of frostbite. Biting cold and noisy too, as the wind moaned and the waves crashed against the giant steel hull, and the spray hissed and spat up at the watchers in the night.

He craned his neck, trying to see the decks below, but the black of the night defeated him. A pace away the Captain's murmured order was relayed by the First Officer and relayed again, until a muffled bell sounded in the far distance. Action stations! He tensed, feeling the vast ship pitch and knowing that all over the giant hull men were scuttling into position. How many times had they practised this manoeuvre? Two dozen, three perhaps? All those rehearsals for just one performance – a performance he hoped played without an audience, an act done once and never repeated.

He looked at his watch. 3.22 am. Rendezvous time and still no sign of them – but on the screen the blip raced onwards and was closing fast.

"There!" One of the Irishmen pointed to a spot on the starboard bow. A thin pencil of light split the darkness, prodding forward like an accusing finger. On, then off – on and off again. He stiffened in alarm. They were *off* course! Suzy was off course. Or else the tanker was? He swung round to the Captain, accusations already forming on his lips. But his panic was unnecessary, long hours of training were paying dividends. Twelve feet below the bridge, a signaller was already clattering out the call sign on an Aldis. The arc lamp bathed the forward structure of the ship in brilliant light interspersed with split seconds of darkness, like a scene in a film shown on a faulty projector; a moment later came the answering shaft of light, already turning, shifting course, homing in on the tanker like a racing pigeon to its loft.

As if in welcome, a sudden pool of light danced on the waves to the tanker's starboard side. The docking lamps swung into position – six telescopic poles suspended beneath a canvas canopy to hide the light from any searching aeroplane. Even from his eyrie on the bridge, he saw only a thin strip of black water as light spilled from beneath the cover of the awning. But it was enough to register the scene, a section at a time. First the prow of the motor launch, then a seaman with a line in his hands, his legs bowed to steady himself as the boat manoeuvred alongside; next midships and more seamen, some still wearing hoods, their eye-slits clearly visible as they looked up to the tanker's deck. Then the girl Suzy, standing with

8

one hand on the wheel, leaning forward to issue an order, absorbed in the detail of command. The watching man caught his breath as he waited for the open hatch to appear. For an agonising second he contemplated failure. All this effort, the grinding practice sessions, the endless planning. To fail now – for the raiding party to return empty-handed? But then, with relief mingled with rising excitement, he saw it. The twelve-foot cube of the rust-red container which meant the raid had succeeded. Sight of it was the only signal needed for the men on the bridge. Muted bells rang, buzzers rasped and all over the ship men sprang forward to perform tasks perfected by months of hard training.

Fresh light appeared – a ghostly green incandescence which lit the tanker's forward decks in a way subtle enough to be almost invisible from the skies above – especially when, as now, black cloud and night mist rolled low over the ocean's surface.

"Mary, Mother of Christ! Will you look at that?" the Irishman hissed.

But the man in Arab costume was already watching the long black crack appear down the centre of the huge forward deck. A split ninety feet long, widening slowly to a gap half as big – a great, yawning crater opening to the very bowels of the leviathan. Now he could hear the hum of machinery and he began to count the seconds, knowing that sixty-eight should pass before the whine of the hydraulics swamped everything. He pictured the frenzied scene below decks as the crew cleared the restraining tackle needed during the voyage. Still counting, he turned to starboard and peered down to the deck below, dimly visible now in the light cast by the docking lamps. The crew from the launch had disembarked, half a dozen of them sheltered from the wind at the top of the gangway, talking and smoking and beating gloved hands together to keep warm. He watched the girl clamber up to the deck. She paused to share a brief word with the crew before glancing up at the bridge, then waved and hurried away. His count reached forty-two. The First Officer was telephoning again, this time with orders for the scuttling party, so that a moment later six men walked briskly across the deck and disappeared from view down the gangway onto the launch. For them too, time was precious.

The unmistakable whine of the hydraulics interrupted his count at sixty. Either he had been a fraction slow or the crew below decks had set another record? He checked his watch and smiled, sharing their triumph at producing something special on the big night. Ahead – from the gaping hole in the forward deck, the long white tip

9

of a spar emerged. It rose slowly, purposefully, at the precisely controlled speed of a foot for every fifteen seconds. His gaze travelled forward to the prow to estimate the rise and fall of the ship as she stood into the sea. Four feet, five maybe? He prayed it would stay that way – at least for the next thirty minutes. Beneath him the spar was well clear, below that he distinguished the shape of the deckhouse and behind that the raised storage hatch, with the wooden crates of fish roped securely into position.

Suddenly he was distracted by a noise and a gust of wind as the door to the bridge slid back on its runners. He swung round and every man on the bridge turned with him. For a moment Suzy just stood there, in a pool of light inside the door, her raven hair glossy and damp from the spray and her dark eyes widening as she took in the details of his costume. Then she was in his arms, his fingers stroking her hair, his strength already steadying her.

"Oh Abou, we did it!" she pulled away, her eyes shining with excitement. "We did it – we did it!"

He exulted at her dependence on him. It had taken time; time, cunning and money, but now she was his, programmed on drugs and sex, and kindness and cruelty. Withhold one, substitute another, subject her will to his until she was no more than a puppet.

He was about to answer her when the whole ship shuddered with enough force to throw them off balance. Collecting themselves, they looked down to the floodlit forward decks. The hydraulic lifts had reached their full upward thrust and the huge locking mechanism had clamped into place. Now, sitting in a cradle high above the steel decks, higher even than the guard rails, was a seiner, an Irish fishing boat. Eighty feet long and thirty-eight feet wide at midships, with a sixteen-foot beam and measuring sixty-eight feet from the tip of her mast to the edge of her keel, the seiner *Aileen Maloney* was almost ready to begin her historic voyage.

"Was ever a sight more beautiful?" asked the Irishman of nobody in particular.

Abou cast a critical look over the restraining cables, examining the chocks and the steel hawsers which held the fishing boat in position. If anything worked loose, if the launching party had been careless, if just one of the safety checks had been overlooked, danger lurked for all of them. Especially for the two seamen who hurried around the apron of the tanker's decks and began the ascent of the rope ladder which swung from the seiner's bows. Abou checked his watch. Sixteen minutes since the floodlighting had been switched on. They were forty-two seconds ahead of schedule. But still to come was the perilous task of launching the *Aileen Maloney*. Meanwhile they were at their most vulnerable – exposed to a search-plane dipping from the cloud, or a patrol vessel slipping through the mist to find them.

The shortwave radio crackled as the seaman now in the deck-house of the seiner commenced the countdown. Below decks huge valves opened and the high-speed pumps began transferring two thousand gallons of crude oil from portside tanks to those on the starboard. A minute passed. Rapid-fire dialogue continued between the First Officer and the *Aileen Maloney* as the countdown progressed. *Five* minutes passed. The Second Officer nursed the radar and the Captain drummed nervous fingers on the chart table. The tanker began her controlled list to starboard as the shifting crude changed the centre of gravity. A bell sounded and the crew member to the Captain's right answered a telephone. The scuttling party had finished and were rejoining the tanker. Abou glanced down to the starboard rails, the angle already different from when last he looked. Now he was twelve feet nearer the waves and the launch alongside was fully visible as the telescopic arms of the canopy withdrew into the tanker's superstructure. For a moment nothing happened to the small boat. It rose and fell rhythmically in a parody of the huge ship. Then, quite suddenly, its bows rose sharply and the stern settled more deeply in the water. It stayed that way – suspended, undecided – until those watching began to suspect a miscalculation by the scuttling party – but then it happened – the bows rose clear of the water, the stern fell and the waves broke over the cargo hatch to lash angrily at the precious red container. Quickly the water level rose to the tiny deckhouse and as relentlessly as an auctioneer's hammer, she was going. Going, going, gone! The black waves closed over her and the boat was no more – as if she had never been.

Suzy stirred at his side. "It seems such a waste. The risks we took, and now – just to dump it –"

"It's the safest way," he said gruffly, discouraging discussion. "This way we're certain –"

"A man was *killed* tonight for that cargo."

"Killed?" he stiffened. "You didn't tell me."

"Oh, don't worry," she sounded almost bitter. "Not one of ours. One of the *Marisa's* officers tried to jump me – Kalif shot him – through the head from five feet away." She shuddered at the memory and his arm tightened about her shoulders. Killing would not have bothered him. He had seen enough, done enough, to be immune to the sight of death. Anyway, the stakes were too high to

11

be concerned about the death of one man. But her reaction had to be dealt with.

"Kalif did right," he smoothed her hair. "You could have been hurt – injured perhaps –" he stopped abruptly, knowing it was the wrong thing to say, cursing an uncharacteristic clumsiness. Everyone in the raiding party had known the rules, but knowing never made them easier to talk about, not even afterwards. Knowing that if Suzy had been in danger of capture, the others would have killed her. Just as she would have killed any other member of the crew, rather than lose them as prisoners.

The growl of the buzzer distracted him. The countdown had finished and the *Aileen Maloney* was as ready as she ever would be. She swung in her cradle, buffeted by a strengthening wind which added strain to the hawsers holding her, while below her the tanker increased its list to starboard. Nineteen degrees, twenty, so that standing upright was impossible without holding a rail or leaning against the side of the bridge. The Captain snapped an order and the First Officer punched a button. More hydraulics whined as the specially designed stabilizer slid slowly down from the tanker's port-side hull and into the ocean. From habit, Abou began to count, knowing that twenty seconds would pass before the steel fin, acting as a second keel but sinking twelve fathoms deeper than the main one, reached its full extent. He glanced at the gauge in front of him. Fifteen thousand gallons had been transferred to the starboard tanks. Five thousand to go. The deck tilted another degree and the wind freshened to pitch the tanker an extra foot into the swelling sea.

At last they were ready. The buzzer rasped the final alert. The tanker rode the sea with a twenty-two degree list to starboard and the *Aileen Maloney* swung out from above the steel decks to hover thirty feet above the white-capped waves. Inch by inch the hawsers unwound. More than at any other moment the sheer seamanship of the Captain would be tested to its limits. In theory, the *Aileen Maloney* should be set down ten yards clear of the tanker's starboard rails. In theory. But all the theories in the world never accounted for the unpredictability of the elements. A rising, gusting wind, an exceptional wave, a combination of both and the *Aileen Maloney* with her murderous cargo would be smashed against the giant slab side of the tanker.

Seamen lined the starboard rails, placing fenders into position at one yard intervals, while casting nervous glances upwards as the

12

Aileen Maloney hovered above them. On the bridge anxious eyes measured the pitch of the sea, knowing it ever important as the Captain struggled to manoeuvre the fishing boat down on an even keel. Twenty-six minutes had passed since the phosphorous lamps had first cast their glow over the forward decks. The *Aileen Maloney* swooped nearer to the ocean. Twenty-seven. Now she was level with the starboard rails and the crew clustered there could see their two compatriots on the deck of the smaller vessel. Twenty-nine minutes. The drop to the boiling sea had shrunk to less than twelve feet. The worst was over.

Then, as tensions eased, the hawser snapped. It was one of eight running to the bows of the *Aileen Maloney* from the cradle above. Nobody ever knew why it snapped. It was doubtful that the seaman forward on the fishing boat even knew what hit him. But tightly-bound strands of steel weighing twelve pounds to the foot cut the air like a stock whip. Just the end of the hawser reached him, the very tip. Had he been a foot nearer the deckhouse it would have missed him completely, as it was it caught him just below the chin, snapping his neck like a broken match and tossing his body the length of the boat.

The Captain slammed a lever and the *Aileen Maloney* dropped like a stone. With one hawser gone, the others would fracture like rotten gut. A plume of water rose thirty feet high, drenching the men on the rails like an exploding shell and signalling action everywhere. The First Officer threw the high-speed pumps into reverse. A seaman punched buttons to withdraw the stabilizer. Below, on the rails, men threw themselves down ropes to the fishing boat to release the hawsers. The pulleys atop the cradle began to rewind at full speed. The hydraulics screamed as the cradle itself began its descent to the bowels of the ship and thirty seconds later it had disappeared from view. The huge ship began to correct its list and the steel forward decks started to close. Five seconds, ten, fifteen. The green light faded as the phosphorous lamps were extinguished. Decks met with a thump like a guillotine chopping bone, and once again the tanker lay in almost total darkness. It had taken exactly thirty-one minutes and five seconds to launch the *Aileen Maloney*.

The First Officer hurled questions into the radio, interrupted by Abou's shout of, "What about the cargo?"

An agonising silence which seemed to last for ever. Then the radio crackled: "Undamaged. Not moved an inch. The restraining ties held good and even the crates of fish are intact."

"And the boat?" queried the Irishman.

"Nothing really – superficial damage to the deckhouse, but very slight."

The Captain turned from the instrument panel, his face lined with fatigue, skin pinched tight around his eyes. "And the crew?" he asked.

The radio barely hesitated: "One dead. One with a fractured arm."

The Captain nodded. He had seen the blow delivered by the hawser. It had *looked* like a death blow. As it was, only one death was a miracle. He glanced at the man known as Abou, choosing his words carefully. "Perhaps it is appropriate to baptise that boat with the blood of a countryman. Anything less would have seemed trivial."

Even so, both men knew that the death would be read as a sign of bad luck. Bad luck for the *Aileen Maloney* and all who sailed in her. Seamen universally are superstitious. But Abou was grateful for the remark. It might help steady Suzy and the two Irishmen, and the seven commandos who would sail with them. Anyway, what was one life against the future of fifteen million? He held out his hand. "Our country's thanks Captain, for getting us this far. Now it's up to us."

The radio interrupted with its last message of the night. "Ready for you to embark on the *Aileen Maloney*."

Abou shook hands with the other officers and turned for the door. "Good luck," called the Captain. Abou paused and looked down at his *djellaba*, trying to think of a suitable reply. Finally he smiled wryly, "May Allah go with you, too." One of the Irishmen grinned hugely as he followed the girl and the others out into the black of the night. "Up the Republic," he whispered, and softly slid the bridge door back on its runners.

"Whose bright idea was that?" I asked. "Transporting plutonium on a scheduled shipping route. It's madness. An invitation to –"

"A hell of a lot of material gets moved around that way," Ross interrupted. "You'd be surprised. Every government does it. It's the easiest way of avoiding publicity."

"Until something goes wrong!" I snapped.

We had been arguing for over an hour. The English policeman had long since gone, Ross as good as dismissing him once the introductions had been completed. I wondered just who the hell

Ross was? And what authority was vested in him that he could handle an Inspector from Special Branch quite so casually.

LeClerc remained. He had one of those sharp-nosed Gallic faces with quick brown eyes, altogether a bit like a fox, mobile, alert and watchful. By comparison Ross seemed almost sluggish. "There's hardly any danger to the public," he was saying comfortably. "And it's nearly impossible to convert fuel for atom plants to nuclear weapons."

"That's *nearly* comforting."

He ignored me. "Katoul and her crowd face the real peril. There's a fifty per cent death risk just in opening that container."

"And a thirty per cent death risk in bomb manufacture," LeClerc chimed in.

"Ten little Indians," I said. "At the end of the day one terrorist might be left clutching an atom bomb. That's what really frightens you."

"Doesn't it frighten you?" Ross countered quickly.

Even then I wasn't absolutely sure that I believed what I was hearing. "Are you telling me it's *possible*?"

For answer LeClerc asked, "Do you know how an atom bomb works, Mr Brand?"

I shook my head. Third form physics had floored me and, God knows, that was a long time ago.

"In its crudest form it's simply a matter of bringing two chunks of plutonium together with sufficient force to make it go critical," he said. "Once the mathematics have been worked out the rest is easy. It could even be done with an alarm clock mechanism and a chemical explosive primary charge."

I stared, prepared to have misunderstood. "So any trained terrorist could do it?"

Ross fidgeted, clearing his throat to interrupt. He wore a glove on his left hand like a golfer. Except that his was made of shiny black kid and was long enough to disappear up the sleeve of his jacket. And now that I looked at it, the fingers were shaped differently from those of the right hand, long and tapered as opposed to short and stubby. "Let's just say that nuclear physics aren't much of a secret anymore," he said.

"And knowing that, governments still move the raw material in unguarded containers?"

"I've already said there's no real danger," he snapped irritably. "But it's an emotive issue. All governments would prefer to ship the stuff under armed escort, but that would alert people to what's going on. So to avoid public outcry, it's moved this way – in secret."

"Some secret," I snorted. "Whoever raided that ship knew exactly which container to take."

"That's for the Brits to worry about," he said with evident satisfaction. "Their boys are kicking it to death. My job is to find Suzy Katoul."

"If it *is* Suzy."

"It's her all right. Her handwriting's all over it."

I fell silent, thinking about Suzy and what I had been told. But Ross barely gave me time to digest it. "Look, nobody's going to make a nuclear device on a kitchen table, but whoever hit the *Marisa* had a lot of muscle. Maybe *enough* muscle to overcome the scientific problems involved in putting a bomb together. All they need now is time – weeks, more likely months, but someday soon a terrorist organisation will have an atomic bomb – unless you get off your butt and help stop them."

The room went very quiet. Ross and I stared at each other and LeClerc studied his whisky while the ormolu clock ticked our lives away. Finally I heard myself ask: "And where do I come in exactly?"

Ross smiled. Not a nice smile. The kind which said *I knew you'd see it my way in the end*. He even took time to sip his whisky before answering. "You probably know more about Suzy Katoul than any man living. We want *everything*. On tape – for our people to analyse. Dates, places, friends, contacts, the whole damn shooting match. Understand? Then when we make contact with her, you'll be the courier."

"Courier?"

"Courier. Go-between." He stared at my baffled expression. "Well, you don't think she'll let my boys anywhere near her, do you?"

"I don't know. I mean I hadn't thought about it." Which was true, but the prospect of telling complete strangers everything I knew about Suzy disturbed me. Made me feel dirty, like a police informer, a spy. I said. "I'm not sure I like the idea."

"I don't give a shit what you like!" He was suddenly blazing angry. "Get it straight Brand – we're working together, no matter what. And if it's any consolation, I don't like it either. People like you – your whole concept of what goes on in the world sickens me. You're so – so bloody naive. All that lily-livered crap in your newspaper column. Fifty dollar words, that's all."

It was quite an outburst. As calmly as I could I said, "Flatterer.

16

Where did you learn your technique, Major? Running press conferences at the Pentagon?"

"Listen buddy boy!" he jabbed a finger under my nose. "Some screwed-up bitch is out there with the makings of a bomb big enough to kill at least half a million people. And you're on the sharp end for once, instead of shooting your mouth off from behind a typewriter. For once you'll be protecting democracy, instead of knocking it."

"Whose idea of democracy, Major? Yours or mine?"

He almost threw his glass at me. He would have, had it been empty. Instead he scowled, "I'll give you another thought to hang onto. Your relationship with this Katoul woman is known. Not just to us, but probably to every flea-bitten political outfit in the Middle East. If it gets out that Katoul's involved, you're in danger. Reprisal killing, taken hostage, just about anything could happen to you. At least by coming with us you'll get protection."

"Coming with you? Where? I'm due in Bonn tomorrow and –"

"That's what you think!" he held his right hand out to LeClerc. "You're on indefinite leave – as of now. Cleared this afternoon by your office."

LeClerc extracted an envelope from an inside pocket and passed it to Ross, who handed it to me. The letter inside stunned me. All of it, but most of all the warm message of good luck from Joe Haines, Chairman of Crusader Press. Someone from a high place had got at Joe. A very high place. I wondered what they'd hit him with. Maybe they threatened to revoke his licence to publish newspapers, or something.

I said, "There should be a government health warning on you. 'Contact with this man is dangerous' – stamped across your forehead."

"Half a million people, Brand," he said grimly. "Any city in the world reduced to rubble. New York, London, Paris. Think about it."

I did. Earlier, the enormity of the idea had numbed my mind, and the sudden aggressiveness of Ross's manner had generated enough hostility to blind me to everything else. But if he was *right*?

"As for government health warnings," he growled, "we're going to just the right place."

I looked at him.

"Spitari's Health Farm," he smiled. "At Delimara Point."

"Where in hell's that?"

"You'll find out. Meanwhile, let's just say it's a step nearer the Middle East."

Including the two Irish Provos, there were eleven of them aboard the *Aileen Maloney*. It was a familiar situation, being the only woman in an all-male environment. She was untroubled by it, well used to the smell of men, accustomed to their talk and their way of looking at things. It was better than being with women, especially Arab women, or even Europeans. Women copped out, consciously some of them, but half the silly cows never knew what it was about to begin with. For some reason the thought provoked memories of touring British universities eight years ago, raising funds and finding friends for the Palestinian refugees. At night she had stayed with the girl students, eaten in their cafés, shared a joint, slept with their men. "Oh yes, we want to do something *worthwhile*," some of the girls had assured her. "We're going to be social workers." She laughed aloud at the memory.

"Something funny?" Reilly asked.

The two of them were alone in the deckhouse, the others asleep or playing cards below. The *Aileen Maloney* pitched into the wind at a steady twelve knots as the skies above darkened again and the sea below hurried in the teeth of a cold north-westerly wind.

"I was thinking of the English," she said.

"Were you now?" He squinted through the windscreen, giving the wheel a slight touch as he did so. "There's a wondrous source of amusement for you."

"Your enemies amuse you?" she looked at him. A man of about forty, thickset, curly hair still brown, blue eyes, clothes smelling of fish and those foul cigarettes.

"Our enemy is the British Government," he grunted, then half laughed and half sighed. "And sometimes our own."

After thinking about it she nodded, "It's like us and the Jews. We're not against them as an ethnic or religious community. We're against Israel as the expression of colonisation based on racist and theocratic principles of Zionism."

"Is that a fact now?"

"It was one of the seven points of the '69 manifesto."

"Ah," he nodded, his serious expression betrayed by a glint of amusement in his eyes, "that explains it."

"Explains what?"

"Why a nice girl like you uses language like that."

Temper flushed her cheeks. "Don't be so damned condescending! Or so sexist." She simmered for a moment, burning with anger and indignation. Then she said; "Anyway – what sort of remark is that from a political activist?"

18

"And I thought I was paying you a compliment," he grinned.
"And is *that* what I am? A political activist?" He shook his head.
"And there's me not knowing. It's lacking in education I am –
thanks to years of British repression."

"We had our share of that."

"Ah, but you got rid of them. Half Ireland's still owned by them."

"The Jews own *all* Palestine."

He was silent at that, his eyes searching the deepening gloom
while his thoughts took refuge behind an expressionless face.

"Anyway, is that *all* you're fighting for?" she challenged. "To beat
the British Government?"

"Is that all?" he mocked. "And I thought it was for a united
Ireland. Ireland for the Irish! God's own country for God's own
people."

"*God's own people*," she mimicked. "The Chosen. You're as bad as
the Jews. And what if you win? What about the social revolution?
What about the fundamental alterations to society?"

He threw his head back and roared with delighted laughter. "Will
you just listen to the girl? Haven't we been fighting the English for
two hundred years? Will you give us a chance to sort that out first?"

She lit cigarettes for both of them, her face still dark with temper.
"You'll *never* win – not without joining the international movement.
People all over the world are fighting imperialist aggression – that's
what you've got to realise. They'll help if you ask – but you Irish are
so – so bloody insular!"

"Pigheaded you mean," he puffed the cigarette. "Going to hell in
our own sweet way and getting there fast enough without other
people's help."

"You do take help," she objected. "But from the wrong people.
Look at the money you get from the States."

"Used to get," he corrected. "It's been a bit thin the last year or so.
And anyway, what's wrong with money from the States?"

"They're not revolutionaries."

"Ah!" he was openly amused. "Is that where we're going wrong?
We should mix more with the revolutionaries. Like those on the
tanker back there?"

She stiffened. "Meaning?"

His smile faded. "And there was I thinking you were a big girl
now. Someone with all the answers."

"They're brothers in the revolution," she protested.

"*Big* brothers," he scowled. "What do they care about the
Palestinians? Or the Irish come to that? What's in this for them –

19

that's what I'm asking myself?"

She stared at him, not answering.

He shook his head, "There was never a whisper of them before. Pat and I were to go to Copenhagen and hang around till you contacted us. After that we'd take the *Aileen Maloney* to Conlaragh and hide your lot up for a few days. Our payment to be the boat, one hundred Kalashnikovs and fifty thousand rounds of ammo – with you paying all expenses."

"And that's what you're getting, isn't it?"

"That and a lot more."

"Such as?"

"Such as meeting five men on the bridge of that tanker and your lover boy the only Ay-rab amongst the lot of them. Such as a trip out past the Orkneys at dead of night and a laden boat which came back empty."

"So now you've seen it all," she sneered.

"Including you committing piracy and then dumping the spoils in the middle of the ocean – boat and all. What the hell was *that* all about?"

"That's our business."

"Not when we're involved, it isn't," he said, grim-faced and with a determined edge to his voice. "Something's going on we weren't told about. Something big. There'll be some talking to do back at Conlaragh, I'm telling you."

"Not by you there won't. You're to tell nobody what you've seen – that's part of the contract."

"I'll tell nobody outside the movement," he corrected her. "But I'm a soldier. They'll want a full report when I get back."

"Abou won't like it," she warned.

His frown gave way to a grin. "Well now, you'll just have to be *extra* nice to the man, won't you. To take his mind off his worries."

Her eyes blazed with anger. "Screw you, Reilly."

His head went back with another delighted peal of laughter.

"There now and isn't it a thousand pities – but even with you burning your bra an' all, that's a thing you'll never do."

20

2

THE SECOND DAY

"Politics is war without bloodshed,
while war is politics with bloodshed."
Quotation from Chairman Mao Tse-Tung (1966)

03.00 Wednesday

The mist was drenched in the scent of the sea. Abou sucked it into his lungs until the cold air caught in his throat and choked him into a fit of coughing. His eyes blurred as he looked at his watch. Almost twenty-three hours aboard the *Aileen Maloney*. Twenty-three come and gone – two or three still to go. Below decks two of his men had been sick and the rancid smell of their vomit had driven him up to the rails for the early morning air to blow the fog from his brain. The sleep had relaxed him. Now he felt strong and confident for what lay ahead. It was up to him now. Whatever happened now, the men aboard the tanker were too far away to be of any help. Strangely the thought comforted him. Being alone had become a way of life. At least for the past four years. Ever since he had suspected that their allies might betray them. And the consequences of *that* were worse than death itself. So the Plan had been devised and he had been chosen to implement it – should the day ever come. And now it had.

His thoughts turned to the others aboard the fishing boat. To the seven commandos, whose oath of allegiance to him and their country could lead them to their deaths. To the two Irishmen fighting a war fifty years out of date, and to Suzy Katoul with her half crazed babblings about a Palestinian Marxist State. He smiled at the irony of his life – of pretending to share her politics while devoting his entire existence to saving his country from being compelled to adopt them. It was that bitter devotion which had led to the formation of the Plan. And it was the Plan which had sent him first to Switzerland for plastic surgery and from there to the very private school in the mountains, where he had learned Arabic and many of the

21

customs of that ancient race. For two years he had toiled there, half hoping that he worked in vain, half pretending that the Plan would never be needed, but knowing in his heart that it would be. Watching and waiting and listening, as their powerful allies edged ever closer to the day of betrayal. Until, almost two years ago to the day, the ruling families had grown alarmed enough to send him to Paris – in search of Suzy Katoul.

He made his way forward to the deckhouse. The wind had dropped and the mist clung to his hair and clothing. Reilly was there, leaning in one corner, sharing the inevitable cigarette with Suzy while Brady, the other Irishman, took a turn at the wheel. Suzy was asking about Conlaragh.

"What's it like?" Reilly answered, surprised, his eyes softening as he thought of his answer. "Conlaragh Creek? Like all Ireland. A place so lovely that the sight of it brings a lump to your throat and a tear to your eye."

Abou checked the compass bearing, while behind him Suzy encouraged Reilly. The Irishman chuckled gently and spoke in a coaxing voice, as if to a child. "Try to imagine a wash of water as quiet as the grave, moving slowly through a winding creek. Trees crowd one bank and bend their branches to ripple the surface while their roots rest in the water itself, knotted and gnarled like old men's feet on a hot summer's day. There's a jetty opposite, with a boat tied up and nets and lobster pots spread over the cobbles like they'd been there a hundred years. And a cluster of cottages with green doors and white-washed faces under thatched roofs, smelling as sweet as a meadow on a spring morning. And along a bit there's a grey-topped church scowling at a red-faced pub, with a thin white road running between on its way to Cork. All framed by the sweetest green hills that you ever did see. Imagine that and that's Conlaragh."

The girl stared, wondering if it was more of his dry humour. No revolutionary spoke like that. They only talked about the rights of men – committees and resolutions, repression and vengeance. Reilly had talked of a *place* not an idea. She said, "You should have been a poet, Liam Reilly."

"And shouldn't I just," he laughed. "But didn't the Lord Almighty make me an Irishman instead."

Abou's gaze was fixed on the scanner. "There's a boat coming," he said abruptly. "Will that be them?"

Reilly jerked out of his corner. "No – not for an hour or more at the earliest." But the blip was unmistakably closing, coming out from

22

the shoreline on a course dead set to intercept their own.

"Coastguard," Brady said gruffly, his hands steady on the wheel, holding his course.

"Sure and why not?" Reilly asked himself. "Wasn't it about here we expected them?" He turned to Abou, "Get her below now – and yourself. We'll do the talking for the lot of us. Keep your men quiet, but ready – and God help us all if they're needed."

"No," Abou had a hand on Suzy's elbow, already steering her towards the door. "God help the coastguard." He slid the door open with his free hand and stepped out into the darkness.

Reilly closed the door. "I've met all sorts, good and bad. Most lacked the devil or the wit to be either, but that's a murdering bastard if ever I set eyes on one."

Brady's answering grunt could have meant anything. He was used to Reilly doing the talking, it was why they worked well together. Mechanically he checked the charts in front of him, rehearsing again the details of their false course and reassuring himself about the fake entries in the log. A moment later he said; "Here they come Liam – lights on the port quarter."

But Reilly had seen them already. He too glanced around the deckhouse, making sure everything was as it should be, and that only what they wanted seen was on show and visible. It would be up to that murdering bastard of an Ay-rab to take care of the rest.

The searchlight broke through the mist and swept fore and aft across the decks of the *Aileen Maloney*, until it reached the deckhouse where the Irishmen screwed their eyes into slits against its brilliance. Brady cut the speed to three knots and waited. The gurgle of sound increased to a throb as the patrol boat came alongside and the searchlight darted back to the stern. Reilly guessed that men in the other boat were reading the name painted there and a moment later came the shout, "Ahoy there, *Aileen Maloney*."

Reilly stifled an oath as he slid the door back. He answered and then listened to the shout of, "Shannon coastguard. Request permission to come aboard."

He resisted an urge to tell them where to put their request and shouted instead, "Come aboard and welcome."

Moments later grappling hooks drew the boats so close that two men were able to swing over the gunnels and board the *Aileen Maloney*. Two men in naval-style duffel coats under peaked caps who hurried directly to the deckhouse. "Morning skipper," the leading figure thrust a hand towards Reilly. "The name's O'Brien. Tim O'Brien. And this here's Wally MacPherson."

Reilly shook hands, studying the baby-blue eyes in a fresh-complexioned face, topped with a thatch of straw hair too long for the cap to contain. God save us, he thought, but they get younger every trip. But he greeted them warmly. "Liam Reilly, and this is my mate, Pat Brady." He turned to the second man. "And what's an Irish coastguard doing with a name like Wally MacPherson?"

The boy, barely in his twenties, hid his blush behind a grin. "My father was a Scot, but my mother came from Kerry. I've lived there the best part of my life, Skipper."

Reilly's eyes twinkled. He turned back to O'Brien. "A Scot and a colleen from Kerry. He'll have the devil's own temper then, this lad of yours."

O'Brien chuckled while Reilly turned away, already busying himself with a bottle and four glasses.

"A fine craft, Skipper," O'Brien nodded approvingly at the instrumentation. "Is she your own?"

"And do I look like a millionaire?" Reilly handed him the whiskey. "Wouldn't I need to be running contraband for twenty years to afford a boat like this?"

According to her papers the *Aileen Maloney* was owned by Inishmore Fishing, a limited liability company with a registered office in Dublin. The company had a subscribed share capital of half a million pounds and owned four boats, of which the *Aileen Maloney* was the latest. The business traded with all of the principal fish markets and made a modest, but respectable, profit according to its annual accounts. Reilly related some of these details in the manner of a raconteur propping up the bar in a favourite pub, knowing that O'Brien would check them later despite his apparent casualness.

MacPherson finished his drink. "Mind if I have a look round, Skipper?"

It was standard procedure. O'Brien would keep the Skipper and the Mate talking while his number two gave the boat the quick once over. "Help yourself," Reilly grinned. "Though you'll oblige me if you let the crew sleep. They've had a hard few days of it." He watched the boy go, knowing that if he as much as sniffed their real cargo he would never live to celebrate another birthday.

"You've had a good trip then?" O'Brien accepted another tot of Jameson's.

"The best in months," Reilly answered truthfully. "Nothing much for the first two days, then we ran into cod off Beaker's Sound." He leaned casually against the chart table and traced the line of their falsified course. "Attacked us you might say," he grinned. "Fair jumped into the boat. Exhausted the lads just packing them."

"Cod?" O'Brien's surprise was genuine. Seiners were near and middle water trawlers, generally out for a week at a time to fish for herring off the coast of Southern Ireland. The recognised fishing grounds for cod were at least two hundred miles south of Beaker's Sound. And well Reilly knew it. But he could hardly admit to being that far south when the fish were caught, nor that the crew of the tanker had lashed crates four deep around the eight foot cube resting on the *Aileen Maloney's* aft deck. Nor would he explain that the fish and ice overflowing from the hold concealed a much more valuable cargo. One hundred Kalashnikov rifles.

"And weren't we as surprised as they were," Reilly warmed to his story. "Of course, there's herring and a spot of dog amongst it all – but it's mostly a goodly load of cod we'll be landing for tomorrow's market."

"For which you'll collect a goodly price, eh?"

They chuckled and the talk drifted, the convivial atmosphere helped by generous measures of Jameson's, and by the time Mac-Pherson returned, the conversation had turned to the weather as it invariably does amongst men who live by the sea. MacPherson's search had been superficial. O'Brien had already given him the nod to be quick about it. After this they would head for shore and an early breakfast. So he had checked the hold, inspected the crates of fish, been surprised to see so much cod in the beam of his flashlight, and taken a quick squint at the crew's quarters to count the sleeping bodies. "You've a big crew, Skipper?" he said casually, having seen nine where he would have expected seven at the most.

"No I've not," Reilly contradicted him quickly. He glanced over his shoulder as if afraid of being overheard. "I've a crew of seven and two layabouts, who'd try the patience of a saint. Relatives of the owners along for a spot of *practical* experience," he pulled a face. "And wouldn't both of them be as sick as dogs on a boat ride up the Liffey."

MacPherson's expression cleared in understanding and O'Brien grinned in sympathy as Reilly launched into a string of abuse about wet-nursing youngsters not fit to sail a boat in a bath-tub. Ten minutes later and still chuckling at some of Reilly's saltier expressions, the coastguards returned to their patrol boat. They hailed farewells until the gurgle of the Rolls Royce engines swamped their voices as their boat pulled away into the black swirling mists of the night. Reilly grinned with delighted satisfaction and tilted the whiskey generously to celebrate. And he was having another tot when Abou returned, Suzy Katoul at his heels like a lap-dog.

"There now," Reilly grinned at them. "That wasn't so painful, was it?"

"No problems?" Suzy asked anxiously.

"Not a thing to worry your pretty little head about."

She glared and Abou said, "It was a pity we ran into them though."

Reilly shrugged. "It was always on the cards." He nodded approval to Brady, who was already manoeuvring the boat back onto course.

Abou checked his watch. "An hour before pick up, isn't it? What's the signal?"

"They'll meet us three miles up from the creek. Just before dawn. Another seiner. She'll show two lights, one above the other, the bottom one flashing. We'll do the same. When she's identified us, she'll turn for the creek and we'll follow."

Abou frowned. "No radio contact?"

"Not in these waters, Mister. Not a word till we're safe ashore."

Arrangements which could not have suited Abou better, but his face remained impassive as he absorbed the information. After a moment he muttered something about the crew and then he left, motioning Suzy to remain in the deckhouse.

Reilly's cheerful face puckered into a grin. "Well now, how shall we pass the time? You could sing us a song perhaps? Or give us a recitation? That would be nice – something out of the Little Red Book perhaps?"

But she resisted the bait. Her earlier clash had taught her enough about Reilly's politics to dismiss him as a hopeless romantic. Now all she felt was relief at the departure of the customs men and anticipation of two nights alone with Abou in Ireland. So she smiled. "That's old hat. There's been a whole cultural revolution since then. Today it's Gaddafi's book – and that's green."

"Green is it?" Reilly nodded. "Sure and what a colourful bunch you revolutionaries are." He broke open another pack of cigarettes, chuckling hugely at his own joke.

His laughter brayed in her ears. How different from Abou. Abou who rarely laughed. Abou with his black predator's eyes that saw everything. Abou of the aquiline nose and thin cruel lips that gave him the look of a hawk. Her desert hawk she had christened him, and the name had stuck. Just thinking about him excited her enough for her body to moisten. Strange, she had slept with dozens of men,

26

four in one night in Paris when a student; sex had been a food like rice, you made a meal of it and two hours later you were ready for it all over again. Sex and drugs. Only Abou made them different. Both were better with him. Trips with Abou – floating high above the bed, so that she could almost look down on his shoulders as he made love to her. Christ, she could do with him now. And a shot. The nembutal were wearing off and they were all Abou would allow until they reached Conlaragh. So the time dragged. Thirty minutes, thirty-five. She helped herself to another of Reilly's cigarettes and watched a thin crack of grey appear low in the eastern sky. Forty-five minutes, fifty. Then Abou returned.

"We've had some trouble with the cargo," he said. "Some of the crates have shifted. The men are re-stacking them now."

"Shifted?" Reilly sounded surprised. "And how could that be?"

"Maybe the coastguard nosing around," Abou shrugged, apparently dismissing it. "It's nearly time, isn't it? Shouldn't we see the signal soon?"

"Oh, they're out there all right," Reilly answered quietly. "Picked us up minutes ago. They'll be making sure, that's all."

"Making sure?"

"Sure the coastguard are tucking into eggs and bacon, sure there's not another boat within five miles of us," he smiled. "Sure we're not being followed and that Conlaragh's as quiet as an empty crib when we arrive."

Abou's dark eyes searched Reilly's face in search of a lie. Not finding one he turned away to peer out into the darkness, and a few minutes later they saw the signal; two lights, the lower one blinking as steady as a pulse. Reilly touched a switch and lights on the *Aileen Maloney's* own main mast responded by splashing pools of white about the deckhouse. "Follow her in," he growled.

"I'm going aft to check the cargo," Abou said. "Skipper, I'd like your advice on it."

Reilly nodded. "I'll be a minute then, Pat," he said, following Abou to the door and out into the darkness. They moved slowly, edging towards the stern, bending their bodies into the biting wind and treading carefully across a deck made treacherous by the icy spray. Reilly gritted his teeth to stop them chattering and reached out to test one of the ropes holding the crates in position. It was as taut as a bowstring. He tried another and found it the same. He started to count the crates, thinking that the stack seemed as secure as ever and wondering what the problem was. And just as Liam Reilly realised there was no problem, the knife went in. Driven

27

hard, it pierced his body just above his kidneys, tearing upwards through his gut and into his heart. Even as the vomit of pink froth spilled from his lips, Abou's free hand clamped over his mouth.

"Get the other one," Abou grunted, breathless under the weight of Reilly's sagging body. Two shadows detached themselves from behind the stack of crates and moved like cats towards the deck-house. "The weights," Abou gasped. "And the explosives." Another commando slipped forward, dragging an oilskin-covered case on the end of a length of rope. A loop was passed quickly around Reilly's ankles and tightened about an unresisting body. Liam Reilly was already dead. Abou checked the knots which secured the oilskin-covered case and straightened in time to greet the two men returning from the deckhouse. Between them they dragged the dead Pat Brady, like a carcass in a slaughterhouse. That too was fitted with weights and then roped to Reilly's body.

"The buoy," Abou commanded. "And someone get forward to the deckhouse. Keep station on the other boat."

He worked quickly, tying a ten foot length of rope to the buoy before fastening the other end to Reilly's ankles. The knots were checked and double-checked, then grunting with effort, Abou and his men pushed both bodies towards the guardrails. The heavy oilskin-covered case hit the water first, followed by Reilly, then Brady, and last of all the orange-coloured marker buoy – all connected like links in a chain. The icy black water closed over them like a satisfied god accepting a sacrifice, and only the marker buoy bobbed to the surface, a dancing insignificant dot in the vastness of those seas, soon lost from sight as the *Aileen Maloney* pulled quickly away.

Abou hurried to the deckhouse to mark the spot on the charts.

"You didn't tell me," Suzy challenged, white-faced and trembling.

"It was necessary," Abou busied himself with the charts. "They would have talked –"

"You *should* have told me," she reproached, trying to still her shaking hands and fighting down the bile which rose in her throat. "You should –"

He hit her without a moment's hesitation. A powerful sweeping blow which caught her across the face and sent her sprawling backwards across the deckhouse. It was done quite without compunction and his bleak eyes betrayed no emotion. The commando at the wheel stared directly ahead and, without another glance at the

28

girl, Abou snatched up the half bottle of whiskey and returned to the aft-deck.

"Cut the stacks free," he shouted above the moaning wind. "Scatter the crates about the deck – make it look like an accident." He stood in the lee side of the deckhouse and watched the shadowy figures respond to his orders. A man dropped a crate onto the deck a yard away, splintering the boxwood and spilling fish. Others did the same, breaking crates open and creating chaos out of order. Abou's right hand closed over the crowbar, retrieving it from its hiding place. Nearby a man crouched over a fallen crate, one hand clawing the top to splinter the thin wood. Abou aimed for the wrist, hoping for a clean break, one that would set easily later. But, as if sensing danger, the man released his grip and straightened up, so that only for the briefest moment was his hand still on the crate, his palms downwards and his fingers splayed. The iron bar traced an arc through the air just in time to catch the knuckles, smashing bone and pulping flesh like a rotten apple caught in a threshing machine. The man screamed and swung round, agony and surprise mingled with shock in his face, and pain coming in thick red waves as his legs buckled on the pitching deck. Abou hit him again, this time with his fist, catching the point of his jaw and sending him plunging backwards into the broken crates.

"Here," Abou pulled the bottle from his pocket and handed it to the nearest man. "Get him below and give him this when he comes round. Enough of it might deaden the pain until we can get him to a doctor." And without another word he turned on his heel, his face set in grim lines as if to suggest indifference. Yet despite the chill wind, tiny beads of perspiration lay across his forehead and along his upper lip. He wiped his face with the back of his hand as he entered the deckhouse. Nothing matters, he told himself bitterly, nothing matters except the success of the Plan.

06.30 Wednesday

Spitari's Health Farm was quite handy really. An ambitious estate agent might even have claimed it was within easy commuting distance of Kensington – quite truthfully too, so long as Ross & Co. handled the travel arrangements. LeClerc even carried my bag down to the unmarked police car waiting on the double yellow lines. Then we drove up through Chiswick, along the Western Avenue to Northolt, and straight onto an R.A.F. Valiant. No customs clearance, no passport control, no hassle with boarding cards. Thomas Cook's couldn't have lived with it. Even the Valiant was bigger than I imagined, four seats facing each other across a low table set ten feet back from the pilot. Noisy though, and no pretty stewardess dripping drinks and cleavage to relieve the boredom. But Ross did his best to be hospitable, fishing half a dozen whisky miniatures from his briefcase and sharing them equally among us.

The mystery tour ended two hours later when we landed. Not that Ross or LeClerc said anything, but even late at night I recognised the place. Luqa Airport – still shared by civil airlines and the R.A.F. I had been there dozens of times – though less often since Mintoff took to throwing disrespectful British reporters out of Malta. A black Mercedes met us on the apron, driven by a dog-faced Englishman called Smithers, who greeted Ross respectfully before frightening us half to death with his driving. Not that it took long, we were there before midnight local time, an hour ahead of G.M.T. Ross showed me straight to my room. "We'll be starting early in the morning," he explained. "Say around six. Get some sleep – we've a hell of a day tomorrow." So I did, and in the morning I got the grand tour.

The Health Farm was really four large villas grouped around a central courtyard and strung into a single entity by a connecting corridor. One villa was exercise rooms, steam baths and saunas; another was rest areas, dining-rooms and kitchens; and the third was administration. Ross and his people lived in the fourth. The whole enterprise was tucked away in a ridge in the hills high up above Delimara Point and hidden behind walls ten feet high and electronically-operated gates. In point of fact, there actually was a Joe Spitari and the place really could function as a health farm. It suffered local taxation, paid lip service to the principle of Maltese co-ownership, had a Negro masseur and possessed a security system to rival Fort Knox.

"Why this place?" I asked Ross.

We were in the first floor room which he used as office cum sitting-room cum dining-room. It was big enough; a vast expanse of marble floor, squashy black Italian sofas, a rosewood desk and matching conference table with eight chairs. One wall was built-in bookshelves and a bank of television sets, with a couple of Akai reel-to-reel recorders next to a wall map. The large window opposite revealed the swimming pool and beyond that, over the boundary wall, the parched brown hillside as it slipped down to the Mediterranean. When in residence Ross as good as lived in that room. He

30

even took his meals there, served on a tray by an assistant called Elizabeth. *Elizabeth*, not Beth or Lizzy or Eliza. She was English too, which I found comforting, her vowel sounds adding a touch of reassuring normality to the place. I guessed her at about thirty, tall, good figure, fair hair bleached and golden skin bronzed by the Mediterranean sunshine; attractive rather than beautiful, but with compelling green eyes. Right at that moment she was distracting Ross by serving him his third orange juice of the morning.

"Why a health farm?" I persisted.

"Maybe it keeps me that way," he said mournfully. "A lot of people die in my business."

"What is *your* business, Major Ross?"

"Security."

"My uncle was in security. Night watchman at Glaxo's until they installed a burglar alarm."

"Machines are taking over everywhere." He looked sad to the point of tears, but he comforted himself by patting Elizabeth's bottom as she turned to fetch my coffee from the sideboard. The gesture was so absent-minded that I think only I noticed.

"C.I.A.?" I tried.

He scowled. "Since Watergate? Are you kidding? Washington put their eyes out. Now they're like the three brass monkeys – blind, deaf and impotent. It's more democratic – only trouble is nobody told the K.G.B."

In twelve hours of knowing him I had learned to expect that kind of remark. Ross was John Wayne in *True Grit*. Rough and tough and prepared to die for what he believed in – which in Ross's case was the infallibility of western democracies and the sanctity of their institutions. Anyone who questioned any part of them was instantly labelled subversive and watched carefully. Whereas I was Henry Fonda in *Twelve Angry Men* – sceptical about almost everything and fumbling about in search of the truth. It is a condition induced by watching too many politicians and learning to distrust them. Even their language is full of weasel words with the meaning sucked out. Try listening to an East German explain about the democracy he lives in and you'll know what I mean.

"This set-up's international," Ross waved a hand possessively at the room. "I think Schmidt and Callaghan were among the prime movers back in seventy-six. Terrorism was getting too organised, crossing too many frontiers. What with Gaddafi sending arms to the I.R.A. and the Japanese Red Brigade linking up with Black September." He shrugged. "And the P.L.O. opening more branches in

Germany than Woolworths. Something had to be done."

"And you're doing it?"

"We've rolled a dozen up already," he said with some satisfaction. "We get a lot of help of course – C.I.A., Secret Intelligence Service and the German GSG9 squad –"

"No Israelis?"

"No one from Moscow Centre either." He gave me a sharp look. "Mossad co-operates, but doesn't participate directly. You know what *they're* like."

I didn't, but telling him wouldn't help. "Why Malta?"

"Good access to the Middle East. The Sixth Fleet in the Med. Help from the British base. And we're halfway between Italy and Libya."

"And that's important?"

"Sure," he seemed surprised. "The Italian Red Brigades are the most active in Europe, and Gaddafi sends them arms like care packages."

"So you're stopping the gun-runners?"

"Trying to," he smiled. He looked tired, despite the vitamin C soaked up in a gallon of orange juice.

The white telephone buzzed and Elizabeth walked to the desk, swaying her hips in a way which explained why Ross looked tired after an early night. "The doctor is ready for you." She replaced the handset and looked at me. Mention of the doctor turned my stomach. The doctor *and* the studio downstairs. LeClerc had explained it earlier. The subject – me in this case – sat in a chair and talked into a microphone. Not that the microphone could be seen, but it was there – several probably, set into the walls or the ceiling – safe from interference and automatically controlled. The doctor would lead the conversation, prompting where necessary and encouraging a tired memory to recall incidents long forgotten. Difficult names should be spelled when used for the first time – letter by letter – so that the computer linked to the tape machines could hunt for cross references. If Suzy had been in London on a wet afternoon in June, who else had been in town that day? Carlos perhaps? Richard Nixon? The Rolling Stones? Don't worry about it – the computer would know. I sipped my coffee and struggled towards a decision.

"There's no lie detector," Ross encouraged. "No pentothal. No bright lights or electric shocks. Just a quiet room and a well-stocked bar. And LeClerc and the doctor."

"The deal we made," I reminded him for the tenth time. "I co-operate and I get to Suzy first, right?"

He sighed, as if I was trying his patience. "Right, Harry. Like I said, we just want the whole situation deactivated – quietly, understand?"

Ever since we left London I had been weighing the chances of him keeping his word. That, and asking myself what alternative I had.

"Harry, she's being used," he said persuasively. "We know she's selling the Palestinian ticket but the mainstream movement – Arafat and his boys – are playing it cool right now. They need this like a hole in the head. Why should they? Half the governments in the world are beginning to recognise the P.L.O. as a political force. And with the oil weapon forcing the States and Europe to re-think the Middle East, Arafat's getting a better press than Israel. Where's the percentage?"

"Perhaps someone's patience ran out?"

"I don't buy it," he shook his head. "But I think your girl did. She thinks she's helping the Palestinians, but she's wrong Harry – wrong by a goddamned mile. And Israel's sitting on a stock of atom bombs into two figures. Are you prepared to risk setting them off?"

Funny the way Ross made everything my fault. I finished my coffee and rose to leave, watching Elizabeth dimple a reassuring smile in my direction. The door opened and the doctor stood framed in the entrance, wearing enough black mohair and crisp linen to do justice to Harley Street. He smiled, myopic behind pebble glasses, grey-haired and stooped from bending over too many bedsides. I had a feeling that I wasn't going to like the doctor. But then, as I wondered where I would begin my betrayal of Suzy Katoul, I had a feeling I wasn't going to like myself too much either. We went downstairs and I began at the very beginning – just as the doctor ordered.

It was October 1947 when I first went to Jerusalem. Young, curious, and on the day I arrived racked by a toothache which threatened to split my jaw open. The tooth had been acting up before I left and I would have fixed it in London, but for allowing my sense of duty to be exploited by an editor's sense of urgency. He wanted me on the first flight to Palestine, so I left him in Fleet Street and took my tooth with me, though by the time I booked into the Imperial I wished I had done it the other way round.

Funny sort of place the Imperial. Part hotel, part officers' mess, part gentlemen's club. Still, I guessed it would make interviewing easier, just prop up the bar and get to know the entire British administration in no time flat. But that first evening I planned differently. More than a couple of whiskies were needed to deaden the pain in my jaw, so I went in search of a dentist.

"It's turned six old boy," a young subaltern complained, as if King's Regulations stipulated set times for toothache. "You won't get any of our chaps now – not until morning."

"But there must be *someone*?"

"Maybe the civilian sector?" He sounded like a Harrod's floor-walker recommending a visit to Woolworths.

I enquired at the desk and did some market research in the lobby before accepting defeat and adjourning to the bar. Whisky was going to have to get me through the night, and I was on the point of ordering my third when she arrived. I jumped, startled to hear my name in a place where I was a stranger.

"Mr Brand?"

She was wearing a green two-piece suit, linen I think, with a lemon silk scarf at her throat. "You *are* suffering from toothache?"

I nodded ruefully, thinking it a childish ailment to admit to, especially to someone as attractive as she was.

"My father is a dentist." Perfect teeth spoke volumes for the family business. "I'll take you to him if you wish?"

I should have accepted immediately but didn't, influenced no doubt by the lieutenant's deprecating manner.

"He's a very good dentist." She added another quick smile as if reading my mind. "As a matter of fact he qualified in London."

The flicker of amusement in her eyes had me blushing the shade of an over-ripe beet, but I finally recovered enough confidence to take her arm and we left.

Her name was Haleem. Haleem Katoul. Dark, vivacious and Arab. And a lot more than I bargained for. For a start she was much more emancipated ("liberated" was a word with different connotations in those days) than I expected. Not only did she drive the car we journeyed in, but owned it as well. And she worked for the British at the King David Hotel, largely taken over for administration. "Clerk B2," she announced with a wry smile, as if surprised by the realisation that the job was important to her. She talked in the same easy manner as she drove, balancing small disclosures about her own life with casual enquiries about mine, so that by the time we reached "home" I felt I knew her quite well. And home in Katamon turned out to be as comfortably middle-class as my parents' house in Guildford.

She was certainly right about Nadi Katoul. He was a good dentist. Fifteen minutes later the tooth had gone, taking the pain with it and leaving behind a vacuum which barely ached. Nadi took me off to the sitting-room where Haleem served thick black coffee and joined in her father's invitation to stay for dinner. I declined as graciously as my anaesthetized face permitted, feeling that I had intruded enough for one evening, and Haleem drove me back to the hotel and then disappeared back into the gloom of the night.

Jerusalem in 1947 took some getting used to. Like an explosives factory with everyone chain-smoking for fear that the whole place would blow up at any minute. Superficially it was normal enough; the market places were crowded and the shop windows were stuffed full of Persian rugs and Yemenite silver and Hollywood records. Delicatessens stocked Rhison wine and Tnuvah cheese and florists blazed gold with the roses of Sharon. But there was a tension running through the place which fairly crackled.

Most of the press corps collected neat gins and embellished stories from the same place – the bar at the Imperial or sometimes the Royal for a change of scenery. I joined them occasionally but not often, distrusting officials even then and preferring to search out my own explanations for what was happening. Which was far from easy. For a start I was English and if that wasn't handicap enough I was as near being an atheist as makes no difference. Not the aggressive argumentative kind, just someone whose natural sceptism left little room for anything mystical. Whether that made *understanding* harder or easier is difficult to say, but to my twenty-three-year-old eyes Jerusalem was cursed not by a lack of faith, but by an abundance of it. Judaism, Christianity, Islam; the City was held sacred by all three and everyone from David and Pharoah to the Crusaders had fought and burned and pillaged inside its walls. And all in the name of religion. And as for being English, the British *were* the occupying power – even if they did so like sullen-faced men who remain seated while standing matrons glare at them. The truth was that most of the city – most of the country come to that – wanted the British out. And the sooner the better.

There were exceptions. The Katouls for instance, or so it seemed at the time. The British had ruled Palestine for thirty years – more summers than Haleem's lifetime. Her worry was not what would happen if the British stayed, that was as predictable as the British themselves, but what might happen if the British left. *If* they left, never when, for like many Arabs Haleem believed the British would stay for ever – despite the wireless broadcasts and the newspaper gossips – despite the snatches of conversation overheard at the King David.

I saw a lot of the Katouls to begin with. Nadi was an Anglophile who liked nothing better than to yarn about his years in London, and Haleem was lively and good-looking – so it was no hardship. She became my guide, first to Jerusalem and then the villages beyond. Through her I met Jew and Arab alike, for she had friends everywhere and saw nothing odd in it. "We're all Jerusalemites," she laughed when I asked her about it, shrugging her shoulders in a mild parody of her Jewish friends. And she was always with them. On Friday evenings she would let herself into their houses to kindle the oil lamps which Jews were forbidden to light themselves on the Sabbath, and once I saw her going from house to house in the Jewish quarter laden with trays of bread and honey to welcome her friends at the end of Passover.

But not all were as gentle. Jerusalem had its darker spirits. Men who maimed and killed from the gloom of alleyways or the escape route of rooftops. Men who, as October slipped into November, stepped up their activities with the steadily increasing rhythm of war drums.

I suppose it's true that the British made a mess of Palestine. The 1947 tragedy was that the world was about to make it even worse. In a sense it was all a hangover from the First World War, when Britain grabbed Palestine to secure the northern approaches to Suez and to edge closer to the new buried treasure of oil in Iraq. After the war, British rule was formalised by a League of Nations mandate. The British promised to succour the wandering Jew, promised to tutor the native and to rule with Christian enlightenment. Promises were the root of the problem I suppose, there were too many of them. First the Balfour Declaration: "His Majesty's Government view with favour the establishment in Palestine of a national home for the Jewish people." And then, separately and at a different time, a promise to the Arabs to support their claims to a vast independent state. And finally – as if enough wasn't enough – the French were promised a "sphere of influence" in much of that area already pledged to the Arabs, and to the Jews come to that. So at the end of World War Two, Britain found herself at the church with three bridegrooms – all of them furious. The United Nations weren't too happy either, but *somebody* had to decide what the hell to do with Palestine. And while the General Assembly debated the matter, a hundred thousand British troops struggled to maintain a crumbling semblance of law and order in the place the world still called "the Holy Land."

With all that happening Haleem was either mad or braver than Joan of Arc just to be seen on the streets with me. But she was always there when I needed her, though when I realised the risks she took I found ways of making my own contacts and of finding my own way to meetings. Which was just as well considering that half of them preached open rebellion and all countenanced sedition as a way of life. But they gave me what I was looking for, stories about what was *really* happening in Palestine. Which was how I ran into my first spot of bother.

I filed a story about the clandestine build-up of arms, a few column inches which won me headlines in London and a place on the mat in Jerusalem – the mat belonging to the Chief of Police. The argument was new to me then – now it's as old as the hills around Jerusalem. Reveal my sources of information, or else. The "or else" fluctuated between threats of deportation and promises of imprisonment. I said nothing a dozen times over and spent a week in the cells before being confined to my hotel for another seven days. Irksome and uncomfortable for the first week, but Haleem was allowed to visit me despite the raised eyebrows at Police headquarters. And my spot of bother did me a favour in a way. News of my refusal to "name names" leaked out, no doubt by the Jewish Intelligence Agency, the Shai, and afterwards I was less widely regarded as a police spy, so a few doors opened to me which otherwise might have remained closed.

One such door led to a simple stone house in the new Jewish quarter. I spent hours at that house, drinking endless cups of coffee in the smoke-filled kitchen, listening to excited people laugh and curse and live their dreams aloud – all presided over by the most famous hostess in Jerusalem. More approachable than Ben Gurion, more likeable than the extremists, Golda Meir was the best public relations officer the Zionists ever had. I never doubted the kind of conversations which took place during my absences, never once fooled myself that "all had been revealed", but equally I never left that house without being impressed by the driving urgency of the people I met there, nor doubting their determination to build a brave new world.

By contrast, the Arabs lacked cohesion, their leadership was fragmented and divided, and even then I thought them politically naïve – at least fifty years behind their Zionist neighbours in their nationalistic aspirations. A dozen or more times I picked my way through the myriad dishes of an Arab *mezze*, listening to the argument roll on all sides of me. "How many Jews are there in the whole of Palestine?" someone would demand. "Answer that!"

Liquid brown eyes stared back. "Half a million, more maybe."

"Well then? And how many are we? How many Arabs?"

A shrug. "Twice as many."

"Hah, isn't that my argument?" a satisfied smile, followed by: "And who owns the land?"

Hesitation, heads shaken in bafflement, then, "Who knows anymore – the way the Jews are taking it from us? Who can say these days?"

But the questioner would persist. "Is the land not ours *by right*? Is the land not sacred? How many times have we been overrun – once – twice? Three times in my lifetime – but the land is always ours."

Heads would nod as the talk drifted to the inevitable conclusion – that even if the British did leave, the Arabs of the surrounding lands would come to the aid of the Palestinians if called upon to do so. It was always such a *comforting* note to end on.

That was Palestine in '47. A sliver of land on the eastern rim of the Mediterranean, half the size of Denmark, with a population no larger than Bristol. Arab by inheritance, Jewish by future and in trust to the British. But British rule was coming to an end. The delegates at the U.N. were edging towards a decision. Like latter-day Solomons they proposed to dismember the body, part for the Arabs and part for the Jews – and by November 29th they were ready to vote on it.

Jerusalem seethed all day. The British doubled their patrols and fanned their secret police through the vaulted alleyways and into the hidden passages of the ghettos, in a final despairing attempt to forestall trouble, or at least to pinpoint where it might first erupt. The soukhs boiled with rumours and counter-rumours. Black-coated orthodox Jews bobbed to the rhythmic sing-song of ancient prayers and mounted perpetual guard on the Wailing Wall. The Church of the Holy Sepulchre rang with the prayers of the Christians; Greek and Russian, Armenian and Chaldean, Syriac and others, all kneeling together in mutual aversion. And above it all, the piercing unending call of the minarets drew the Moslems to their own devotions.

I spent most of the day in the streets, listening and watching, storing information in the back of my mind to write about later, until at mid-afternoon I drifted up Julian's Way to the King David, keen to sniff out official reaction to what was happening in the city. Half way down the west corridor I bumped into Haleem as she made an exit from an office, laden with files which threatened to scatter as she struggled to close the door.

"Carry your books for you?" I took care of the door handle.

"It's all right, I'm only going to the next room." For once her smile was less than radiant. She lowered her voice, "Will I see you tonight?"

I hesitated. "I'm not sure, I've a feeling it could be quite a night."

She seemed anxious, perhaps her mind was more on what would happen six thousand miles away in New York than on seeing me later, but she said, "Our door is always open to you." She lowered her eyes, "Whatever the hour."

"Then I'll come."

She smiled shyly, nodded and turned away. Somebody opened the door to the office from the inside and closed it after her, so that I was left watching her shadow disappear behind a pane of crinkled glass.

After my meeting with officialdom I went back to the Imperial, still thinking about Haleem. We had seen a good deal of each other during the weeks I had been there. True she no longer accompanied me on the meetings circuit, but that was at my insistence, not hers. I was a constant visitor to their villa, and as they were Christian Arabs I was permitted to return their hospitality, often taking Nadi and his grown-up sons with Haleem to dinner in the Arab quarter. So mostly we met in the midst of her family, Nadi so trusting that he almost adopted me as his eldest. But sometimes Haleem would flash me a glance which made me think of her in a way no brother feels for his sister, and I was beginning to seek those glances and respond with looks of my own.

At the Imperial I took a bath and read myself the riot act. A lot of stuff about keeping her at arm's length and being in no position to get involved with anybody, let alone an Arab girl. And afterwards I climbed into a fresh suit and went down to the bar for a drink.

Pierre Moreau was there before me. Moreau was a know-it-all Frenchman who wrote for *Le Monde* when he was sober. Mostly he buttonholed people in the bar and bored the pants off them with his solutions to world problems, his complexion and his politics turning a shocking pink with successive martinis.

In the bar I bought Moreau a drink and he bought me one, and then some of the other Press boys joined us – so that by the time we left for the wire room of the Palestinian Broadcasting System all of us had had a few.

The first surprise was the street, the street outside the Imperial. Pulsating with life a couple of hours earlier, but now as quiet as a ghost town. We stopped in our tracks at the sight of it and just stood there – listening and straining our ears for sounds of the living. A few minutes passed, then a sound like distant thunder reached us and a British half-track emerged from behind the building line. It shuffled crab-like round the corner, pointed its muzzle in our direction and crept down the road to meet us. We waited for it to pass before walking slowly towards a forbidding compound outside the general post office, fenced with barbed wire by the British for security reasons and christened Bevingrad by the Jews. Nobody spoke, we were all too damn puzzled. I think I imagined the whole city at prayer, it was the only explanation I could think of until we reached the café. Then it clicked. The place was full of Arabs. Normally their laughter and argument would fill the street for twenty yards in all directions, but now they just sat there, sipping coffee or with heads cupped in their hands – listening to one voice. The voice of the Arab broadcaster relaying the news from Flushing Meadow. Then I realised the Jews were doing the same – the whole population was huddled over its radio sets. The threat of division had succeeded in creating a rare moment of unity – perhaps the only such one in Jerusalem's two-thousand-year history.

But if the streets were quiet, the wire room was bedlam. News of each vote was ripped from the teletype, one copy was snatched by a Jewish runner who raced across the courtyard to the Hebrew service, while the Arab boy rushed his copy a few yards further to "the other channel" next door. Early in the evening the rest of us greeted each vote with muttered approval or groans of dismay, and there was a good deal of good-humoured argument and heated speculation. But as the night wore on, we became less noisy and the grim-faced runners competed all evening without exchanging a word. Perhaps it was their tension which finally gripped us – or the chattering urgency of the teletype – or just the realisation that the Middle East would never be the same again. But whatever it was, we fell quiet until the final vote was cast and the verdict was known. The General Assembly of the United Nations, by thirty-three in favour, thirteen against and ten abstentions, had voted to partition Palestine.

The City was a blaze of sudden light and alive with noise. Windows were flung open, doors wrenched back on their hinges and the Jews – many still struggling into whatever clothing came to hand – took to the streets. Faces struggled to express a whole gamut of emotions. Initial disbelief – dazed that something dreamed about, prayed and sacrificed for, was really happening. Then fear – fear it was a rumour, fear it was a trick, fear that they would wake to discover a dream passed in the night. Followed by the slow dawning realisation that it was *true* – real – had happened and couldn't be snatched back again. Until finally they felt a joy too rich for laughter, too stifling for words, too overpowering for cheers. The Jews were so happy that they cried.

The streets overflowed with a people radiant with joy. They kissed and hugged. Neighbours, strangers, wives and lovers, wiping each other's tears away before turning to embrace somebody else, anybody, man, woman or child, anybody and everybody. By two o'clock every Jewish bar and restaurant in the city had opened its doors. Everywhere was open house. Every street corner had its group dancing the hora, every thoroughfare its procession singing the Hatikvah. By three the synagogues were open, packed with worshippers offering thanksgiving before slipping joyously back to the streets. Officially one hundred thousand Jews lived in Jerusalem, but that night they seemed twice as many, all convinced that after the terrors of the Holocaust the Jews of the Diaspora would come home to the Promised Land. And so they linked arms and squeezed and danced and laughed and cried their way to the building of the Jewish Agency, with its searchlight-washed balcony and wide open courtyard. I arrived just in time for the explosion of noise which greeted the blue and white Zionist flag as it fluttered to the masthead. And just in time to watch a woman's bulky figure appear above me.

"For two thousand years we have waited for our deliverance," Golda Meir fought against her tears. "Now it is so great and wonderful that it surpasses human words," her voice broke to a sob. "Jews!" she cried. "Mazel Tov! Good luck!"

It was very late when I remembered my promise to Haleem. I hesitated, not wanting to go and wishing I hadn't committed myself. Haleem had said I was welcome at any time and I had warned that I might be late, but *this late*? I struggled with my conscience, knowing the store they set by promises. Finally I decided to walk up to Katamon – if there was a light in the window I would knock – otherwise I would turn and flee.

Nadi was waiting up for me. "My family are in bed asleep." He seemed strangely embarrassed. "They hope you'll forgive their bad manners."

I looked at him, sensing a rebuke and cursing my decision to call at

41

so late an hour. He looked old. Even allowing that he was tired, in three days he seemed to have aged ten years.

"Haleem says the British have betrayed us." He used the excuse of pouring coffee to avoid my eye. "She is very upset. She's young, of course, inexperienced in life, but –" he shrugged, and then in case I thought him disloyal, he added: "But usually she has a great understanding of these matters."

I nodded but remained silent.

"What will happen now?" he asked simply.

"Perhaps very little," I ventured, trying to sound hopeful. "After all, although Palestine is to be partitioned, Jerusalem is to become an international city – administered by the United Nations."

"You believe that?"

"It's what the U.N. has decided."

"But can they do it?"

I struggled. "I believe they'll try."

"And if they fail?"

"How can they?"

"Was the League of Nations so successful?"

"This is different, Nadi, surely? A different organisation – different men – different times. The world must try again."

He smiled that tired patient look which the very old reserve for the very young and gently led the conversation away from politics to more general matters. He asked my plans, and I told him that I hoped to be allowed to stay in the Middle East for a while – and then, quite suddenly, he said: "Harry, I lied to you. Haleem is not upstairs. Nor are my sons."

What the hell do you say when somebody says something like that? Nadi of all people. Kind, civilised, gentle, urbane. It was so out of character. My mind slipped a cog between analysing his motives and speculating on the whereabouts of his children, but I held my tongue and said nothing.

Eventually he sighed and asked, "Do the initials E.G. mean anything to you?"

The question was almost rhetorical. "Emile Ghoury?" I asked and he nodded.

Ghoury was leader of the Arab Higher Committee. A Christian Arab, educated at Cincinnati University and powerfully persuasive. I had attended one of his meetings once, or at least tried to. Half way through I was discovered and thrown out.

"An hour ago a messenger brought this," Nadi passed me a scrap of paper. It was grubby and creased into a million wrinkles, as if whoever had carried it had screwed it up to make it much smaller than it was. On it were the initials "E.G." and the sign of the crescent and the cross.

"Other men were waiting outside," Nadi whispered as if afraid of being overheard. "They had a car, a truck perhaps, it was dark so I'm not sure. Hemeh took the man into the other room, Negib and Haleem joined them." He shook his head in bewilderment. "In my own house, Harry. Have I so little authority that I have lost the respect of my children?"

I told him his children loved and honoured him and encouraged him to continue.

"Fifteen minutes later the messenger left, taking Hemeh with him. When the car had driven away Haleem came to see me. We had –" his face folded into a grimace of misery. "We had an argument. Haleem says the Jewish terrorists will never accept partition without Jerusalem. That soon they will attack us. That Arabs all over the city must be prepared to defend themselves."

"But Haleem has so many Jewish friends?" I protested.

"Who hasn't?" His eyes were closed and he sounded tired enough to be talking in his sleep. "But Haleem says all of our friends will follow the terrorists. They will have no choice in the matter, if they remain friends of ours they will face reprisals from the entire Hebrew community."

"So you argued?"

His hand rose and fell limply in a gesture of defeat. "Negib joined sides with her. Said the Mufti was right after all – we should never have trusted the British. Arabs everywhere must be ready to defend themselves against murderers like the Stern Gang."

"What happened then?"

"They left. They'll be back before dawn they said. Also, if you arrived, it would be best to tell you they'd gone to bed."

"Why didn't you?"

"Yes, why didn't I?" his eyes opened wide, as if the effort of answering had jerked him into wakefulness. "Perhaps because a father worries for his children, Harry. Even when they ignore his advice. Even when they treat him like –" he struggled to find the right expression. "Like a United Nations." He lapsed into silence for a moment, as if trying to reach a decision. "Harry, they like you. All of them. Especially Haleem, she never stops talking about you. Perhaps – I mean, I thought – well if *you* were to talk to them? You're nearer their own age, only your experience makes you appear older. Tell them that only trouble can come of it – explain to them –

persuade." The words ran out until he gathered himself for his final plea. "They're only children after all."

I promised to do whatever I could and offered to wait for their return, but he didn't want that, preferring me to seek them out in a day or two, and sound them out without letting on that he had confided in me.

He embraced me at the door. "May all your feasts find you in good health."

"You too – look after yourself."

"Harry, those men," he clung to my arm. "They all had guns."

I walked back to the Imperial, pulling my coat tight against the cold, surprised to realise it would be dawn in half an hour. In the streets the Jews still celebrated, their ranks thinner now, reduced mainly to the young Sabras, the first generation Palestinian Jews, still singing and dancing, intoxicated by the hour and fortified by the free drinks which had bathed their throats all night. Some of the British soldiers joined in while others looked the other way and pretended that nothing unusual was happening. But not an Arab was to be seen.

Back in my room I rummaged through the pockets of my jacket, looking for my notebook before settling down at the typewriter. Perhaps it was prophetic, but the first quote I found was that of the Syrian delegate immediately after the vote at the U.N.: "The Holy places are going to pass through long years of war, and peace will not prevail there for generations." I shivered. I watched the cold grey dawn slide through the window, and wondered if Haleem had yet returned to the safety of her father's house.

07.00 Wednesday

There was no mistaking Conlaragh. A hundred yards in from the sea the creek twisted and Reilly's birthplace was laid out before them. The early morning mist had given way to soft rain which dimpled the water as the *Aileen Maloney* followed the other boat up the estuary, and a minute later the liquid sun broke through the clouds to wash pale light over the countryside, turning the grey road to a silver ribbon. The road to Cork, Abou remembered. He followed it down from the brow of the hill, past sheep grazing dew-wet grass and beyond a knot of cottages to the other buildings which lined the jetty. He saw the church with its grey slate roof, and at his side Suzy looked at the pub and thought of Liam Reilly. She imagined him at the bar, his provocative blue eyes emphasising the sardonic twist of his mouth. Reilly would have been popular, she thought. Strong enough for men to like and with enough of the devil to be attractive to women. Fearfully she glanced sideways to her own devil and anticipated the crisis facing him when they landed.

Unexpectedly the other boat went past the jetty and on up the creek. Abou stiffened, ever suspicious of a trap, always on guard for a sign of betrayal. But a hundred yards on he saw the boat-houses and the little wharf beneath a sign which read "Inishmore Fishing" in letters a foot high. The buildings slid down to the water, a corrugated iron roof supported by concrete pillars jutting out thirty feet from the bank. The boat ahead slowed and manoeuvred then disappeared beneath the cover of the roof. Bare electric light bulbs winked out from the gloom and half a dozen men congregated on the jetty to meet them. Reilly's friends had come to welcome him home.

Abou grunted to the helmsman to follow. The port side door slid open and one of the commandos entered armed with a Kalashnikov. Abou watched others take up positions, one in the prow and another alongside the deckhouse on the starboard side. Three more would be aft next to the cargo while the last man nursed his wound in silent agony below. The next few minutes would be critical. As critical as any so far. Get through them and you've a chance. The Plan has a chance – a chance to succeed where all else has failed. A chance to safeguard the future of fifteen million people. Abou gritted his teeth and clasped and unclasped his hands to ease his tension. The helmsman cut the engine and the *Aileen Maloney* drifted beneath the iron canopy. On the jetty men sprang forward fore and aft to secure the boat quickly and a big man jumped across to her decks and hurried forward to the deckhouse. The waiting was over.

"Right on time, Liam," the man said, the door only half open. He stopped abruptly, his eyes flicking from face to face, pausing on the man with the carbine before coming to rest on Suzy as she watched him. He was big, taller than Abou and broader, a white seaman's sweater straining across his shoulders and around the massive bulk of his chest. Dark hair was flecked grey and a scar on his cheek showed with a blue tinge to it, the way flesh sometimes heals from a bullet wound. "Well now?" he growled softly. "What's this, a British gun boat?"

"Shouldn't you identify yourself?" Abou asked coldly.

The man opened the door to its full extent and stepped forward, his very bulk threatening everybody in the cabin. "The name's

Reilly. Big Reilly to most – to separate me from Liam," he looked at Suzy. "And you'll be Suzy Katoul," he jerked his head at the commando. "And if you've an ounce of sense you'll tell him to put that thing down – before I wrap it round his bloody neck."

"Reilly?" she saw the resemblance immediately. It was in the eyes. Except that these lacked the amused irony so characteristic of the other face. These were cold and pitiless.

"Where's Liam?" he looked straight through her. "I'm his brother."

"There's been an accident," Abou said, needing to assert himself quickly. "A bad one. We've lost some men and we've a badly injured man below."

"Liam," Big Reilly said, dead-voiced and threatening.

"The cargo shifted," Abou lied in a firm strong voice. "We were turned over by a Customs boat a few miles out. They interfered with the crates. Afterwards one of the stacks collapsed. We thought we'd got it under control, but then another stack fell on top of it. I was below and Liam was helping. By the time I got up one of my men was overboard. I'm not sure what went wrong, it all happened so quickly. More crates toppled – Liam and Pat Brady were round the back – we heard a shout – it was dark – when I got there they were nowhere."

"Nowhere?" Doubt and incredulity were written all over Reilly's face.

"They must have been unconscious when they hit the water," Abou said. "Knocked out by the falling crates. We put a boat down and searched for half an hour," he paused, knowing the worst was said and watching the other man's face for a reaction. "We lost one of our own men as well – and we've another badly injured."

Reilly's eyes went as dead as the last embers of a dying fire. "And you found *nothing*? Liam, falling off the stern of a boat? Liam, who's been at sea all his life?"

"Not falling," Abou corrected. "We think he was knocked overboard by the collapsing cargo – in the dark on a choppy sea in a howling wind. It's all that could have happened, isn't it?"

The "isn't it" was the hook. A test to see if Reilly had swallowed the lie.

"You're telling me Liam's *dead*?" Reilly said.

"We searched," Abou said, and carefully went through the story again.

Listening, Suzy thought he might have been comforting a child. It was his dark brown voice, all soothing and reassuring, the one he used on her when they had argued or after he had beaten her. When he explained it was all for her own good. Oh Christ, why do I feel the way I do about him, she thought.

Abou finished, "We searched for at least half an hour. Three men lost in the space of so many minutes. Three brave men."

"You put a boat down, you say?" Reilly's bleak eyes bored into him. "And Pat Brady, too?" he shook his head like a fighter recovering from a blow. Expressions flickered across his face, comprehension mingled with shock as he paled and the scar on his cheek throbbed a deeper shade of blue. Liam *dead*! Liam *and* Pat Brady! And one of their men? His gaze wandered around the deckhouse, past the radar scanner and the depth sounder to the chart table. A pack of Liam's cigarettes lay open beside the sextant, four remaining from the original twenty. He stared, then reached for one as his other hand fumbled through pockets for a match. He smoked in silence, withdrawn, alone with the memories of a lifetime, while the pungent tobacco smell filled the cabin like incense in a church. Abou began to say something, but Reilly's look chilled him into silence.

The cigarette in Reilly's hand was almost finished when he spoke. He cleared his throat noisily. "Liam left a wife and two kids. And Pat supported a widowed mother. My grief can wait its turn, now's a time to be practical."

Abou needed every ounce of self-control to suppress his excitement, inwardly he shook but no hint of his feelings showed on his face. "We've had a rough trip," he said. "I'm sorry it's you we've had to break the news to, but I'd like you to know we're all in debt to your brother. It was his quick thinking which saved us. The coast-guard would have taken the boat apart if he hadn't convinced them otherwise." He paused, judging the effect of his words and allowing time to lend weight to their meaning. "Debts should always be paid to brave men. Do I make myself clear? We've access to funds and would like to show our gratitude. We'll make proper financial arrangements – you have my word on that."

Reilly's head lifted slowly and he stared at the other men, keen-eyed despite his grief. Abou submitted to the searching inspection without flinching. He sensed Reilly *wanting* to believe and exulted as he watched lingering suspicions begin to fade. Convince this man, he told himself, and there'll be no trouble. Convince him, *convince* him. Aloud he said, "We're all soldiers. We know how tragic it is to lose brave men. But we've the living to answer to now. My men are desperately tired, the man below needs a doctor and your men are in danger so long as this cargo remains out in the open."

Big Reilly straightened. It was right to think of the men, it was as it should be. "Very well," he growled, "we'll talk later. It makes sense to get the cargo out the way. Tell your men to put up their guns Mister, they'll need their hands for other work."

Abou nodded, his grave face showing none of his triumph. He signalled to the men outside while the commando next to him carefully set his carbine down next to the chart table. Big Reilly turned to the door with Abou a pace behind him. The Plan had docked safely in Ireland.

14.00 Wednesday

Ross made a sound like wire scraping tin by scratching the side of his jaw with his gloved left hand. It was artificial of course. Only the thumb and forefinger worked, like a claw, a shiny black skincovered claw. He said, "Okay Archie, where are we at?"

Archie Dorfman stared back across a table still littered with the debris of our lunchtime meal. Beads of perspiration stood out on his forehead and his well-muscled frame would need all the help Spitari's Health Farm could give it in a few years' time. Even in the air-conditioned chill of Ross's office the heat was getting to him. Or maybe Ross was.

"We're nowhere," he answered miserably. "At least we weren't an hour ago."

Swearing softly Ross heaved himself up from his chair and walked to the wall map. He pointed to a dab of blue just out from the English Channel. "The *Marisa* was hit around here, right? About three in the morning. Then it ran like a scalded cat to Cherbourg where it docked at six. LeClerc was there three hours later and had a general alarm out by ten. So the raiders got a seven hour start, right?"

Dorfman still looked unhappy. "That was some boat they had. Forty-five foot, hairy engines, could make twenty-five knots on a calm sea."

"And was it?"

"It wasn't rough."

Ross calculated. "So they could have been two hundred miles away when the balloon went up?"

Dorfman nodded.

"Hell, they still had to cross some of the busiest shipping lanes in the world. Someone must have seen them?"

"We've traced every ship known to have been in the vicinity.

48

Even interviewed some of the crew." Dorfman shrugged. "Not much so far."

"Anything at all?" Ross demanded.

"The description of the launch could have been better," Dorfman grumbled. "Trouble was the *Marisa's* crew were kept well clear of the rails, so nobody's been that specific. But the harbour authorities of seven countries have been circulated with the best possible description. If it shows up almost anywhere in Europe, we'll know about it."

"And?" Ross persisted.

"We're checking all angles," Dorfman sounded as tired as he looked. "Lloyd's Register, coastguard reports, the Royal Navy, yacht clubs, fishermen, marine service yards," he gestured helplessly. "It's a lot of territory, but we're covering it."

"We?"

"Indirectly – we've got cover through the various national narcotics agencies. Story is we're looking for a boatload of cocaine."

Ross returned to the table and slumped into his chair. "You got anything, Paul?"

LeClerc busied himself with the files laid out in front of him. "Suzy Katoul's apartment is under observation. Nobody's been near it in twenty-four hours, no mail, no phone calls, no –"

Ross snorted. "Stable doors. The horse bolted forty-eight hours ago. How's the ident going?"

"Suzy Katoul has been positively identified by the *Marisa's* First Officer and two of the crew."

"And the men? The three in the life-raft?"

LeClerc shook his head. "No positive I.D."

"What about voice prints?"

"They've heard all we've got – nothing so far."

Ross scowled. "So Suzy's working with hired hands. Not known members of any Palestinian organisation."

"Maybe," LeClerc sounded doubtful. "But the voice print library is still limited," he hesitated. "Even the one at Langley."

Ross shifted his gaze to the next man at the table. "Any political noises?"

"Nobody's claimed credit for the heist yet, if that's what you mean," the man said.

"No, that's *not* what I mean," Ross growled. "*That* would be too much to hope for. That would be a positive lead for once," he shook his head. "Anyone been speaking out of turn, shooting his mouth off more than usual?"

49

The man squared a dozen sheets of loose paper into a neat pack before answering. It was characteristic somehow – everything about him was neat. Neat linen shirt under a grey lightweight suit, silk socks worn with suspenders inside black shoes. He had arrived just before the meeting and Ross hadn't introduced him.

"Arafat's in Moscow," he read from the papers, "and hasn't made a public speech in weeks. George Habash is in retreat in Lebanon; Mahamed Achmed is in South America, probably Cuba; Begin is on holiday; Sadat is –"

"Not *where* they are," Ross interrupted. "What they're saying."

"Nobody's saying anything," the neat little man shook his head. "At least not within the last forty-eight hours. Nothing worth reporting anyway."

"Any Russian moves?"

"Not apart from Arafat being in Moscow. But that may not be significant. He's been angling for an invitation for years now. So far it's all low key – as least so far as we know."

Ross frowned and looked out of the window. He was quiet for a moment and then he flicked a wad of typescript with his thumb nail. It was the transcript of my recording session with the doctor. "I've read this," he looked at me. "Only thing missing is Noah's Ark. What the hell are you doing down there – giving a history lesson?"

I nodded at the doctor two places away. "I started where *he* wanted. I can stop just as easily."

Ross and I played our game of staring each other down and the doctor said, "Start half way in these things and you risk missing something."

"Oh?" Ross turned to him. "Well can't we speed it up a bit? You're supposed to be giving me a profile on Suzy Katoul. Knowing her grandfather belched in church isn't going to help."

The doctor was lost for an answer to that, so we adjourned to the studio downstairs. LeClerc shuffled behind the bar and grinned at me from across the mahogany counter. The shelves behind him carried enough booze to stock a night club. In fact, the whole place had that kind of atmosphere. Dim lights with the occasional spot behind potted greenery, the smell of sweat doused in cologne, deep padded chairs and a thick carpet which stopped a foot away from a small stage.

"Drink?" LeClerc upended a glass.

"Only if you take American Express," I hooked myself over a stool and watched the doctor emerge from the shadows. He was still wearing his Harley Street suit and plastic smile. "It's on the house, Mr Brand."

I accepted a scotch and nodded at the platform. "Very intimate. Who's on tonight? A big name or a local tart?"

The doctor contrived to look shocked, which was difficult with a face like his.

Israel, 1948. The birth of a nation. At the time, journalists poured words out by the thousand and since then historians have written fifty times as many. The stink of the gas chambers still fouled the air of Europe and the world's conscience cried out at the fate of the Jews. For many, what happened in '48 was a sequel to the Second World War. To me, even looking back, it was a fragmented nightmare, a sick joke, orchestrated by Lewis Carroll without his marbles, the Maddest Mad Hatter's Tea Party of all. There had been a chance of peace in '47. Slim, but a chance all the same. Something worth hanging on to. But thanks to the apathy of the watching world, the incompetence of politicians, the greed of vested interests and the sheer breathtaking bigotry of a few – the Holy Lands were once again to be plunged into war.

After the U.N. vote, I stayed on at the Imperial for a while, watching the pus bubble up from Palestine's open sores. Arabs attacked Jews, Jews attacked Arabs. There was violence even in Jerusalem as a hundred and five thousand Arabs swapped more than nervous glances with a hundred thousand Jews – all of them living in the shadow of the British guns. And as the rest of us prayed for some more positive U.N. involvement, Christmas came and went and Palestine stumbled into the new year like a drunk in a minefield. Only the lingering presence of the British prevented open warfare – and the British were leaving in May. Friendships which had endured generations strained and then snapped as both communities accepted the inevitability of war.

During those months I saw a lot of the Katouls. Time changed all of them. Nadi aged a year for every passing month, his sons turned militant and Haleem became even more beautiful. She flowered, somehow the tension-charged atmosphere boosted her adrenalin, quickened her step and put a flush to her cheeks. Unlike most Arab women she had always refused to accept a passive role in things, and as the weeks ticked past her political activities increased by leaps and bounds. If the Jews were to have Golda Meir then, it seemed, the Arabs would have Haleem Katoul. Not that Haleem ever joined the extremists – not for her the cry of "we'll drive them into the sea." But she desperately wanted to stay at Katamon and live in the house of her forefathers, in peace with her friends, Arab and Jew alike.

But she struggled in vain. I remember one day in particular. Pierre Moreau and I were driving from the Jewish Agency to the French Consulate, through King George Avenue and Wauchope Street and along Julian's Way. Heavy firing had started and bullets were flying along most of the route, so that the car swerved and zigzagged like a stag outrunning a wolf pack. Even when we reached the Consulate, the atmosphere was heavy with tension. The Truce Commission was in session. The U.N. had sent a Belgian, an American, a Frenchman, a Norwegian and a Spaniard to sort things out. Dodge City might as well have hired a cripple for sheriff. I watched the Frenchman jump up and down while the Belgian twittered and the American pontificated and I remembered Nadi Katoul's sad little question on the night of the vote: "Was the League so successful?" I began to share his doubts. Not that he harboured them for long. Two days later he was dead.

I had gone up to Katamon to visit, guessing the boys would be out but expecting to share a midday meal with Haleem and her father. In a few short weeks the place had become a battleground. The districts on either side were controlled by the Hagganah, and Katamon itself was on a ridge of high ground overlooking the Jewish positions. The strategic importance of the place was so obvious that the Hagganah had adopted a policy of trying to persuade the Arab families to leave, even offering armed escorts for families as they moved through the Jewish quarters to the Arab districts in the north-west of the City. Grimly I wondered what would happen if the persuasion failed. Or if the Hagganah ran out of patience – or even worse, if the Irgun or the Stern Gang took over.

I parked against the villa's high wall and as I climbed out of the car Nadi came down the steps laden with wicker baskets. He embraced me as always and when I asked where he was going he simply replied: "To feed the ducks." He meant the Jews of course. By then Jerusalem was a city of shortages as far as the Jews were concerned. The Arabs controlled most of the surrounding countryside and in spite of the British had begun to lay seige to the Jewish districts in the City. Except that Nadi was waging a one-man crusade to break the seige. No Jewish friend of his would go hungry – not while there was food on his table.

"Take my car," I said. "It's safer." I pointed to the U.N. emblem daubed on the doors, no guarantee of immunity, but it improved the odds slightly.

He shook his head, smiling up at the warm skies. "A day like today? The walk will do me good. Go, Haleem waits for you."

So I went – and behind the cedar-wood door his daughter melted into my arms as I kissed her. It had been like that between us for weeks. God knows what sparked it off – maybe the whiff of cordite in the air or the ever-growing feeling that life was precious and short. Or perhaps the realisation that the only relief from a harsh world was to be found in the love which men and women sometimes share with one another. I don't remember either of us saying much that day. We just sat down and devoured each other with our eyes, holding hands and smiling with the trance-like contentment of people in love. And then the explosion rattled the shutters and tinkled the chandeliers, and white flakes of plaster showered all over us.

I had opened the door and was down the steps before she even as much as moved. What sixth sense told me it was Nadi I never knew, but the scene outside confirmed it. Fifty yards away a car lay on one side, wheels still spinning and flames belching so fiercely from its underside that it would be gutted in minutes. Nadi knelt in the roadway nearby, cradling a man in his arms. Even from that distance I could see blood on the man's face and the dark red stains on his shirtfront. One of Nadi's wicker baskets rolled in the dust and a dog ran away, its barking suddenly drowned by a burst of rifle fire. Hemeh, Nadi's eldest son, rounded the far corner, running and half turning at the same time, scuttling like a crab, his attention fixed behind him. He carried one of those old Lee Enfield rifles in one hand and a bandolier of cartridges bounced on his shoulder. Nadi saw him in the same split second as I did and shouted something, but the words lost themselves in the breeze. Hemeh called back, something about getting off the streets I think, but I missed most of it.

By this time I had reached my car and was starting the engine – it was the quickest way to get to them. After that it all happened so quickly. I glimpsed men on the rooftops, half seen from the corner of my eye as I shoved the car into gear; just two or three shadows moving quickly. Then the crack and splutter of gun fire. Hemeh was lifted a foot in the air and sent spinning backwards. Nadi was up and running towards him. Then he too was caught in the hail of bullets, sudden blotches of red perforating his shoulders to throw him face down in the dust. I slewed the car across the road with some crazy notion of putting it between Nadi and the line of fire from the rooftops, but I need never have bothered. Hemeh was dead when I got there and Nadi was dying fast. I propped him up, hugging him in the wild hope of trying to save him. But my first glance had been right. At least three bullets had passed through his chest and blood pumped out in gushes. Just once he looked at me, a moment's flickering recognition in his fading eyes. "Haleem – and Negib." It was all he said. I nodded and promised to take care of them and his eyes brightened, but then went so dim he might have been blind. He tried to smile, but blood spurted from his lips like vomit. Then, thankfully, he was gone.

Haleem ran all the way. She either stumbled or threw herself into the dust beside me, her arms reaching for her dead father, cradling his shattered body against her breast. I watched some of his blood transfer itself to her white blouse and felt my heart break at her sobbing. Doors opened up and down the street and people scurried to help. I looked up at the rooftops, deserted now, just empty parapets, so much white stone against a cloudless blue sky. The *incident* was over. It had lasted all of two minutes – three at the most.

I suppose I took over that afternoon. I remember carrying Nadi's frail body back to his villa. Every step of that fifty yard walk is etched in my memory. Neighbours carried Hemeh between them while others supported Haleem and tried to comfort her. Relatives were fetched from far and wide and half an hour later Haleem's younger brother Negib returned from some guard post or other. He was seventeen then, big and strong, an uncomplicated boy whose proudest possession was his black moustache which had taken six months to grow. Helplessly I watched his solemn eyes fill with tears and his body shake with grief. But not all were so quiet, and the villa groaned with wails of grief for hours afterwards.

By evening most of the mourners had returned to their homes and families. The men were needed on and off during the night to stand their turn on guard duty. I forget who suggested I stay the night, but I suppose it was logical enough. Someone had to watch over the bereaved and I was the only non-combatant. So eventually I closed the door after the last of them and let the silence of the house close over me. Haleem and Negib had retired to darkened rooms to nurse their personal miseries, and the bodies of Nadi and Hemeh lay in state in the next room, washed and cleaned and ready for the funeral in the morning.

By ten I had finished the whisky Nadi would have offered me had he been able to and, feeling drained and worn out with the hope-lessness of it all, I went up to bed. Crossing the landing outside Haleem's door I hesitated, drawn by the sound of her weeping. There was so much pain and loneliness in those sobs, so much suffering and sorrow, like a child's misery, defenceless and hurt, vulnerable and alone. I *had* to comfort her. She was face down on the bed, still in her bloodstained clothes. I bathed her face and stroked her hair and held her. Words would have been an intrusion even if I had trusted myself to speak. So I held her and let her cling to me. She cried for a long time, but gradually her sobs became inters-persed with long periods of silence. At one time I thought she had fallen asleep, and I began to ease from the bed, but her arms gripped me with all the urgency of somebody drowning. It was as if she was scared to lose contact, or perhaps she was just terrified of facing the hours of darkness alone. So I stayed.

When I awoke, pale shadows were squeezing under the shutters and Haleem was moving gently in my arms. Her blouse had come undone and my hand was inside the silk, cupping her breast and feeling her trembling response. There was no plan to it – no seduc-tion – no conquest. Just an overwhelming sense of relief as our hands removed clothes and our bodies joined our minds in a state of union.

Was that blasphemy? Was that disrespect for my dead friend and his murdered son? To make love together on her bed, in his house, for the one and only time in our lives. Was it wrong to seek release from the agonising terrors of those last few hours? I've asked myself a hundred times, but never have I believed that one single act deserved such terrible consequences.

Neither of us heard the door swing open. There was no sound, no movement other than those we made ourselves. Just a growing light flooding in from the open door. Haleem stirred under me, her legs splayed, our bodies still moist, hearts pounding and my chest heavy on her breast. And Negib stood framed in the opening, his face contorted with misery.

"Whore!" he screamed. "Fucking British whore!"

I can hear him now. Full of outraged suffering. His father and brother killed and now *this* – the final betrayal. He threw himself at us, punching and kicking, wanting to hurt her every bit as much as me. I *had* to stop him. Not to harm him, God knows he'd been hurt enough, but just to *stop* him. Otherwise he would have gouged her eyes out. It was a nightmare, wrestling with Negib, trying to calm him, Haleem weeping in the background with a sheet hurriedly pulled from the bed to cover her nakedness. Finally he threw me to the floor and stormed from the room and out of the villa. But not before he had ripped the cover from her trembling hands and spat at her. She stood shaking like a leaf, weeping, his spit running down the side of her face as the front door crashed shut behind him.

Negib missed the funeral. There were questions of course, and dark looks, and afterwards the uncles moved one of their number into Nadi's villa, so I was free to return to the hotel. I felt disgraced and sick and baffled, and my mind was spinning because so much had happened so quickly. But Haleem *wanted* me to leave, I sensed it, so I went.

Back at the Imperial I concentrated on getting drunk. I would have succeeded too – but for the Jews. A Jew in the bar at the Imperial was a rarity, but two of them joined me as soon as I got there. I told them to shove off, leave me alone, let me drown myself in whisky. But no matter how I insulted them they stayed their ground, all the time talking quietly and gently of Nadi. Other Jews joined them, all come to praise their dead friend. A steady procession, Jew after Jew. They gave me the words they were afraid to give to his family for fear they would be shot down by the extremists – Arab extremists *or* Jewish extremists, Arab *and* Jewish extremists. It was the Jews who put me to bed in the end, because despite their entreaties I had put away more than a bottle of Johnny Walker. They got me to my room and helped get my clothes off. Then I fell asleep, to dream of Haleem and Nadi, Hemeh and Negib – and the whole sorry mess that was Palestine.

3

THE THIRD DAY

"Politicians are the same all over. They
promise to build a bridge even where
there is no river."

Nikita Khrushchev, comment to reporters,
Glen Cove, N.Y., October 1960

07.00 Thursday

Liam Reilly had forgotten to mention the rain. But it had rained all
night and as dawn lit the creek with a flickering light it was still
raining. She stood at the window and watched enough shadow lift
to reveal the fishermen's cottages on either side, single-storey buildings with high-pitched roofs and ghostly white faces looking down
to the boathouses.

She shivered suddenly and wondered why? True she was quite
naked but the room was warm, peat still smouldered in the hearth,
whisps of smoke still floated up the chimney. Perhaps it was Ireland? Perhaps it always rained here? Twenty-four hours and every
minute raining. Perhaps it was last minute nerves? They were so
close now, so near the end of the road. Two years she had waited for
this. Her chance to free an entire people – her chance to avenge the
Catastrophe – to return to the Palestinians that land stolen by the
Jews. Listening and watching and learning as Abou had put the Plan
together. She glanced to the bed where he lay sleeping. He was two
people she thought – three really. Abou her lover who could make
an animal of her whenever he chose, who made her crave the things
he did to her and made her do in return. And then Abou the planner
– the cold remote man who had listened to her dreams for the
restoration of Palestine and given her the means to bring about a
miracle. One single act that would make the world gasp at its
audacity.

She smiled as she imagined her triumph. It was the prospect of *that* which made her shiver. To succeed where so many had failed. To create unity while others squabbled. The bitterness between Arafat and George Habash, the ineffectiveness of the Palestinian Communist Party, the futile P.F.L.P. killings, the endless accommodations offered by Sadat. And above all the never-ending whining of the *mullahs* who wanted nothing more than to turn the clock back to an Islamic Brotherhood. And all the time Arab fighting Arab as the Jew stood back and laughed.

Abou stirred and rolled over on his back. She thought about the third Abou, the even more shadowy Abou, the almost invisible Abou. Abou the non-Arab, Abou the agent of a foreign power, Abou who would rip her tongue from its roots if ever he thought she would betray the little she knew. Oh, cruel, cunning, vicious, wonderful Abou – as if I *ever* would?

A sudden commotion outside the door spun her round and the guard's shouted warning was drowned by Reilly's throaty bellow as the door burst open and the big man's bulk filled the entrance.

His eyes focused on her body silhouetted against the grey morning light. "Well now? And isn't that a fine sight to start the day with?" His gaze flicked sideways to where Abou reached under his pillow. "Leave that, Mister, if you know what's good for you." Abou froze. Reilly looked back to the girl at the window. His lips curled as his eyes explored her body. "And they call you a terrorist? What do you do to them my pretty puss – screw them to death?"

She fought the urge to cover herself and stifled her angry words. Instinct overcame fear, or perhaps merged with it, so that she shifted her weight, slowly and deliberately, moving her feet a yard apart and turning to face him squarely.

"Sometimes," she said, smiling. "When they're man enough." Even in that poor light she saw his eyes widen. She laughed. "Well, Big Reilly – did you just come to look or are you man enough to touch?"

She heard the sharp intake of breath and in the same split second saw the gun in Abou's hand.

"Cassidy's been taken," Big Reilly ignored the gun. "At two this morning."

"Taken?" Abou shifted his weight onto one elbow, the revolver still in his hand.

"By the police. They've got him in the Holy Cross Jail."

"Will he talk?"

"No," Reilly growled with more conviction than he felt. "Anyway, it's next to nothing he knows."

58

But it was the *next to nothing* that worried Abou. "Why Cassidy? Are they on to us?"

"Impossible. It's routine harassment. He's arrested on suspicion that's all."

"Suspicion of what?"

"Of sympathising with the movement – of being one of us." Reilly's huge shoulders rose in a shrug. "Police intimidation, that's what it is. They've been this way ever since Ewart Biggs got his. It's the Dail's way of humouring Westminster."

"Will they hold him?" Abou asked.

"Maybe. They could do – under the new regulations – anything up to fourteen days."

"Fourteen days!" Suzy was halfway into her robe. "But we need him on Saturday."

"And isn't that what I came to tell you," Reilly snapped. "I'm away to Cork now to find a replacement. And that'll not be easy. Not with him their most trusted driver."

"But is it *possible*?" Suzy asked.

"We made a bargain didn't we?" Reilly said angrily. "The guns you've delivered are no damn good without the –"

"You'll get the ammunition," Abou cut in. "When we get our driver – and his lorry."

The girl watched the two men stare at each other with open hostility. Big Reilly still nursed a suspicion or two about his brother's death. That was obvious. But what good were suspicions when Reilly only ranked as a local commander and had to take orders from Dublin? And Dublin said to co-operate. Abou had seen to that.

"So we'll send our cargo to Pallas Glean today," Abou said, "as arranged."

"Reckon so," Reilly nodded. "The truck will load up in an hour's time. Four of your men travel in the back – the rest wait here, indoors and out of sight, until I get back."

"And when will that be?" Suzy asked, the robe gaping open as she moved to the bed.

"Tonight some time," Reilly eyed her carefully.

She let the robe slip from her shoulders and stood facing him. "Well," she smiled, "we'll see you then. And if you could *knock* next time – I'd be grateful."

Reilly left the room, scowling furiously and slamming the door to drown her mocking laughter. Abou pulled the girl down on top of him, gasping with pain and pleasure as her hands reached under the sheets to cover his body. Minutes later he was delighting in the only pleasure he allowed himself since meeting her. The pleasure of making her body respond to his wishes. But even in those moments of mounting ecstasy, one part of his body remained aloof. That part of his mind which was ever the Plan. Even as he entered her, his thoughts were miles away – at a Health Farm on an island in the Mediterranean. Then Suzy's desires demanded all of his concentration and for a while he gave it to her.

10.30 Thursday

Ross was very angry. I had seen him throw tantrums before, but they were giggling fits compared to this. His face fairly tensed with fury and a line of spittle edged his lower lip. He thumped the desk with his tin fist, so that the coffee cups tinkled with fright and the ash rearranged itself in the ash-tray. I wondered if he knew he was foaming at the mouth.

"It came this morning," he snapped. "In the ordinary mail – two hours ago."

I looked at the letter on the other side of the desk. More than a letter really, a couple of dozen sheets of A4 creased once down their length the way lawyers fold writs. The envelope next to it was heavyweight manilla and I could see Ross's name and Spitari's address scrawled across it in green ink. The writing looked vaguely familiar, but I was the wrong side of the desk to see it properly.

Ross was still boiling. "Addressed to *me*! Here!"

"That would explain it," I said.

Elizabeth walked behind his chair and began massaging his shoulders. She stared at me reproachfully from above his head, and my eyes bobbed like cork floats, choosing whose face to focus on. They chose Elizabeth's because she was prettier.

Ross said, "We've been penetrated."

I leered at Elizabeth and said, "I bet," but she didn't even blush.

"It's from her," Ross said.

"Her?" I said absently. Elizabeth's eyes fascinated me. They really were the greenest eyes I had ever seen. Liquid pools of green. A man could drown in them. If he broke the ice first.

"That bitch of a goddaughter of yours!"

"Suzy?" I snapped out of it. It was after ten in the morning and the three of us were alone in Ross's office. I had slept late after being dragged up and down memory lane for half the night by LeClerc and the doctor. "You've *heard* from Suzy?"

"I just said so, didn't I?"

"Is she all right?"

"She didn't say," he said drily. "It wasn't a postcard wishing I was there."

"Where's there?"

"Libya. Post-marked Tripoli, yesterday morning." He pulled a face to show his disgust. "Gaddafi country – wouldn't it just *have* to be?"

I was still frowning, trying to make sense of it. Not that Suzy in Libya was any more surprising than me in Malta really. The whole thing had me punchdrunk.

"One mad dog," Ross growled. "That's all it needs. And they don't come madder than Gaddafi." He seemed a shade calmer, the result of Elizabeth's soothing touch no doubt. I wished she would have a go at me, my nerve ends were like frayed shirt cuffs. Ross cupped his head in his hands and squeezed flesh into his eyesockets until he looked like Confucius. "I'll tell you a story about Gaddafi," he said. "It happened back in '73. Israel was twenty-five years old and throwing a party, so five hundred British and American Jews boarded the Q.E.2. and sailed to Haifa to celebrate. Remember?"

"Yes." I could even guess which story he was going to tell me.

"The papers were full of it," he jeered. "Remember the headlines? Bomb scare aboard Q.E.2. Well, we swept that boat cleaner than a Hilton hotel room and found nothing. So the trip went ahead. Everyone had a ball in Haifa, returned to Southampton, wished each other *mazel tov* and went on their way. The real story didn't leak out till later." He took a long pull on his orange juice. "How two submarines seconded to the Libyan Navy tracked the cruise ship all the way from Gib. Submarines with enough torpedo power to sink Cunard's ship twice over – skippered by Egyptians but under the direct command of Gaddafi. It was Gaddafi who ordered them to sink the Q.E.2." He laughed. "Can you *imagine* those submarine commanders? Anyway, they signalled Base for confirmation and Sadat did his number – told them to get the hell out of there and get back to harbour." He scowled, shaking his head from side to side. "Could have been another Titanic – even worse – could have started another war."

I nodded. "Sadat told the story himself, later – when he fell out with Gaddafi."

"Gaddafi," Ross echoed in disgust.

"And he's involved with Suzy?"

"He runs Libya, doesn't he? And this Suzy Katoul dame writes from there. To this place. Using *my* name!"

"Well, you *are* an interested party."

"Smart ass!" he growled, but his heart wasn't in it. He was too busy worrying about his security leak. He sighed. "Hell, we were bound to close this place down soon anyway. Next year probably, when the Brits pull out," he shrugged. "Gaddafi will probably take Malta over anyway, unless Mintoff raises the money in Europe. Turn the whole damned island into some crazy Arab Disneyland – no booze anywhere, but kebabs on sticks at every street corner."

"Suzy," I reminded him. If Mintoff threw the British out and faced a twenty-eight million pound budget deficit because of it, that was his problem. Suzy Katoul was mine. "What did she say?"

"Suzy," he mimicked, "will let us know her next move in twenty-four hours."

The door opened and LeClerc entered with less noise than a cat. He sat on a sofa and watched us.

"Anything?" Ross asked him.

"We've got three men touring the Tripoli waterfront. So far they've seen nothing like the launch we're looking for." He watched the scowl darken on Ross's face and tried to lighten the gloom by adding, "but they've only had an hour – there's still hope."

Ross winced. "Hope? What are you – some kind of salvationist?"

LeClerc inspected his fingernails.

"Any political noises?"

LeClerc shook his head. "None so far."

Ross stared into space. "I suppose our masters have been informed?"

"Half an hour ago," LeClerc mumbled. "Simultaneous transmissions. Washington, London, Bonn and Paris."

Ross held his head in his hands. "Jesus. Now the shit really hits the fan."

"It's the rules," LeClerc apologised. "You know standing orders say –"

"I know standing orders by bloody heart!" Ross bit his head off. I was beginning to feel sorry for LeClerc which was something of a miracle considering the hours he kept me in front of those microphones.

I nodded at the sheaf of papers in front of Ross. "Is that *all* Suzy said? All that paper just to say that?"

"No. This little note says that." Ross tapped what looked like a compliment slip pinned to the top sheet. "The rest says something entirely different."

"May I see?"

"Why not?" He unclipped the compliments slip and tossed the rest of the papers to my side of the desk. "Forensics have been all over it. You can't damage anything."

I braced myself as I unfolded the sheets of paper. But the anticipated shock turned to surprise as I tried to read them. Sheet after sheet was covered with equations and what looked like scientific formulae. But I recognised Cyrillic characters when I saw them.

"Want to know what it says?" Ross asked in a flat, dead voice. "It's full instructions on how to convert plutonium to fissionable material. A do-it-yourself kit. How to make your own atomic bomb in five easy lessons."

The moment of truth, I suppose. All along I had told myself that it couldn't happen. That whatever Suzy's politics – whatever, whoever she had become – she wouldn't contemplate this – this mass murder. Ross sat watching me with Elizabeth motionless at his side. I suppose they expected some reaction, but I could think of nothing to say – nothing constructive anyway.

After a long pause Ross said, "The technology's perfect, according to the Atomic Weapons Research Establishment boys – within two years of current work."

"But written in Russian?" I said, baffled.

"What do you expect, Arabic?"

"But what did Suzy's note say? Are you *sure* it's her?"

Ross sneered and handed me the compliments slip. I would have known Suzy's scrawl anywhere. She had written – "We hold the cargo from the *Marisa*. Our ultimatum will be communicated to you within the next twenty-four hours." And it was signed simply "Suzy Katoul – the Deir Yassin Memorial".

"Deir Yassin Memorial," Ross growled. "One of the oldest tricks in the book. Arafat's pulled it a dozen times. Form a sub-group with some fancy title, commit some mindless atrocity and then claim it has nothing to do with the P.L.O. I can list dozens of them – Black September, the Eleventh day –" he stopped in mid-sentence. "You okay?"

I must have gone white or shown something in my expression, because Ross stopped in full flight. Thirty-year-old memories revived with such searing clarity that I felt sick. Sick to the pit of my stomach. Deir Yassin! After all these years. Suzy still remembered! My voice shook as I answered. "Yes, I'm okay. It's just that it reminded me of something, that's all."

"Yeah?" Ross extracted a wad of paper from his "in" tray. "Well, that reminds *me*." His thumbnail flicked through the pages of the transcript of my last session in the studio. "Don't get me wrong Harry. I like it. I can't wait to see the film." His sarcasm gave way to temper as his face flushed. "But we've only got another twenty-four hours for Chrissakes!"

The door opened and the doctor arrived to collect me. LeClerc had already risen from his chair and shuffled from foot to foot as he waited. Arguing seemed pointless, so I just allowed them to lead me away.

"He's a bit strung up this morning," LeClerc explained in the corridor.

"I know," I nodded. "He's all heart underneath."

And LeClerc seemed pleased to meet someone who made allowances.

We had been in the studio for an hour. For some reason I was sitting up on the stage with the three of them grouped in a semi-circle facing me, Elizabeth in the centre and the doctor and LeClerc on either side of her. The lights were dimmed as usual, so although I could see Elizabeth clearly, the others were partly in shadow and when they spoke their voices seemed strangely remote and disembodied. It was becoming a bit of an inquisition and the strain of answering their questions began to tell on me.

"Nadi's relatives," the doctor was asking. "His brothers and cousins who attended the funeral. Would you recognise them?"

"After thirty years? For God's sake be reasonable. Even the youngest brother would be an old man now – if he lived through it."

"Yes, of course," he humoured me. "But we'll show you some photographs later, just in case."

"So what happened the next day?" LeClerc wanted to know. "After the funeral?"

"After the funeral was over," I echoed. It sounded like an old music hall song. Odd word, funeral. To have a *funeral* right at the beginning of a war, when so many others were destined to die.

It was three days before I returned to Katamon. Why three I can't remember. I think I hoped Haleem would contact me when she recovered enough strength to come to terms with the living. But not hearing from her I went to seek her out. Getting into Katamon had become a problem. With only a month or so left of their Mandate, the British were struggling desperately to keep Arab and Jew apart. A cordon had been flung round the entire area and the British troops were stopping everybody, examining papers, conducting body searches, even stripping the seats from cars in an unending search for arms. It meant waiting hours in the sticky heat and arguing about the reason for my visit with some snotty-nosed officer, who complained that journalists were a bloody nuisance, forever getting in the way. And all the while Arabs flowed out of the district, their belongings heaped onto carts or in the back of lorries for those lucky enough to scrounge petrol. A long steady stream of people, their eyes averted, women crying, children protesting, the men sullen and bitter. Finally it was my turn to go the other way, and I was allowed to walk up the hill, while a Lance Corporal drove my car to Bevingrad for safe keeping.

I think I was afraid. Negib was certainly armed and had wanted to kill me three days earlier. I climbed the hill, my gaze constantly straying to the rooftops, expecting every minute to see his outline dark against the sun, so that by the time I turned into their row of villas I was bathed in sweat, not all of which was from the heat of the day. Up the steps to knock on the cedar-wood door, bracing myself to meet Negib, preparing to face his anger and bunching my fists in case of attack. But nobody answered. I knocked again and waited. And again. Then I sensed someone watching me and I heard the scuffle of feet behind me. I swung round, expecting Negib, my fists rising to protect myself. But the man standing just inside the gate was a stranger. Beyond him, next to an ox-cart overloaded with possessions, stood an old woman, her dark eyes watching me carefully.

"Excuse me," the man said in English. "But they are gone."

"Gone?"

He nodded.

"But where? I mean, when will they be back?"

He shook his head, and then cautiously, in case I was a police spy, he asked, "You *know* the family?"

"Yes, we're friends."

Doubt and suspicion hardened his expression. He was sorry to have involved himself now, I could see that. He half turned away to where his wife waited patiently at the gate.

"I was here the other day," I said urgently. "The day – the day Nadi and Hemeh were killed."

"Ah! You are *that* Englishman." Suspicion vanished and he almost nodded with approval. I breathed a sigh of relief, until he said, "Haleem left yesterday with her uncle."

65

"Uncle? Which uncle? Left for where?"

"Who knows?" he shrugged. "Perhaps for somewhere in the city, perhaps –"

"Perhaps?"

Still shrugging and shaking his head he said, "Forgive me, but truly I do not know."

I pressed him, desperate now, my panic so strong that it was all I could do not to shake him. Finally he said, "It is the truth. I do not know where she went, but her uncle was not of Jerusalem. A man of the villages, a *mukter* perhaps?"

It meant nothing to me. "Which village? Where?"

But his gaze had turned inwards like a blind man's. We walked to the gate, me keeping pace at his side. Some money found its way into my hand as I pleaded with him, but he shrugged me off, the way I turned beggars aside. The ox-cart lumbered into movement and they were away, the woman's black skirts sweeping the dust as she followed the cart. Out of sheer desperation I tried the door again. Haleem *gone*? I couldn't believe it. That she might leave Katamon was understandable – but to go somewhere and not tell me? To *avoid* telling me? We had shared something – an understanding – some sense of a future together – unspoken perhaps, but real for all that. And I was still asking myself questions when the woman returned.

"Haleem," she said urgently, out of breath and speaking in no more than a whisper.

"Haleem – yes?"

She eyed the money still in my hand until I thrust it at her. A claw clutched the notes and withdrew into the black folds of her shroud. "Haleem in the hills. To the west of the city."

"West? How far west? Which village?"

But she didn't know. She turned and scuttled away. There seemed no point in chasing her, both she and the old man had told me all they knew, I felt sure of it. I tried the door again, but of course there was no answer and after a while I went back down the hill. Funny, but on the way back I never once looked for Negib on the rooftops. It was not until afterwards – when my brain got into gear again – that I realised neither of them had mentioned Negib. For all I knew he was still in Jerusalem.

Elizabeth watched me closely. Even in the gloom of the studio it was impossible to remain unaware of her eyes. They watched without blinking, as green and as still as a cat's.

"I never saw Haleem again," I said.

The doctor snickered with laughter. "Ships that pass in the night, eh, Mr Brand? A bit on the side with a nice little wog girl and –"

It was as far as he got. I was out of the chair without knowing it, my left hand at his throat as my right measured the punch. But LeClerc moved as swiftly, looping his arms around mine in a bear hug. For a split second we remained like that, the doctor swaying backwards out of reach and LeClerc on my back like a limpet. Then Elizabeth's voice cracked like ice on a pond. "That's enough! You'll apologise for that remark, doctor. At once!"

His eyes never strayed from my face. Nervous eyes, full of surprise. "Of course," he said. "Figure of speech that's all. No harm in it."

I glowered, not believing a word, detesting him. Even Ross was better. Ross was as blunt as a five pound hammer, but you knew where you stood with him, whereas the doctor made my flesh crawl.

"It's all right," I hissed. "I was just going to get a drink. That is, if they're *still* on the house."

"Paul," Elizabeth said.

LeClerc unwrapped himself and went to the bar, while I flopped back into my chair and looked at Elizabeth. For an *assistant*, she pulled rank with an astonishing sureness. She looked back at me, cool, unsmiling, and very much in control. "But you *searched* for Haleem," she said, "didn't you Harry?"

Searched? Hell, that was a joke. Jerusalem was a bloody mess. Under seige with no proper communications with the outside world, reporters bribing stray politicians to smuggle copy out and facing a bullet round every corner. Searched? Yes, I searched – I asked *everybody*! Most of the press boys knew her anyway, and they helped. Someone thought he'd seen her in Jaffa, but I hoped he was wrong. The Irgun had bombed the hell out of Jaffa for three days solid, until on the fourth those Arabs still alive had panicked and fled. They were the first I think – the very first Palestinian refugees. Yes, I searched all right – and I listened to the bar gossip and the rumours, the British statements all stiff upper lip, U.N. Press Handouts so much waffle, the Americans changing position faster than a high-class whore. And then on April 9th came Deir Yassin. My blood ran cold when I heard about it.

Not many lived through the massacre, but a few witnesses survived to tell a tale of unparalleled savagery. Entire families – women and children and babes in arms – were dragged from their homes and murdered in barbarous ways. The stomach of a pregnant woman was ripped open with a butcher's knife. Jewellery was torn from the throats of women and young girls – then they were raped – then they were killed. The slaughter was still in progress when Jacques de Reynier led the first Red Cross column into the village.

Deir Yassin – a village to the west of Jerusalem – attacked by the combined forces of the Irgun and the Stern Gang. More than two hundred and fifty Arabs were murdered – most of them women and children or the elderly – and most of them brutally. When the Hagganah arrived, the Commander was so sickened by the sight that he refused to let his young Jewish soldiers enter the village, and when *his* commander arrived there was even talk of shooting the killers. Jew had killed Arab, now would Jew kill Jew? But instead the Hagganah rounded up the terrorists and made them clean the village. They carried the mutilated bodies down to Deir Yassin's rock quarry and laid them on the stones. And when they had finished, they poured petrol over them and set them ablaze.

It was a lovely spring day. The blue skies were warm, birds sang, the almond trees were in blossom, the flowers were out – and everywhere there was this stench of the dead, the thick smell of blood, the terrible odour of corpses burning in the quarry.

"The Deir Yassin Memorial," Elizabeth said slowly. "Thirty years later." She sat forward in her chair, knees tight together, hands clasped in her lap, an expression of total concentration on her face. "Is that what this is all about? Revenge?"

LeClerc snorted. "Revenge against whom for God's sake? The entire state of Israel because of a single atrocity thirty years ago? Almost every Jew in Palestine condemned Deir Yassin."

"But it happened," Elizabeth said thoughtfully. "An atrocity that went unpunished. Is that what we're up against Harry? Are the Arabs now going to claim *their* Nazi war criminals?"

"I don't know." I shook my head. "But as far as Suzy's concerned it's more personal than that – at least I imagine *she* thinks so."

Maybe the tiredness and strain sounded in my voice, and some of the sadness too, because Elizabeth looked at me shrewdly. "And I guess it's more personal for you too, isn't it? What *did* happen to Haleem Katoul, Harry?"

It was years before I found out. 1957, the year after the Suez fiasco. The Middle East was playing the Big Game in earnest then. Civil war threatened in Lebanon, so the Sixth Fleet landed nine thousand marines in Beirut. "Invasion," screamed the Russians to the United Nations. "Mutual defence pact," answered the Yanks. Britain sent the paras in to prop Hussein up in Jordan. Nasser was arming Egypt with Russian tanks. Israel bought new French fighters and shiny British guns with good old-fashioned American dollars. And the C.I.A. finally shoved Mossedeque from power in Iran and put the Shah there in his stead.

The funny thing was that there was all this brave talk about *self determination*, but it was all guff. Small states everywhere were manipulated by larger ones in a never-ending game of chess – and the cheapest pawns on the board were the Palestinian refugees. They were all over the place. Half a million in Jordan, thousands in the Lebanon, thousands more in Syria and Egypt – and shanty villages by the mile along the Gaza strip. More than one and a half million refugees. Conditions in the camps were appalling – over-crowded, insanitary, disease-ridden – the sheer stench of some of them was enough to take your breath away. People died in those camps and entire families conspired to keep the death a secret from the officials, because to reveal it meant the loss of a precious ration book. There were always a few doctors of course, working them-selves to the bone, stamping out one epidemic before drawing breath to start on another one. But it was a hopeless task. There was no work for the men and no pride of home for the women, so whole tracts of land became breeding grounds for resistance groups, whose bitterness boiled over with the passing years as the world forgot about them. By the late fifties they had ceased to be news altogether, though now and then, when I was looking for a filler piece, I would visit a camp and write about them. Which was how I came to meet Negib Katoul – after a gap of nine years.

It was Beirut in '57. I was staying at the Hotel Normandy on the seafront at Ras Beirut. The bar was quite large and cool, and as far as meeting anyone was concerned it was about as discreet as anywhere in Beirut. Arabs were admitted in any state of scruffiness and I remember a side door which opened directly onto the street for those who wished to avoid someone in a hurry. It was a sort of journalist's gossip shop. Everyone knew everyone else and for those who wanted to yarn about Middle East politics it was the best place in town. Kim Philby was always there. By then he had sur-vived his "third man" inquest and had arrived the year before,

69

complete with a new cover job as correspondent for *The Observer* and *The Economist*. I never knew him well, but most of the boys did – probably because he was always buying the drinks.

On that particular day I had been to two camps in the south and arrived back at the Normandy with a splitting headache. Nothing would induce me to involve myself with the crowd at the bar, no matter how amusing they might be; all I wanted was a shower and an early night, so I went straight to my room – and Negib was sitting on my bed, pointing a revolver at me.

"Come in Harry, and don't make a sound."

There was no escape. I had as good as closed the door and anyway he was only a couple of yards away. "It's been a long time," I said, once I had recovered from the shock. I was nervous and I turned my back on him to pour a drink, the coward's way of facing a gun. "I looked for you, you know."

"I heard. I looked for you too – for a while," he said. I turned round and indicated the bottle. But he shook his head, half smiling, the gun still pointing at my chest. "It's against my religion," he said.

That surprised me. "You used to be a Christian. You changed?"

"A lot's changed, Harry – an awful lot. But as you say, it's been a long time."

I thought that he sounded tired, more tired than angry, despite the gun. I sat in the only chair and swallowed some whisky, trying to think of something to say. "I've been to the camps today."

"I know. I saw you."

Another surprise. "You *saw* me? But you're not on the register. I looked, I always look."

He laughed. It was a dry rattle of a sound, quite without humour. "No, I'm not a resident. But that's the trouble, isn't it? I'm not a resident anywhere since the Jews stole my country." His eyes flashed with a warning of temper. Right at that moment I think it could have gone either way. Something told me that he hadn't come to kill me, but a careless word might spark off feelings beyond his control. I finished my drink and sat looking at him, wondering what he was going to do.

He sneered. "So you've seen the camps today. What now?"

"I'll write about them and the paper will run it or spike it – according to how they feel."

"And you're satisfied with that?"

"You're not – I can see that." I turned my back on him to replenish my drink. I was screwing up courage to ask the question which burned in my mind above all else, and not too proud to take courage

70

from the bottle if it helped, not with a gun pointing at me. "Negib," I faced him, phrasing the question a dozen different ways in my mind before blurting out, "Haleem? Do you know where she is?"

For a split second I was sure he would kill me. His mouth tightened and his dark eyes blazed in his face. All the time the gun stayed steady in his hand and I wondered what the hell he wanted from me? Remorse, guilt, fear? Then I saw the pain creep into his expression and I *knew* that Haleem was dead, even before he told me.

"It was years ago," he began quietly. "In the Catastrophe. My uncle was taking her to Bet Hakerem, I think. I was in the hills with some of the others – we were making our way there separately. But it went badly for us and we got held up – we never made it – not in time anyway. My uncle and Haleem were also delayed and they stayed overnight with relations. At *Deir Yassin!*" His voice flared with sudden temper. "And everyone in Palestine knows what happened there, don't they? The whole rotten world should know. Why don't you write *that* in your filthy capitalist press Harry? Or would they spike that too?"

I was too shaken to answer, but enough of what I felt must have shown on my face. If he had come to inflict pain then he had succeeded. He knew it too I think, because a moment later he slipped the revolver into his pocket and just sat there, finishing the story.

"We were in the hills for months. Raiding the Jewish convoys on the roads and trying to stop the flood of refugees. But it was hopeless. After a while we fell back to Lydda on the Syrian border, hoping we'd meet Arab troops on the way, but there was nothing, no troops anyway, just thousands of refugees. The U.N. had got some kind of ceasefire going which helped while it lasted, but on July 9th the truce ended and an hour afterwards the Jews stormed the town. Loudspeaker vans toured the streets, ordering all Arabs to leave within half an hour. *Leave?* Go where, we asked? Anyway Lydda was in the Arab sector according to the U.N. We were *supposed* to be there. The town was full of thousands of our people, sheltering in doorways, alleys, on the steps of mosques – women and children – thousands and thousands of people, but no bloody U.N. Just Jews armed to the teeth with grenades and rifles and machine guns. Some of our men started to fight, but by then we'd nothing left to fight with – and the Jews quickly rounded them up and drove them away in trucks. We never saw them again. After that it was just one mad panic. Fleeing across open country in the burning heat to the nearest Arab village across the border. Ten miles

71

it was – ten miles of running – harassed by mortar fire as we ran – weaving and ducking, scrambling for whatever cover we could find amidst the bare rocks – women screaming, children petrified, the elderly dropping like flies."

He accepted a cigarette without even looking at me. At that moment he was so gripped by his memories I might not have existed. "Thirty thousand were driven out of Lydda that day – and it was the same all along the Syrian border. The Catastrophe doesn't begin to describe it – doesn't begin. . . ." His voice trailed off and his face twisted in pain. For a moment he seemed close to tears, but then he pulled himself together so that only bitterness sounded in his voice. "That's where I found Haleem – running from the guns at Lydda. You wouldn't have recognised her – even I didn't to begin with. She was dressed in rags, her face was dirty and she hobbled along on a badly-sprained ankle. The worst part was she wouldn't tell me what had happened to her. No matter how often I asked. She would never *talk* about it. Not even when we reached Damascus and I knew she was with child."

I swore aloud. I felt ashamed. Before I had been frightened and horrified, but at that moment I just felt sick with shame.

"Haleem had the baby in October." He stubbed the cigarette out as if he'd lost the taste for it. "It was a difficult birth, she was six weeks premature. The doctor may not have been the best either, I don't know. I was seventeen then and not very knowledgeable. Afterwards he said she just hadn't been strong enough – and he thought she'd been raped. I don't know. I *never* knew. When Haleem died I was almost alone. The Jews had killed my father and brother, and finally they had taken my sister. I swore then that I would avenge their deaths – *all* their deaths!" His face suddenly paled and his eyes blazed with fury. "And I have – ten times over!"

I was stunned for a minute, then I said, "You said you were *almost* alone?"

"I met a cousin. Older than me, a qualified dentist like – like my father. His wife had lost a little girl – blown to pieces by a bomb a couple of months earlier. Idris, my cousin, offered to take care of the baby – to preserve his wife's sanity I think as much as anything. Still it worked out. It was like watching her come alive again when we gave her Haleem's baby."

"And the baby?"

"Was a girl. Idris and Farida called her Suzette."

"Suzette. That's not an Arab name?"

His look was half amused and half contemptuous. "You wouldn't understand. Those were the early days of the Catastrophe. We feared that we might be chased beyond Syria. Where was it going to end? We had nowhere to hide. Farida had friends in France. She wanted to live there if they could get out of Syria. At the time it seemed safer to give the baby a European name."

Big Reilly drank sweet tea from a chipped enamel mug and pretended not to notice the woman's hostility. She sat on the other side of the kitchen table, her thin yellow hair bound in pink curlers and her plump white body encased in a grubby blue housecoat. He remembered her once as pretty, as lively a colleen as could be found in the whole of Cork, with flashing eyes and swinging hips that had jerked the heads like balls on a string. But that was twenty years ago. Before her father drank himself to death, before she had nursed her mother through the long black months of a terminal illness, and before Mick's *accident* had left him half the man he used to be. Now everything in the cramped little kitchen mocked the wreckage of her life, everything from the unwashed pots and pans to the fly-blown face of the cheap alarm clock which looked down from the dresser. Clothes lay airing in the hearth beneath a mantelpiece cluttered with the bric-a-brac of a lifetime, and on the wall a framed sampler next to a plaster cast of the Virgin Mary asked God Bless This House in faded yellow silks.

"And how's that boy of yours?" Big Reilly asked. "Michael, isn't it? He must have grown a yard taller since I last saw him."

He tried his smile on her and felt a pang of remorse as he remembered Liam. Liam's smile would have got through to her. Liam would have charmed her, had her laughing and joking about the old days, when they were all young. And as for her son Michael, hadn't Reilly seen him himself not more than an hour ago? Hadn't he waited at the bottom of the street, watching the bleak row of houses until the boy left for school?

"Michael's all right," she said ungraciously. A wisp of hair escaped from a curler and she brushed it away from her eyes. Reilly noticed her hand, red and swollen, bloated like a body recovered from the sea. Liam's body, he thought bitterly, if ever they found it.

The woman looked at the clock. "It's as good as ten now. Mick might not get back. Some days he's too busy to get away." Hope swelled in her breast and the words rushed out. "I'll tell him you called – perhaps another time – if you'll let us know when you're coming."

Reilly shook his head and watched the hope die in her eyes. "Sure now, he'll be along in a minute or two. I'll wait. It's a long way I've come and –"

"And it's always the devil you bring with you! Mick's not a well man Big Reilly and it's you should be knowing that better than any man living."

Reilly thought back eight years. They had been moving gelignite across the border, Mick and him, driving an old Austin van stolen two days earlier from a builder's yard in Dublin. They *knew* the sticks were sweating, but they had wrapped them in old blankets and hoped for the best. Sure hadn't they done it a dozen times over? But their luck ran out that night. Two miles from the border the gelly had blown, ripping the back of the van open and sending it arse over tip down a gulley. The explosion had been heard in Ballyconnell and within an hour police were thicker on the ground than fag-ends in Patrick's Bar. Reilly had been lucky, two fingers of his left hand severed to the bone and a few other cuts from flying glass. But Mick's back had been blown in and the side of his jacket drenched with blood. Sweet Mother of Christ, it wasn't the first time Reilly had seen blood, but he'd never seen a man lose so much and live through it. They got clear of the wreckage somehow, Reilly carrying the other man for a mile and a half before Liam found them.

"Mick's finished with all that," Molly stretched her determination to its limit. "How many times do you need telling? Leave it for the younger ones. If they care enough they'll do their share of the fighting. These days Mick is –"

"Mick's a soldier," he interrupted roughly. "Once a soldier *always* a soldier. You know the rules."

"Oh no!" she banged the table angrily. "Not *that* all over again. Hasn't he done enough? Enough for Ireland, enough for the Movement, enough even for the high and mighty Big Reilly himself?"

He took the money from his jacket pocket and laid it on the table. "There's five hundred pounds there Molly. Think of all you could do with that. Think of the boy – think of Mick – of –"

"And who else would I be thinking of? Them and the price you'll be wanting for your money!" She fought to steady her voice. "Can't you get it into your thick head Big Reilly, we don't *want* your money – we don't *want* the worry of it – we don't *want* you!"

"*Molly!*" Mick Malone rebuked from the back door, his arrival unnoticed by either of them. "Is that any way to talk to an old friend?" His gaze shifted slowly to the pile of notes. "And you'll have won the sweepstake itself Big Reilly to be carrying that much money about with you."

Reilly turned to greet the man he had grown up with, and tried hard to stop the shock from showing in his eyes. Mick Malone was less than half the man he used to be. Even in the six months since last they met he had shrivelled. His body, once as tall and broad as Reilly's own, had stooped and bent itself, so that now he stood a foot shorter and weighed half as much. And his face was the colour of putty with lines enough for a man of seventy – and a sick man at that.

It had been Big Reilly's decision that night eight years ago. Liam had wanted to leave Mick for the police to find. "It's the only thing to do," Liam had pleaded. "That way he'll get doctors, a hospital, an operation, whatever's needed." But Big Reilly had roared back, "That way he'll get twenty years in jail and you damn well know it." So they had stolen a car and raced to Dublin, arriving at the safe house at four in the morning, only to wait another twenty-eight hours for that quack of a doctor to get there. And ever since Mick's damaged kidneys had been slowly killing him, forcing him off the hard stuff and onto a diet fit only for mewling infants.

Mick's eyes sparkled as he wrung the other man's hand. "It's good to see you. Have you been here long?" He shuffled to the dresser before Reilly had time to answer and rummaged in a drawer. "Ah! And wasn't I saving this for a day like today?"

"Mick no!" Molly was out of her chair and around the table, one hand grasping for the green bottle as Mick swung it beyond her reach.

He caught her with his other arm and squeezed her. "Just a spot in my tea Molly, that's all. Big Reilly can drink his neat, the way it should be taken."

Molly brewed a fresh pot and watched the men settle in front of the fire, trying the while to keep her eyes from the money on the table. Taking his tea Mick added a finger of whiskey and handed the bottle to Reilly, telling him to finish it. Then he said, "Isn't it your sister you're seeing this morning Molly?"

She could have argued. These days she was almost as strong as he was. But it wasn't her way. Not in front of people, even people like Big Reilly. God and she knew there was little enough left of Mick for her to shame in front of his friends. So she climbed the narrow staircase to her bedroom, brushed her hair and put on a clean dress, picked up the coat new twelve years ago and went to her sister's place in O'Connell Street.

In the kitchen the men finished talking about the old days as soon as the door banged behind her. Reilly raised the reason for his visit. "It's Steve Cassidy, Mick. He was taken this morning. Did you know that?"

Mick finished his tea. "I heard. He's in the Holy Cross Jail." His grey face darkened to near black. "God knows what the murdering bastards will do to him."

"Will he talk?"

Mick smiled sadly. "If they hold him long enough. If they give him the full treatment. There's not a man born who can swallow his tongue, however hard he tries. You know that. But he'll make the bastards work for it."

Reilly sighed. Mick always gave it to him straight. Whether he liked it or not. Mick was like that. Once, a couple of years ago, when Mick's condition was obviously worsening, Reilly had asked him outright. "Mick do you blame me? Liam wanted to leave you, leave you for the police. Reckoned they'd get you to a hospital. Maybe if –" But Mick had interrupted him, "They'd have killed me on the spot, like as not. Don't fool yourself they'd have wasted fancy surgeons on the likes of me, Big Reilly. I'd have done as you did, so would any soldier. Liam's well enough but the lad's a poet and we've known that a long time."

A dead poet, thought Reilly bitterly. Aloud he said, "Steve Cassidy was going to do a job for us, Mick. Saturday. If he's not out by then we're in trouble, bad trouble."

Mick's eyes narrowed. He jerked his head at the table. "Is that what all the money's about?"

Reilly gambled. "No, that's for old times' sake."

Mick chuckled until his breath rasped and his chest heaved in a spasm of coughing. When he recovered he said, "So now the Movement's got funds enough to pay pensions to the likes of me? That's good news for a change." He sat looking into the fire, his breath still wheezing. "What's the job, then?"

"Steve was due to take a load over to Cologne this week. Isn't that right?"

"A load from *our* factory you mean?" Mick's eyes widened. "What the devil's that to do with you?"

Reilly smiled. *Our* factory belonged to the English, a company called Exide Ltd with a fancy head office in London and other factories at Birmingham and Manchester. Mick had worked for them for years – one way or another. He had been a driver with them until his "accident." Then he had not worked for anyone for three long years. Three years for his back to mend itself as best it could. Three years without a wage coming into the house. Three years living on the handouts and help from his friends, debts building into a mountain of despair until finally, when he could get about on sticks, the factory had given him another job. Now he sat in a shed in the yard and was called a transport supervisor. Every morning he left home at six to get the lorries away by ten, when he slipped back again for his breakfast.

"It's a fair bit we know about your factory, Mick," Reilly was still smiling. "Like for instance most of the export loads going by containers these days. Isn't that right now? But this time you've a lorry going all the way – all the way to Cologne."

A faint flush added a touch of colour to Mick's face. "And how the devil did you know that?"

Reilly tapped his nose. "Isn't it enough that we know?"

Mick stared, trying to work it out. "I only knew myself a week ago. There's some stuff to come back to us. That's why we're sending a forty-footer. It's cheaper."

"I know."

"You know that *too*?" Realisation dawned slowly. "You *arranged* it?"

Reilly let the idea take hold, then added. "Steve was going to make a call first, Mick. This side of the water. Then he was going on like nothing had happened."

"In one of *our* lorries?" Mick made it sound blasphemous. He looked back at the fire. "And *that* was the job?"

"Nearly. Except in Germany he was to miss the Mercedes plant at Cologne and go on down the road a bit."

"Mary Mother of Christ! What's the Movement doing with a truckload of batteries in Germany?"

Reilly shook his head. "That's none of our business. It's a job we're doing for – for some friends," he smiled grimly. "We're being well enough paid for it though and that's a fact."

Mick eyed the money carefully. "And Steve was getting the five hundred pounds?"

"No. Steve wasn't coming back. If he got away with it, he was going to the States. It was all arranged."

"Not coming back. To Ireland? Ever?" Mick's astonishment faded slowly. Cassidy was a single man. His mother had died a year ago and he had no close family left. Not here. Uncles and Aunts by the score, but all in America; hadn't he heard tell of enough Cassidy's in New York to drink Guinness dry? That made sense right enough. But the rest was a puzzle. How much did it cost to make a man vanish in Germany and fish him up again in America? A packet of money, that's for sure. And for what? He looked steadily at the man in the chair opposite. "Big Reilly, we've been friends as long as we've lived. Are you going to tell me what this is all about or aren't you?"

Reilly barely hesitated. He would *have* to tell him. Without Steve Cassidy, Mick was the only man who could make the plan work. "I'll tell you what's in it for us," he said, "or at least part of it – but I'll not pretend to know about Germany."

They smoked cigarettes while Reilly talked about the one hundred Kalashnikovs and the promised ammunition – and of the people hidden back at Conlaragh. And last of all about Liam and Pat Brady. Mick listened thoughtfully, coughing now and then, but otherwise in silence. When Reilly finished Mick carefully praised Liam and muttered a prayer for his memory, then asked, "And what are you wanting from me Big Reilly?"

"Another driver. A man we can trust."

Mick thought about that for a very long time. Ten minutes passed as he smoked another cigarette and stared into the fire, preoccupied with his own thoughts. Then, in a quiet precise voice he listed the other drivers at the yard, telling Reilly a little about each of them before systematically ruling them out, one after the other. But he had made his mind up minutes before. Mick *knew* who the driver would be, and as the idea grew in his mind he felt an overwhelming sense of relief. For the first time in months he felt at peace with himself.

"I'm thinking it's a dangerous job we're talking about," he said slyly. "Stands to reason. There's so much involved. And if someone's powerful enough reason to want that lorry a few miles extra then they'll be others wanting to stop it. Wouldn't you think so?"

Reilly nodded, half guessing what was coming next.

Mick grinned and straightened his cripped body in the chair. "You know, I've half a mind to take that load over myself. Maybe a breath of German air is what I'm looking for," he gave Reilly another sly look. "That is, *if* I'm compensated for my troubles."

It was Reilly's turn to look into the fire. He forced himself to ask, "But are you strong enough, Mick?"

"You want me to take you out to the yard – to thrash you to prove it?" Mick flushed.

Reilly's smile disguised his sadness. "What about the factory? Will it be all right with them?"

"And isn't it my job anyway? Transport supervisor and relief driver."

"But long distance?"

Mick looked very determined. "I'll fix it."

"Got a passport?"

Mick nodded.

Reilly scratched the blue scar on his cheek as he thought about it. Then he said, "It's the truth I told you Mick, about not knowing what's happening in Germany. But Steve wasn't going to America just to join relatives – he was going there to hide. Whoever drives that truck will be a wanted man. Whatever the job's about, the police will know he was part of it – d'you understand?"

Mick had already guessed as much. He was completely relaxed when he answered. "I'll *not* be going to America Big Reilly. And I'll *not* hide either," he gazed steadily at the man opposite. "And then again, I'll *not* be taken. Do *you* understand?"

Reilly wished that the half size bottle of Jameson's had been full when he started it. Now it was completely empty. He looked away, pretending to search his pockets for another pack of cigarettes.

"It's Molly and the boy that matter," Mick said. "I've only a few months left in any case. Follow me?" He chuckled as he watched Reilly's face. "Don't look so gloomy. Tell me what the compensation's to be – better than a collection at St. Joe's I hope."

Reilly thought about the money back at Conlaragh. Fifteen thousand had been earmarked to set Steve up in New York. All that would be saved. He searched his mind desperately for other ways to cut expenses, wanting to give all he could to the man watching him. Maybe it would ease the guilt he felt.

"Twenty thousand," he said in a hoarse whisper.

Mick smiled. Twenty thousand pounds! Enough for Molly to buy a small shop perhaps? Hadn't she always wanted one? And enough for the boy to finish the schooling – maybe even enough to get him to the University at Dublin later on? Twenty thousand pounds was a powerful enough sum for any man to leave to his family. Twenty thousand pounds would make up for the years of grinding poverty. A sudden pain reminded him of the Jameson's but he shrugged it off. What was a little pain now and then to a man providing for his family's future.

"And when do I get the money?" he asked.

Reilly shook his head. "I'll have to talk to them – the others back at

Conlaragh. It'll need some arranging. But I'll try to make it some before you leave if you like?"

Mick shrugged. "Arrange it how you want – so long as Molly gets it afterwards and never knows where it really comes from."

"And how would we do that?"

"Find a way. It'll need to be damn good though. If Molly as much as thinks –"

"We'll find a way," Reilly said quickly. He frowned, wishing he could see an answer there and then. It would need thinking about, that was for sure.

"Molly must never know. *Never*. You understand that, don't you?"

Reilly nodded thoughtfully. It was beyond the wit of the likes of him. It would be up to the Ay-rab. But he smiled with feigned confidence, "Rest your mind. Molly will never know. I promise you that."

Mick breathed a sigh of relief: "Is it a deal then?"

It was a deal. Mick brewed more tea while they discussed the details and at eleven o'clock Reilly slipped quietly out the back way and returned to the multi-storey car park five streets away. He climbed the steps to where his driver waited in the old Ford on the second floor, trying all the while to rid himself of the feelings of sadness which clung to him. Liam and Pat gone already. Now Mick. Soon none of the old faces would be left. What had Molly said? Leave it to the younger ones? Sure now, and soon there'd be damn all choice.

When Molly returned, the kitchen was empty. The money had gone from the table and she wondered which of the men had taken it. Big Reilly she hoped, taking his blood money elsewhere. She hurried upstairs to change before tackling the dishes and preparing the midday meal, beans on toast for the boy and an apple to follow, thin soup as usual for Mick.

They arrived together, the boy demanding food and relishing the prospect of it, the man welcoming only the warm strength it would lend to his body for a few short hours. She served them both, her anxious eyes searching the man's face for a clue about the visitor earlier. There would be no mention of him in front of the boy, she knew that.

Mick grinned at her. "I'm going to Germany. For the factory, on Saturday."

"Germany?" The moon would have meant as much to her.

He nodded. "It's a rush job. With a bonus – not the fortunes *some*

80

get their hands on of course," he winked at her. "But it's a handy sum of money."

Thank God! She breathed a sigh of relief. Mick had sent him packing. Wasn't that plain enough? And wasn't this an answer from the Blessed Virgin herself on the very same day? She smiled and waited, knowing he would tell her more in his own good time.

"I'll be gone for a while though," Mick said to the boy, his face serious, almost sad she thought. "And you'll be the man of the house. What will you make of that?"

The boy squared his shoulders and flashed Molly a shy smile. "We'll be all right, won't we Mum?"

"We'll manage," she said quickly.

"Of course you will," Mick seemed suddenly cheerful. "And we've a couple of nights left before I go – and me with an advance against my bonus that's fair burning a hole in my pocket. Enough for the pictures tonight – and supper after with what's left over."

The boy whooped and rushed to find the programmes in the paper while his mother made the tea. An advance? She had never known that before. Not the factory paying out before the work was done. Still, it *was* short notice. A rush job. Perhaps that was why. Mick was sure to tell her later. She watched them flatten the news-paper over the table, and calmed herself, ignoring the tiny seed of suspicion which had taken root in her mind.

14.00 Thursday

The thick white bath towel had a fringe on one end, like tassels. Draped half way across Nikolai Orlov's ample backside it looked like a lampshade covering a light bulb. Not that it turned me on. But his skin looked a few years younger and shone with the almost fluores-cent pink of lightly boiled pork. Not surprising really, considering the hour it had spent in the steam room. Max, the negro masseur, gently cuffed the upper regions of Orlov's thighs while the Russian sprawled on the massage table and watched us. He rested his chin on his left hand while his right clutched a Monte Cristo cigar and hovered over a half full glass of zambuca. To my knowledge he was the first K.G.B. man I had ever met.

"So, Ross?" he grinned, and two gold teeth winked like hidden transmitters. "Newsboy here," Orlov nodded at me, "your new assistant. Does he have a 'need to know' classification?"

Ross wiped the back of his neck and watched a trickle of sweat disappear into the matted hair on his chest. "As far as this Katoul thing's concerned, Brand's classification is unlimited." The trickle emerged at his waist and dispersed into the towel knotted around his buttocks.

Orlov nodded and turned curious eyes to me as I sat next to Ross on the slatted wooden bench. He looked like Khrushchev, an accident of fate which had no doubt helped him get his job in the first place and hindered promotion ever since.

"So," he said. At long last the famous columnist Harry Brand joins the ranks of the spooks."

"Thank you, I didn't know it was such a cosy club. Do you two go on holiday together?"

Orlov chuckled. "The Arabs have a saying – the enemy of my enemy is my friend."

"That explains their disunity," I said.

Major Nikolai Orlov even chuckled at that. He really was a very jolly Russian.

He had booked in an hour or so earlier, using a Hungarian passport and wearing an English suit and Italian shoes. Not that he had kept them on long; we had adjourned to the steam room almost immediately. Apparently Ross had phoned him last night in Rome, where he was cultural attaché at the Russian Embassy. Old pal networks work everywhere.

"Suzy Katoul," Ross reminded him.

"Oh, yes," Orlov grinned. "If you knew Suzy like I know Suzy."

"You *know* her?" I asked in astonishment.

He shook his head. "American popular song, Mr Brand. Circa 1930. Oscar Hammerstein I think."

"Cultural attachés know everything," I conceded.

"Who's running her Nikki?" Ross asked urgently.

"Not me. You have my word on that," Orlov smiled. Watching the pair of them I was reminded of the two Jewish businessmen who *almost* trusted each other after thirty years of partnership.

"The formula was written in Russian," Ross said.

"So? Solzhenitsyn writes in Russian. Can I help it?" Orlov dismissed it. "The benefit of a good education."

"Good organisation," Ross snorted. "A clean hit on the *Marisa* – the exact container – the complete disappearance of that patrol boat. Christ, it was well planned!"

"*Too* well planned?" Orlov raised an eyebrow. "For the Arabs you mean?"

"Our Arabs or your Arabs?" Ross asked and finished his drink.

Orlov chuckled. "Remember Berlin in the fifties? When it was our

Germans or your Germans? The game hasn't changed has it? Only the venue."

"And the pawns," I said.

Orlov seemed surprised. "Pawns only function to protect the more important pieces, Mr Brand."

"They're holed up somewhere," Ross said grimly. "That blasted girl and her crew – and the cargo."

"But they're in Tripoli," I blurted out. "That's been established."

Orlov gave me a pitying look. "Wherever they are, Mr Brand," he said with chilling certainty. "They're *not* in Tripoli."

"There's not much time left," Ross said bitterly. "That's the problem. Less than twenty-four hours."

"And what then, my friend?" Orlov sounded unconcerned. "Even if they've got the bomb they've still got to deliver it. How do they do that? With an Inter-Continental Ballistic Missile?" he shook his head. "It's a bluff I tell you. A bargaining trick. You'll hear what they want soon enough. Then you can move. Meanwhile, my people are turning the Middle East inside out."

"If it's in the Middle East," Ross said gloomily.

Orlov laughed. "It's got to be. We've already searched Washington."

He was still having hysterics about that when the door opened and Elizabeth came in. She wore a lemon-coloured beach robe over a black bikini over a tanned body. Most of what showed was golden brown. She carried a silver tray bearing vodka for Ross, a Zambuca for Orlov and a scotch for me.

"Elizabeth, darling!" Orlov would have passed muster in the Chelsea set.

Elizabeth darling put the tray down and kissed him. Dropping his cigar into an ashtray, Orlov's right hand wrapped around her bottom until he covered it. Spooks must shake bottoms the way freemasons shake hands, there has to be something special about it.

"Excuse me not getting up," Orlov jerked his head backwards to indicate the towel across his backside.

"Why?" Elizabeth purred. "You got something special?"

"Yes," Orlov yelled delightedly. "My weapon's still on the secret list."

She put a light to the rim of his glass and we sat like children watching the blue flame lick its way across the surface of the zambuca. After a moment she blew it out and handed the glass to Orlov. Then she kissed his cheek again and made her exit.

"Decadent," Orlov looked at the door with shining eyes. "Wild

83

and decadent." He shook his head as if to clear his brain. "You know Rossi – I've still got the same mistress. The one you met in Prague that time. Forty-eight years old and as fat as a barrel."

Ross grinned, "I'm told mistresses of that age have compensations."

Orlov was already laughing. "You mean they don't teli, they don't yell and they don't swell."

"And they're as grateful as hell!" Ross spluttered, spilling his drink.

They fell about. A bell rang faintly in another part of the building, as if to signal the end of school break. I half expected my old headmaster to beckon from the door, but instead it was Bill and Ben the dungeon men, LeClerc and the doctor ready for another session.

"What did Negib Katoul want from you?" the doctor asked.

"A package delivered to Paris."

"What was in it?"

"I don't know. I didn't look."

"But you took it?"

"Yes."

"Why?"

"We made a deal. I took his package and he told me where I could find Haleem's child."

"And that was important to you?"

"That's right."

"Why was that *so* important Mr Brand?"

"I felt I had a duty – an obligation."

"To the living, or the dead?"

"What's that supposed to mean?"

"Negib Katoul was P.L.O." The doctor polished his spectacles with a silk handkerchief and watched me with naked eyes. "We know that much. Did you feel obligated to him, or the cause he stood for?"

I barely hesitated. "Neither, I was just concerned that an eight-year-old child was growing up in conditions which appalled me."

"Because she was your daughter?"

They had to get around to it I suppose. Funny, but it didn't make me feel sick anymore, not the way it used to. When Negib first told me I was tormented for days. Had Haleem borne me a child? A child I had walked out on, deserted, ignored. And even if . . . even if she was *not* my child, she was still Haleem's. I owed it to Haleem. I had promised Nadi. Yet I didn't want the *responsibility* of a child. How could I? With the life I led, rushing from one war to the next? How could I get *involved*? But I was involved and I had to do *something*.

"I didn't say she was my daughter."

"Are you saying she wasn't?"

"I'm saying she was Haleem's child."

"And you went to see her."

"Yes, I went to see her."

"Hello, Suzy," I said. Even as an eight-year-old the child shared some of Haleem's delicate beauty. Dark eyes, oval shaped and bright with curiosity, and a shade too large for her face, lustrous black hair and skin the colour of honey. She snuggled behind Farida and peeped out at me.

"Say hello, Suzy," Farida encouraged.

But the child would have none of it, so we were forced into adult talk in the hope that her shyness might pass. The camp was in Lebanon. Ironically I had even visited it before, inspected the registers, searched for the name Katoul, not knowing then that Haleem was dead and her child bore the name of Suzette Muhair. The shack they lived in was clean and tidy, and the luxury of two "rooms" set it apart from the squalor of the one-roomed sheds which housed most of the camp's population. Idris used a section of the main room as a dental surgery, so they even had water piped in – though toilets and the main washing facilities were in the communal ablutions fifty yards away. A curtain in the smaller room screened Suzy's bed from the one shared by Idris and Farida. The thin plasterboard walls and bare light bulbs contrasted sadly with the book-lined studies and carpeted rooms of Katamon – but that was a lifetime away.

After a time Farida took Suzy to the bedroom, while Idris and I talked. He seemed suspicious, even hostile, which surprised me until I tried to see it from his point of view. Legally I suppose they had no claim on Suzy, and if I challenged their right to keep her what would happen then – in a camp with too many mouths to feed? I tried to explain what a good friend Nadi had been, and how much I had liked the whole family. How they had helped and befriended me when I had arrived as a young man strange to their land. I explained the promise made to the father and something of the debt owed to the daughter. Idris listened politely, his eyes watchful, warily waiting for the trap. There was no *trap*. They wanted to go to France, I would help them: they needed money, I would arrange for some. After a while Farida could no longer bear to

85

listen from the bedroom and she rejoined us. She stood next to Idris, one hand on his shoulder, the other smoothing Suzy's hair. Three pairs of eyes watched me, doubt and anxiety written all over their faces. I found myself wishing Negib had stayed instead of leaving so soon after the introductions. Negib carried authority, not just with them, but throughout the entire camp. I had seen young men stiffen with respect, just at the sight of him. Negib was P.L.O. – or the camp's equivalent.

Idris and I talked for an hour and then I returned to Beirut, not knowing whether he had accepted or rejected my offer. But I spent the rest of the day organising my end of things as a show of good faith, hoping that when next we met we could make plans to get them out of the place. Money was no real problem, the paper didn't pay a fortune but I lived well and mostly on expenses and was able to bank a good part of my salary each month. And the United Nations Relief and Works Agency officials were quite helpful when I went to see them, so by the following morning it was all set as far as I was concerned. All the Muhairs had to do was to pack their pathetic bundle of possessions and come with me. So the next day I returned to that hell-hole not knowing what to expect, but determined to get them out, one way or the other.

Suzy saw me when I was fifty yards away. She dashed into the shack and emerged a second later dragging Farida by the hand. Initially Farida looked astonished to see me, then her expression changed to something like fear. She clutched the child to her body and then pulled her back through the open door. It was as if a signal had sounded. Dozens of Arabs emerged from doors and alleyways to fall into step alongside me, jostling violently, knocking me one way and another – not punching or kicking, not even looking at me, pretending that any contact was quite accidental. But twenty yards from the shack the pressure about me had grown so great that I was lashing out just to keep from being trampled underfoot. Then someone shouted and the whole performance stopped as abruptly as it started, bodies sprang back from mine as if I carried the plague. Ahead of me Negib stood in the doorway and beckoned me in.

"What the bloody hell was that all about?" I demanded angrily.

He smiled. "Palestinian unity Harry, that's all."

Idris emerged from the other room and I could see Farida and Suzy crouched by the curtain between the beds. Without any preamble Negib said: "Idris told me about yesterday. Perhaps he got it all wrong – why don't you tell me what's on your mind?"

So I did and he let me finish before he smiled. "Poor Harry, how simple life is for you."

"What's complicated? I've spoken to the United Nations people and –"

"No, Harry!" Negib flashed with a show of the quick temper I had seen in my room back at the Normandy. "No *damn you*, no! You're as bad as the rest! Will you people never learn? You want to talk about the welfare of the Palestinians? Okay that's fine – you come and talk to *us*. Us understand, not the U.N.! Not the bloody Americans! Not the fucking Red Cross – but US, US, US! Understand?"

He trembled as he shouted and spittle flecked his lips. Next to him Idris looked sick, and in the back room Farida buried her head in her hands.

I allowed a long minute of silence to pass before I said coldly, "All I *understand* Negib is that I want Suzy out of here. And Idris and Farida. And *you* – if you'll let me help. It's as simple as that."

He sneered. "You'd like to think so, wouldn't you? You and your kind. What is it, Harry – some newspaper stunt? Something to run a headline about? Capitalist press saves young girl from fate worse than death. Is that it?"

"Oh, for God's sake! Don't be so ridiculous!" I was angry enough to be on the point of striking him when the knife appeared in his hand. And that cooled me down like a bucket of water. A crude wooden table separated us, and behind me the Arabs crowded into the open doorway, listening to every word we said. I calmed down and tried to make the best of it. "All right Negib – just who the hell *should* I ask?"

"It's been decided," he turned to Idris. "Tell him."

Idris looked like a whipped dog. "We didn't think you'd be back," he began apologetically. "Farida and I – neither of us thought you'd be –"

"*Tell him!*" Negib shouted. "Tell him what's been decided."

Clutching the back of a chair for support Idris threw a quick glance at the bedroom before turning to face me. He licked his lips nervously. "We would like to go with you, Mr Brand. We would like to be free – free of this place – but most of all we'd like to return to Katamon."

I stared at him, not understanding. Next to him Negib shouted, "Or Idris – *or* – tell him the alternative."

Idris seemed on the verge of collapse. "Farida's family come from Beersheba," he said softly. "If we could return there –"

87

"But that's impossible," I interrupted. "Both places are out of the question. Idris you *know* that's impossible. That's Israel now. I could never get –"

"Never get?" Negib shouted. "Never get? Never get what Harry? Permission? Permission from the Jews? Permission for a family to return to their homes?"

"Idris," I said urgently. "I was in Beersheba some time ago. It's changed. Many of the old houses have been pulled down. There are Israeli settlements there now – you wouldn't even recognise the place."

"There's still the land!" Negib shouted. "They can't change that, can they? It's *our* land – *our* land – *our* land!"

They were all chanting it, shouting at the tops of their voices. The noise was deafening in that little room. Only Idris remained mute, misery and despair written all over his face.

I shouted to make myself heard above the din, "Idris, I can get you into France. It's what you wanted isn't it? Think of your wife – think of Suzy – eight years old and never seen the inside of a schoolroom, in danger of –"

Negib gestured with his hand and the mob behind me stopped chanting as if in response to a conductor's baton. "You've had your answer, Harry," he snarled. "Now *get out!*"

His arm swung upwards in a sudden curve, the knife still in his hand.

I heard the hissed collective intake of breath from the doorway behind me as his arm came over and down like a whiplash – and the knife buried its blade into the bare tabletop. In the moment of quiet which followed I could hear Farida sobbing in the back room, while the child uttered small whimpers of comfort.

Helplessly, Idris groped for the words of apology. "We never thought you'd be back – I'm so sorry Mr Brand – so *very* sorry."

Dazed and shaken I turned away. A passage opened in the sea of bodies and I passed through it and out into the fresh air. What *could* I do? I had heard the stories of course. Of how the P.L.O. and the P.F.L.P. and others were tightening their grip on the camps. Of how the refugees were refusing to be integrated with the host countries. Of the doctrine which preached that the refugees would lose political negotiating power if the camps were broken up. But for God's sake, we were only talking about one family! About the future of an eight-year-old child. A *future* instead of rotting the rest of her life away in a camp. *The rest of her life?* God Almighty, was that *really* possible?

I spent what was left of the day in abortive meetings with the U.N.R.W.A. officials, seeking help, action, advice – but while they had been prepared to bend the rules for me before, now their hands were tied. I even consulted a local lawyer who gave me a lot of guff about protracted litigation with only a fifty-fifty chance of getting custody of Suzy at the end of it. Hell, was *that* what I wanted? I was in no position to raise a child. And there was no doubting the love and affection she was getting from Idris and Farida. In the evening I even talked it over with a few of the press boys back at the Normandy, but of course they were no help – so finally I pushed off to bed, bewildered by the whole turn of events and feeling like a beaten man. Then, at one o'clock in the morning, the telephone rang.

"Mr Brand?"

"Who is this?"

"Mr Brand, can you get down to the camp right away? There's been – there's been an accident."

It took me forty-five minutes of fast driving and the officials were waiting at the main gates when I arrived, three anxious-faced men who hurried me into a tiny office at the reception compound. A demonstration was taking place in the camp itself and even with the doors and windows closed in the office, the noise from outside was deafening. All that chanting and singing of "It's *our* land – *our* land – *our* land," over and over again.

The senior official wasted no time in preparing me for the shock. "Idris Muhair was murdered two hours ago. We can only guess what happened, and at the moment our guess is that he changed his mind about the answer he gave you."

"Murdered?" I was stunned. "And they killed him for *that?*"

He shouted to make himself heard above the racket from outside. "We have removed the woman Farida and the child from the main camp. For their own protection, you understand – anything could happen tonight. We've had incidents before, but none as bad as this."

"What can I do?" I shouted. "Is there anything – ?"

"Farida Muhair and the child should be removed to another camp, Mr Brand. Any offer to provide transport would be accepted at once." Without batting an eye he added, "Of course, you would be in a position of trust – but if you fail to arrive at the other camp –" The noise outside drowned the rest of his words. Then he shouted, "In a day or two we should report the matter, but meanwhile our priority must be to restore order here." He nodded energetically, as if convincing himself. "Yes, that *must* be our priority."

Farida and Suzy were in the other room, both unconscious. Alarmed I said, "They're all right, aren't they? Shouldn't we get a doctor –"

"Sedated, Mr Brand. Both are in shock – as would anyone be who watched what happened to Idris Muhair."

"They *watched*?"

"Such killings are ceremonial, Mr Brand. Idris Muhair had his testacles ripped off before he died. It is customary for the family to be made to witness these rites."

17.00 Thursday

Beyond the trees the road would dip slightly, still six hundred feet above sea level, but as if anticipating the sweeping descent to Conlaragh four miles away. Meanwhile, the old Ford wheezed up the incline like an old man climbing a flight of stairs.

Reilly gazed out from the passenger seat and thought about Mick Malone. Sure, wasn't it best this way – for all of them? Best for Molly and best for Mick himself – to go like this instead of lingering on for months at the cottage hospital, with her at his bedside morning, noon and night, watching the strength ebb out of him an inch at a time. And best for the boy too? Reilly exhaled and finally put the thought from his mind – there was a devil of a lot to do before that and hardly the time left to do it.

At the crest of the hill the panorama of the creek was spread out before them. Reilly fumbled in the glove compartment for the binoculars, while the driver checked the rear view mirror, making sure that the road behind them was as empty as a travel poster. Then he cut the engine and bumped off the road, sliding through a gap in the bushes like a rabbit down its hole.

From the cover of the trees Reilly swept the binoculars through a wide arc, starting at the mouth of the estuary and going through the village to reach the Inishmore boat-yard on the other side. Twice he paused to adjust the Zeiss lenses, and both times he began his search back at the estuary to make sure that nothing was overlooked. He ticked off the signs, one by one. Old MacCaffety fishing by the blighted elms on the east bank, wearing a yellow water-proof which shone like a beacon in the fading afternoon light. Then a mile upstream to Callan's Butcher's Shop. Sure, and there it was, the red rosette stuck in the corner of the window like Callan had won it this week instead of a year ago at the County Show. Then along to the boat-houses, with their wide black roofs and Inishmore painted over them in letters a foot or more high, and nets spread out in the yard as innocent as you please, but a sign for all that. Finally he searched the row of white-washed cottages until he found a back window open to the chill air. And then he *knew* that all was well at Conlaragh. A police raid might have been swift enough to stop the boys from taking the nets in, but one of them would have got to that window and closed it. And the bell would have sounded in Callan's cold-store for him to take the rosette from the window. And from where MacCaffety fished he saw the whole waterfront. The sight of even one police car would have sent him scurrying away.

Reilly walked back to the road, checked that it was empty of traffic, waved the driver back quickly and they resumed their journey as if nothing had happened. And wasn't that the truth? Reilly would no more arrive in Conlaragh without reading the signs than cross the border to join the Ulster Constabulary.

Once at the creek he sent the driver away to park the car, then walked quickly across to the cottages, entering by the back way and checking his men on guard duty as he did so. This time the door to their room was open, so knocking never came into it. The man was studying papers by the light from the window, while the girl sat watching him. Both were dressed in sweaters and trousers and they turned to face him as he entered. He caught sight of her cigarette. "Smoking again? It'll be the death of you, that."

"Just so long as you aren't, Big Reilly."

Despite everything he laughed. "You've a bold tongue, Suzy Katoul. I'll say that for you."

She mimicked his Irish brogue. "And you've a bold enough look in your eye to catch the wrong side of it."

He grinned and sat on the bed. "It's a good mood I'm in. You'll not be scolding when you hear the news I've got. It's all set for Saturday. The plan stays. I've fixed your driver for you."

"The police let him go?" Abou asked sharply from the window.

"No, but I've got a replacement."

Abou frowned. Any change in the Plan had to be considered carefully, even a replacement driver. Cassidy had been vetted. He was a single man with no relatives to be held hostage. Besides, Cassidy still in jail was worrying enough by itself. What if he talked and told what little he knew?

"It's a good man I've got for you," Reilly said firmly. "One of the best in Ireland. You'll be proud just to know him."

Abou's attention sharpened. "This man, he's a friend of yours?"

91

"The oldest I've got," Reilly said proudly.

Abou heard the pride and wondered about it. "He understands the risks?"

"Naturally."

"And he's prepared to be smuggled into the States when the job's over? He knows he'll never see Ireland again?"

"He'll never see Ireland again," Reilly's face darkened with sadness.

Abou concentrated, focusing on Reilly's words and manner, analysing the change in his attitude. Something had made the job more *personal*, that much was obvious. "Why?" he asked aloud. *"Why* do you want your oldest friend shipped half way round the world?"

"He'll not be moving anywhere," Reilly said softly. "Not after Germany. He's going to die there." A sad smile flickered at his lips. "Play your cards right and you've another martyr on your hands. How would that suit you – a good Irish Catholic willing to die for the Deir Yassin Memorial?"

Yes, Abou thought – that *might* suit very well – very well indeed. He put the papers to one side, reminding himself that the problem of Cassidy was still to be dealt with and allowing none of his rising excitement to sound in his voice.

"Very well, Big Reilly," he said. "You'd better tell me about this man. *Everything* about him."

19.00 *Thursday*

"Farida Humair and the girl Suzette were stateless persons," Le-Clerc said. "How did you get them into France, Mr Brand?"

"Does it matter?"

Elizabeth crossed her legs. "Everything matters Harry. Everything and anything."

I sighed. "Look, you can buy anything you want in Lebanon. You know that. Passports, papers –"

"You took a risk," LeClerc said.

"Not really. I fixed Farida up with the necessary papers and then simply escorted her on her journey. There was nothing to connect me with the transaction. Anyway, if they were caught what could the authorities do to them? Send them back to the camps? That's not a risk – not for desperate people."

"So you went to Paris?" Elizabeth said.

I nodded. "Farida had friends there who could help, and anyway

Paris had the biggest Arab emigré population in Europe. Over a million, even with the Algerian business going on."

"And then?"

The early years were uneventful I suppose. A child in Paris, growing up without a father, but with a woman she believed to be her mother. Suzy had a lot of schooling to catch up on, but she was a bright and more than willing pupil. Her I.Q. was a hundred and forty-eight if you believe I.Q. tests. Farida had taught her French and English and she just soaked up other languages, adding German in no time flat and even passable Spanish. I was delighted – and relieved that the camp had left no apparent scars. She was quiet and studious, introverted if you like, but she could laugh out loud when things amused her and join in a conversation if it interested her. Farida was devoted to her, of course, and the two of them got along well together. I used to visit two or three times a year, and for me it was like going home. My parents had died by then, and I had no close family anywhere else, so after a while their flat in Paris became a kind of base for me – it *felt* like home. Moneywise they were okay, Farida worked as an interpreter for a French engineering firm with contracts in the Middle East, and what with her income and the allowance I provided, they were comfortable enough.

Then in '65 I was in London and I met a girl at a cocktail party. She was a T.V. producer, documentaries and current affairs stuff, a high-powered go-go type, who had arrived at the top without turning butch the way some do. Anyway, she was doing a series on the Middle East and asked me to do the background stuff for her. Big fat fee and all the trimmings. So I left the paper and turned free-lance. After the first series we knocked out another one, then a third and by then I was rolling in it. I even began to think about settling down. After all, I was forty-two and had been batting round the world almost non-stop for nineteen years. And the girl and I worked so well together that one thing led to another and the following year we were married.

Farida and Suzy came over for the wedding and stayed on in London for a holiday. Suzy was eighteen then, and it was time we started to think of a career for her. But she had worked it out for herself and her mind was already set on what she wanted to do. International law of all things. Still, why not? There was money in it and by then she had added Russian to her list of languages, so what with Arabic and the others she was half way there. Four years at the Sorbonne she said, and I said okay. Elaine – my brand new wife –

was a bit snotty about upping Suzy's allowance, but then Elaine got snotty about spending a penny if it wasn't tax deductable.

Suzy started at the Sorbonne in '67. France was totally different from the France of today. All that Algerian agony and trembling on the brink of civil war, governments in and out like bad actors playing auditions, and De Gaulle doing his Moses coming down from the Mount bit. And it got worse. Riots, strikes, demonstrations, Jacques Soustelle and his lot. All leading up to the student riots in '68. And when they broke out, I grabbed a camera crew and caught the first flight to Orly. The opening weeks were chaos. I really thought France was done for, it seemed *that* close to civil war. Then De Gaulle put riot squads on every street corner and began to get a grip.

Anyway, it was the third week. The black flags of anarchy and the hammer and sickle hung from every window in Paris, and the air shook with the scream of police sirens. We were at Quai des Orfèvres and all hell had broken out. The students had ripped the paving stones up from the road and were forcing the police back, yard by yard, towards the entrance to the Prefecture. The Gendermarie had brought up a couple of water cannons, but somehow the kids had got at the water supply and rendered them useless. And the mob were keeping up such a solid bombardment that the *flics* were virtually trapped behind their own riot shields. Then a company of mobiles arrived and mounted a counter-charge. We were filming from the top of a truck at this stage. Two of my cameramen had been hit by stray bricks, so I was shooting with one of those old Pathe 350s and shouting twenty to the dozen into a taperecorder strapped to my chest. The noise was deafening, the kids screaming and cat-calling, the police bellowing back over loudspeakers, stones and bricks bouncing everywhere and glass smashing as a car had its windows hacked out.

I was trying to keep the camera on Danny the Red – Cohn-Bendit – and his crowd – because they were the leaders and would be at the centre of any police counter-attack. One moment I had the shot I wanted and in the next the crowd would surge forward and I would lose it again. *And then I saw Suzy.* It sounds crazy now, but never once had I expected to see her there. Of course, she was at the Sorbonne and I had *thought* of her, but only in the sense of her studies being interrupted. I had never suspected her of even being interested in politics, let alone imagined that she would be involved. Yet there she was, in the thick of it, four or five away from Cohn-Bendit himself, with one arm linked to the person next to her and the other curved like a javelin thrower's to hurl a stone. Then a squad of Compagnie Républicaine de Sécurité arrived and the battle was joined in earnest. The C.R.S. charged in a flying V formation with the leaders making straight for Cohn-Bendit, while the men at the sides scythed away furiously with riot clubs. A dozen kids went down with split heads before the C.R.S. regrouped. Then a second terrible charge was mounted and another dozen demonstrators were felled, but this time the squad dragged a kid back with them – two of them frogmarching him backwards, while others tried to stop his feet from lashing out all over the place.

Suzy was close to the action then, and I had her in focus. I saw her face when they got this kid's feet under control. Suddenly she *knew* what they were going to do to him. A horrible certainty of what would come next showed itself in her expression. And I think I knew too. By this time the kid was spreadeagled, with his legs splayed so far apart they damn near split him like a chicken. Then the club smashed down into his groin and Suzy was back at the camp watching Idris being mutilated. Her mouth opened in a scream, veins in her throat knotted like rip cords and her eyes bulged in horror. It was as if something snapped inside her brain. She threw herself at men twice her size. Somehow she got her fingers inside one man's protective visor and the next instant his face was streaked with blood. Then the world fell apart as the clubs descended over her head and shoulders. I was down from the truck and running as fast as I could by now, but the crowd blocked me. They panicked, flooding back towards me like a tidal wave as the C.R.S. men launched another strike. Then tear gas canisters started to land everywhere and the rout was complete.

The next few days were a nightmare. The riot squads had taken Suzy *somewhere* but finding her – getting access to her – was impossible. France was shaken to the core. Graffiti daubed every wall and Marcuse's theory about violence being justified for oppressed minorities blazed across Paris in letters six feet high. A state of emergency was declared and the police reacted with a security clampdown as tight as a locked safe. I tried every trick in the book to get at Suzy, but to no avail. In the end I hired a battery of lawyers to help raise hell around the corridors of power, but even with them it was tough going. It took a week to reach her.

"Hello, Harry."

She sat on the other side of a bare table in a cell at the St. Antoine Prison, her hands neatly folded in front of her. The rough grey prison dress was a size too large for her and somehow it added a touch of childishness to her appearance. But there was nothing childlike about her expression. One glance was enough to dispel any notion of vulnerability. Or even of innocence. Her dark eyes were calm and assured, completely without fear and strangely knowing. Suzy was nineteen years old and seemed to have grown up overnight.

"We'll soon have you out of here," I said as cheerfully as possible. "I'm sorry it took me so long –"

"Don't apologise. You're always doing it. Did you know that? Every time you come to see us you say how sorry you are that you don't visit more often."

"Oh."

Her calmness astonished me. I had expected tears, hysteria perhaps, relief at seeing me, fear of her surroundings, all sorts of things. Instead I found something approaching serenity. Her attitude made me nervous and I fumbled for words.

"I didn't realise."

"How's Mama?"

"Worried sick about you of course – but she's okay."

"I'm glad you didn't bring her to this place."

"I didn't know if I'd be able to see you myself. I waited hours upstairs and –"

"It's difficult. It's because they're afraid."

"Afraid?"

She nodded. "Afraid of us, of what we represent. What we stand for and what we'll do when we get out of here."

"I hadn't realised – about you being interested in politics."

"No."

I think that shook me most of all, the way she said "no." Such a flat, unemotional voice. Not reproachful, just indifferent.

I said, "I've hired some lawyers, Suzy. They'll be in to see you tomorrow. They'll want a statement, of course. I've already said you were provoked and –"

"Yes, a statement would be good," her mouth tightened in a way which gave a spiteful expression to her face. "But *not* about what happened at the Quai des Orfèvres."

I wondered if she was suffering from shock. "Suzy, I don't understand?"

"About being raped."

I thought she meant figuratively – the rape of freedom – that kind of thing, the extravagant language of the protest marchers. She spoke with such detachment. But then she added, "The pigs raped all the girls."

96

"Oh Christ! Suzy, *no!*"

She looked right through me. "It's not uncommon. But all the same we ought to issue a statement about it."

"Suzy, for God's sake!"

"Six times. Twice in the van and four times at St. Germain before they shipped us here."

"The *police* raped you?"

If she hadn't been so clinical I might have understood more readily, might have accepted more easily what she said, but her manner confused me. I said, "Can you prove it?"

She half smiled. "After a week? Can you *disprove* it?"

"We need an immediate doctor's report. I'll see the lawyers –"

"After a *week*," she repeated, still half smiling. "Why do you think they kept you away so long?"

We were interrupted by the prison wardress who declared the meeting finished. I protested of course and only gave in when I obtained a promise of being allowed to visit again tomorrow. After which I went directly to the lawyers.

The following day we obtained statements from Suzy and two other girls, all alleging multiple rape. Some of it was a bit vague, but descriptions were given of some of the policemen involved and the lawyers seemed halfway satisfied.

The case made headlines three weeks later. The girls were all good-lookers and there was enough evidence of police brutality elsewhere in Paris for some credibility to be attached to accusations of rape. But on the third day of the trial an especially fierce outburst of cross-examination trapped the youngest girl into first changing her story and then admitting it was a pack of lies designed to discredit the C.R.S. Suzy maintained that the girl had changed her story as a result of police intimidation. Then she embarked upon a bitter denunciation of the police in general and of the conditions of their confinement in particular. But the damage was done and the allegations were rejected.

I went through an hour of misery as I listened to the closing speeches, half expecting Suzy to be sent to prison for at least six months. But in the end the court was lenient and decided that the time already spent in custody was penalty enough, so the girls were released. They posed for cameramen on the court steps and Suzy made a statement bitingly critical of the entire judiciary, declaring the proceedings no more than a whitewash job for the C.R.S. At the time I didn't know what to make of it, still don't I suppose; there were moments when I believed every word she said, but other times when I doubted the truth of it. Her attitude was so changed that it was difficult to recognise her as the same girl.

Farida was heartbroken when we got Suzy home. Neither of us could get through to her. She was polite enough, but as unresponsive as granite. I wanted her to go away for a while, Farida too, to England or almost anywhere for a holiday, but Suzy refused, saying she had too much to do in Paris. And "too much to do" turned out to mean attending endless meetings in cafés and bars and on street corners.

By this time I had been in Paris for almost two months. My work schedule was in tatters and the T.V. crowd were on my back screaming about breach of contract and God knows what else. They were especially adamant about one engagement. I had promised to leave for Algeria with a film crew at the end of the month and the T.V. people were insistent that I go. I hated like hell to leave Paris. Farida was coping as best she could, but Suzy was still behaving in this strangely disturbed fashion, cool and remote about anything not connected with politics. Some of the Algerian dissidents had linked up with the Palestinians and Suzy had joined that crowd, so that after that she was forever talking about the refugees and the sins of Israel. Farida and I were even blamed for taking her away from the camp in Lebanon, as if it had been some kind of desirable finishing school. But in the end I could delay my departure no longer and after making sure Farida was okay for cash, I left for London to join up with the T.V. crew.

Algeria was like a bad horror movie. Too much death, too much torture, too much corruption and barbarity. The only good thing which came out of the trip was that I found *myself* again. Making money and a settled way of life were all very well, but London had been slowly stifling me. It was too far away from the real action and the T.V. thing involved too much team work for my taste. I was used to working alone, digging up my own stories, sniffing out the kind of news officials were trying to hush up. Being met with a scowl was something I could live with, whereas being met with open arms unsettled me. Arriving with a T.V. crew too often meant scripted interviews with the bite taken out of the questions I would have liked to ask, so that the finished product was too often a plug for some politician instead of a report on what was really happening. Perhaps it was just that I had been doing my own thing for too long. Whatever it was, something convinced me to kick the London deal in the head and go back on the paper – if they would have me.

Back in Paris Suzy was making her own headlines. She had

become something of a cult figure in the protest movement and hardly a day passed without some mention of her appearing in *France-Soir* or *Paris Match* or another of the French papers. She was good-looking and sincere and articulate, which makes good copy for any newsman, and she was giving almost daily press conferences at the apartment in the Rue Mouffetard. Even in Algiers her name and face were widely recognised, which was another aspect of the whole affair which filled me with misgivings. Notoriety attracts all sorts, and from Farida's letters I gathered that she and Suzy could hardly get through the front door each morning for the crush of hangers-on who laid siege to the place. It made me anxious to get back to Paris in the vague hope of being able to do something about it – though do *what* was never precisely defined in my mind. I just felt *uneasy*, as if some impending disaster was growing increasingly imminent and that my presence in Paris might somehow avert it. In the event I got back a day too late. Negib Katoul had called before me.

Between tears Farida told me about it. "Suzy went out with him in the morning and when she came home she knew everything. *Everything* Harry – that I'm not really her mother! About Haleem dying in childbirth. Even about Deir Yassin!"

She rocked back and forth in the chair, hugging herself, tears streaming down her face. "What could I say to her? She's more to me than my own child – she's my *life*! What else is there for me? What have I lived for since they took poor Idris away?"

I made her swallow some cognac and did what I could to comfort her, but she was almost hysterical. "Harry, I can't *reach* her anymore. I've tried to explain, but she won't listen. All she wants to know about is politics, politics, politics! France, Algeria, Israel and Palestine – what do I *know* about these things? What does she *know*? Except for what her friends tell her. *Friends*! They'll bring her nothing but grief and disgrace – I've told her, I've warned her a dozen times that –"

"Where is she now?"

"Who knows? Once I knew where she was every minute of the day. But now?"

It took me an hour to calm Farida before I left in search of Suzy. It was mid-afternoon and Paris throbbed with the heat of an unending summer, so empty of breeze that dust settled in layers on the chestnut leaves along the Avenue de l'Observatoire. I worked my way through the rabbit warren of streets and alleyways which make up the Latin Quarter and along the Boulevard Montparnasse, checking the bars and cafés as I went. Paris was still a frightened city. Police klaxons screamed, newspaper placards shouted headlines about Big Charlie's latest crisis measures, graffiti still adorned the walls and pavements. Whenever I saw a café full of students rather than tourists I would stop and ask where I might find Suzy Humair – but if they knew they weren't telling, at least they weren't telling *me*. Twice I telephoned Farida in case Suzy had returned home, but I knew even as I made the calls what the answer would be.

It was almost eight o'clock when I found her. She was in one of those little cafés in Saint-Germain-des-Prés, not far from the Palais Bourbon. There was a crowd of students with her, mostly French, but sprinkled with Germans and a few Algerians. About twenty of them had shoved three tables together and were arguing in loud excited voices. Next to them two old men were trying to finish a game of chess, while in a far corner a middle-aged Englishman explained his wife's shortcomings to a girl half his age.

I took a table along one wall and disappeared behind a copy of *L'Express*. Even if they had lowered their voices I would have heard most of it. Lots of chat about the Algerian war with excited references to Palestine and the rest of the Middle East. There were plenty of Maoist remedies spiced up with the teachings of Ché and Herbert Marcuse, with proper respect being accorded to Cohn-Bendit and Red Rudi Dutschke. Marcuse had preached that the revolution would be led by the students, and I wondered if he would be proved right, especially when all the heady talk of personal freedom prompted the girl in the corner to remove the Englishman's hand from under her skirts.

Suzy saw me half an hour later. I was spreading some over-ripe brie on a crust of bread and thinking about another bottle of Algerian, when the sudden hush in their conversation made me look up. Suzy was watching me, her face white with fury. For a second she just stared, then rose so violently that her chair fell over as she started across to my table.

"Who gave you the right to spy on me?"

"Suzy?" I pretended surprise. "Suzy, how marvellous. I didn't know you used this place?"

It was enough to make her hesitate, and by then I was pulling a chair out for her to join me. She sat down without even thinking.

"*You* know this place?"

"Come here whenever I'm in Paris. Discovered it years ago. Ask the patron – he'll tell you."

The patron stood at the kitchen door, his eyes moving quickly to

100

the crowd of students who watched me with open hostility. You could see what they were thinking – someone was causing their girl trouble, and any minute now they were going to take a hand in the matter, which meant a fight and broken furniture – and maybe the police and more broken furniture. The patron shrugged and flicked some bread crumbs from a table cloth. He turned away – maybe he knew me, maybe he didn't, a man like him serves many customers.

"You've seen Farida?" It was the first time Suzy referred to her as anything other than Mama. I nodded.

"And I've met my uncle," she said defiantly. "Negib Katoul called to see me yesterday."

"So I heard."

"And you've lied to me – for all these years!"

"About what?" I needed to know *exactly* what Negib had told her.

"As if you didn't know!" she sneered, shouting the words and causing the gang at the big table to mutter dangerously.

"Suzy, why don't we go home and talk about this?"

"I haven't got a home. The Jews stole it along with my country and –"

"Your mother's worried sick about you."

"She's *not* my mother! Are you still going to lie to me? Even about who I am?"

"Who does Negib say you are?"

"My name is Suzy Katoul. Katoul, Katoul, damn you! It's a name you should remember, it's a name you helped steal from me. You stripped me of my inheritance, Europeanised me, kidnapped me from my people and –"

"Suzy, don't be such a damn little fool." My own temper boiled over. "Everything that's been done has been done for your own good –"

"Including bringing me to France I suppose? Instead of –"

"Your father *died* so that you could come to France."

Her face went as white as paper. "Idris Humair was *not* my father. He was a weak bourgeois – he was a traitor to his people –"

"He stood up to a mob! A mob that murdered him! He was a brave man –"

"Don't you dare say that! How *dare* you talk of brave men! The brave men are fighting now to win our land back from the Jews."

"Fighting's not the way."

"Tell that to the bloody Jews!" She stood up, trembling so violently that her whole body shook with temper. In a sudden movement she reached for my glass and jerked it upwards. The wine stung my eyes and ran down my face onto my collar.

"Suzy, we've got to talk!" I said desperately, but she was already turning to rejoin her companions. I rose to follow her, but four of the men detached themselves from the big table and surrounded me, hands on my shoulders to push me back into my chair. I heard the click of a switch-blade and a voice in my ear said, "You will sit down and order another bottle of wine."

The patron served it silently. Suzy was already outside the café, flanked by the rest of her companions. The four who remained watched me carefully over the rim of their glasses and we sat for what seemed hours without exchanging a word. And all the while the switch-blade was held an inch from my throat.

Nobody intervened, nobody sent for help. Instead they pretended not to notice. The old men began another game of chess and the Englishman sweet-talked his paw back under the girl's skirt. For all the attention paid to us we could have been some kind of mural. Finally they left, but not without warning me about what they would do to me *next* time.

I paid the bill, complimented the patron on his clientele and went back to see Farida. And six years were to pass before I saw Suzy again.

I felt dog tired. Ross and Elizabeth had joined in, and the four of them fired a never-ending stream of questions at me. Describe this – remember that – dates, names, places, people. My head ached from the relentless demands made on my memory.

"You're telling us that four young thugs *frightened* you off?" Ross demanded. "You gave up as easily as that?"

"I didn't say that."

"It sure as hell sounded that way."

"I *tried* to see her again. I even got beaten up trying if that proves anything."

"Why didn't you go to the police?"

"What good would it have done? She had left home – left Farida's apartment. And shortly afterwards she even left Paris."

Ross nodded, and when he spoke the words came softly, like a sly prosecutor preparing a trap. "And of course if you'd gone to the police they might have been curious about how she got into France in the first place?"

"Possibly – but that wasn't a consideration."

"So what was?" he snapped.

"I told you. I just didn't think it would do any good. And – and there was Farida's position to consider as well."

"Her papers you mean?"

"I suppose so."

"Come on Harry! *Come on!* This isn't some two-bit investigation about a forged passport. We're trying to stop this screwed-up bitch from wiping out a million people! For Chrissakes, get your act together."

"What's that supposed to mean?"

"Stop holding back. Jesus Christ, do I have to spell it out? We want the *whole* picture. That's what that's *supposed to mean*. The *whole* picture Harry. Like were you and Farida keeping house together?"

"If you mean what I think –"

"Damn right I do! Your marriage never worked from the word go, Harry, so who was putting out for you? Were you so busy screwing the ass off Farida that –"

"No I was not!"

"Temper, temper, Harry," he taunted. "So just who *was* giving it to her?"

"Nobody was."

"How can you be sure? Was she a nun or something? Is that what *she* told you?"

"No it damn well isn't. We never discussed it. She was widowed, her whole life revolved around Suzy, she was in her late forties by then anyway –"

"And life had passed her by," Ross sighed. For a moment the tension seemed to drain out of him. He slumped in his chair like a tired fighter at the end of a hard round. Next to him Elizabeth watched me with those curious green eyes, while LeClerc and the doctor waited to pounce. I felt like a goldfish in a tank full of sharks.

Ross hunched forward in his chair. "Shortly after that she turned up in West Germany, you know that don't you?"

"I do now, but I didn't then."

"Where she met Ulrike Meinhof."

"I suppose so."

"You *suppose* so," Ross said heavily. "Dammit, they both wrote for *Konret*, didn't they?"

I nodded wearily. "If you know why bother to ask?"

"What's *Konret*?" The doctor asked.

"It was a magazine," LeClerc explained. "Political articles mixed up with *Playboy* type centre-spread."

"Ché Guevara with tits. Let Karl Marx help your orgasm," Ross

103

summed up. "Secretly financed by the East Germans – they channelled a million marks into it via Prague. Meinhoff used to be *Konret's* star columnist. Married its publisher, a guy called Klaus Rohl and left him in '68 to join Baader in West Berlin."

The doctor looked surprised. "*That* Meinhof. The Baader Meinhof gang. I didn't know Suzy Katoul was mixed up with them."

"She knew Meinhof," Ross qualified. "How much she was involved is hard to say." He turned back to me and injected a note of sarcasm into his voice. "Unless you know all about that?"

I shook my head. "I lost touch with her until '74. Even when we met again, she was reticent about the missing years. And I suppose I was so relieved to have found her again – and found her so apparently normal, that I never probed very hard. It seemed best to – well, best to let sleeping dogs lie."

Ross studied me with brooding eyes. "So you claim you met her again in '74. Where was that?"

November 5th, 1974. In England children celebrated a Catholic terrorist's attempt to blow up Parliament and in France I buried Farida at the little churchyard of St Augustine de la Salle on the outskirts of Paris. Rain lashed down from a leaden sky and the scent of woodsmoke drifted across from a bonfire in an adjoining garden. Dust to dust, ashes to ashes. Grief, loneliness, despair and death – it seemed Farida's life had been that empty. Even death mocked a life so inconsequential that only three mourners stood at the graveside – the Algerian neighbour who had sent for me and the French concierge from the apartment building. They huddled against me as we listened to the priest's teeth chatter in the biting cold and when it was over we trudged back to the church, our heads bowed and eyes slit against the dust flung up by the swirling wind. I thanked them for being there and sent them away in the car I had hired. I can't remember now why I didn't go with them, but I stood on the steps to the church and thought about the one person who might have comforted Farida in her failing years. And when I looked up she was there, half-hidden in the gloom of the entrance with her face turned towards me. For the craziest moment I thought she was Haleem. A trick of the light and the mood I was in, but the resemblance was uncanny.

"Hello, Harry." Even the voice was an echo twenty years old.

I was suddenly angry. "You should have been here."

104

"I was," Suzy said. "But in the church, not at the graveside. I forfeited that right years ago."

By then my surprise had faded enough for me to notice the details. Like the assured way she carried herself and the cut of the black suit under the unbuttoned mink coat.

"It's too late to say sorry to Farida," she said. "But can't I say sorry to you?"

Then the composure cracked wide open and we were in each other's arms. All the anger died in that instant. Perhaps I realised how much I had missed her and just what she meant to me. And maybe how lonely I was – with a failed marriage behind me and a way of life which provided a million acquaintances, but no real friends. The only *family* I had known since childhood had been Farida – and Suzy Katoul.

Her chauffeur drove us back to Paris. The smart car and the mink coat were the first clues I had to her new lifestyle. The apartment at 14 Avenue de Friedland was the next – a Canaletto in the lobby and a Ruoualt *and* a Guardi in the drawing room. When I finished admiring the place she indulged my preference for whisky, served herself a cognac and we settled down to talk. It had just turned noon then, and crazy as it sounds we almost talked the clock round. She prepared a snack lunch and we went out to dinner in the evening and then back to her place. When I got over how grown-up she was, it was time to question the material possessions.

"I'm a purchasing agent," she said. "For half a dozen businesses in the Middle East." She gave me the names of a couple of them but no bells rang – at least not then.

Had my schedule permitted I might have stayed even longer, but I was due to entertain a visiting congressman in London the next day, so at just after midnight I left. But we promised to stay in touch. Finding each other after a gap of six years seemed like discovering another part of ourselves – or at least it did to me. I was in Paris every second month or so and she was sometimes in London – so though we never made a firm date it was on the cards for us to meet again soon. And I looked forward to it.

The following evening I had my first brush with Special Branch. Three of them arrived at my flat with a search warrant. You can argue all you like with Special Branch, but they have a knack of getting what they want in the end – which was to take my place apart and rebuild it.

"So what were you looking for?" I asked when they finished.

The boss man grinned. "Guns would have been best, though any kind of explosives would have been useful. Failing that, forged passports, unexplained stocks of currency, even drugs at a push."

"I'm sorry to disappoint you," I said coldly.

"We'll get over it. Nothing surprises us in this job."

"Is that so?"

"Well, take you for example. You've just been to Paris right? Mind telling me why?"

"Only if you'll tell me what this is all about."

His agreement was less positive than I had hoped, but none-the-less I told him, "I've been to the funeral of an old friend."

"Anything else?"

"It's your turn."

"Suzy Katoul, Mr Brand – you spent twelve hours with her and forgot to mention it."

"So what? Anyway, how do you know?"

"Friends of ours told us. They watched you go into her flat and saw you come out again." He smiled broadly. "It's all very simple."

"You mean her apartment's under observation?"

"Surveillance we call it."

"For what reason?"

He seemed the slightest bit surprised. "Terrorist activities. You're *not* going to tell us you don't know who she is?"

"Of course I know who she is!" As my astonishment faded my temper boiled over. "*Terrorist* activities? You must be completely –"

"You know she's involved in politics," he said sharply.

"She used to be involved in *student* politics, and –"

He laughed outright at that. "I'd say she's graduated, Mr Brand. Suzy Katoul is the European end of the Palestinian Marxist Front – and they're *very* grown up."

"She's a highly successful businesswoman who's –"

"Purchasing agent for some big shots in the Middle East?" he cocked his head to one side. "Oh yes, she's that as well. A very busy little lady isn't she – one way and another."

He had to be telling the truth. Christ, I was angry! Angry with him and his goons for turning my flat over, angry with Suzy for not telling me, and above all angry with myself for not anticipating something like this. All I needed to do was remember the last time I had seen her. All those people in that café – all politicals, every single one of them.

I phoned her when they left. "Why the bloody hell didn't you tell me?"

"Harry, believe it or not I was *pleased* to see you." She hesitated

106

and then said firmly, "But well, is it really any of your business?"

"The police seem to think so."

"Oh *that*," she dismissed it. "That's nothing – harassment that's all. I get it all the time."

"You mean you *know* they watch your apartment?"

She laughed. "Harry, I've even had them in for a drink. It works both ways, you know. Like now – them tapping the line helps establish your innocence. I mean, even *they* can tell outraged indignation when they hear it."

That shut me up so completely that I was still thinking of an answer when she giggled: "Testing, one, two, three. Harry and Monsieur Le Spook – are you both still there? This is Suzy Katoul signing off – over and out." And she hung up.

I got used to it. When I next visited her she even took me to the window and pointed out the guard on duty. He sat reading a magazine in the front seat of a blue Renault parked on the other side of the road. Suzy blew him a kiss and shut the blinds.

"Okay, Harry, I'll make a deal with you. You've got your work and I've got mine. Mine's what I live twenty-four hours a day. Total immersion, got it? I'm not a kid, I'm twenty-seven years old, Charles de Gaulle is dead and there aren't any barricades on the boulevards this year. Since I left home the French have got fat, the British got lazy, the Germans got rich and the Yanks got Nixon. Added together, the West hasn't got a philosophy worth stuffing in a Christmas cracker!"

Her scornful look defied interruption. "Meanwhile, one and a half million people live in camps and are deprived of the most basic right of all – the right to return to their own homes! And the world doesn't want to know. Well, I'm one of the lucky ones. You and Farida got me out and for that I'm grateful – even if I once thought differently. But my life *belongs* to the people in those camps and I'll not stop fighting until the Palestinians return home. And I'll tell you something else – there'll be damn all peace in the Middle East until they do!"

We never discussed politics after that. She was *dedicated* to Palestinian Liberation – it was that simple. We met whenever I visited Paris, shared meals together, exchanged gifts at Christmas and that was that. It was half a loaf if you like – she was my *family* again but on her terms. I can only guess at the kind of life she led – she rarely talked about it, other than places we had in common, cities we had both visited, restaurants we had dined in, those kinds of things. She knew a surprising amount about art and was a collector in a minor way, and while on my travels I would look out for things likely to be of interest to her. We went to the theatre once in London and saw a couple of films together – it was *that* kind of relationship – *non-political*, as I said at the very beginning.

THE FOURTH DAY

"Since a politician never believes what he says,
he is surprised when others believe him."

Charles de Gaulle,
October 1st, 1962

08.45 Friday

Molly Malone was actually singing. She had no voice to speak of and
she sang for nobody's pleasure but her own, but she was *actually*
singing. Such a simple thing, but she couldn't remember when last
she had been happy enough to sing. Days, weeks, months and
years had strung together into a drab backcloth against which they
lived their existence; sometimes, it seemed, without so much as a
spark of joy to lighten the gloom. But this morning was different.
This morning she had already cleared the crockery and washed the
pots and pans, and cleaned the stove and tidied the kitchen. And
this morning she felt ten years younger.

Silly really, to feel like a girl again because of such little things. Yet
wasn't it the little things in life which made all the difference? Mick's
bonus of a few hundred pounds would come in handy when they
got it, God knows the money was needed right enough, but it was
the difference in *Mick* that was important. He had got his self respect
back. It was the importance of the job as much as the money being
paid for it, she knew that. To drive one of those trucks all the way to
Germany and back was a job for a man, a *whole* man, not the fading
husk he'd been turning into for the last year or more.

Yesterday she had worried and harboured fears that his strength
might run out. She had been afraid he would overtax himself, but in
bed last night he had laughed at her fears and overtaxed himself in
other ways. Just remembering made her weak at the knees, so that
she sat down quickly and smiled about her like a cat that had stolen
the cream. It was years since they had made love *that* way, so long

that she had forgotten the excitement of it, so long that his tenderness had brought tears to her eyes.

And this morning she was having her hair done for the first time in years. Mick's orders, so that she looked her best for tonight. And she was to buy a new shirt for the boy and shoes for herself. Money helped, but it was more than that. She knew it was. It was the joy of living with a man again, a husband and a father who was at peace with himself, a man with his self-respect back, who would ruffle the boy's hair and look at her with love in his eyes. That's what mattered. Molly glanced at the alarm clock, counting the minutes until he returned for his breakfast – and she started to sing again.

09.00 Friday

It was my third morning at the Health Farm. It felt like the hundred and third. My head buzzed from the question and answer session which had lasted till midnight, while my mind got busy and counted the number of people searching for Suzy Katoul. But the hunt had only just started.

We were in Ross's office. All of us. Elizabeth, LeClerc, Archie Dorfman and the neat little man from political intelligence. At the head of the table Ross drank orange juice and glared at the transcript of last night's interrogation session. He turned to LeClerc. "What's the computer make of all this?"

LeClerc braced himself for his normal morning bawling out. "Still cross-referencing. People she met at the camps – other refugees who made it to Paris – links with Baader-Meinhoff. It all takes time."

"We haven't got time."

"Another hour," LeClerc pleaded. "That's all."

"An hour too long," Ross growled, forever mindful of Suzy's twenty-four hour deadline. The gold Tissot flashed on his wrist and he grew increasingly restless. "What you got this morning, Archie?"

Dorfman frowned. "Pieces of another guy's jigsaw I think. Not much to fit our situation."

"So tell me."

Dorfman would clearly rather not, but he opened his file and fumbled into his report. "Taking the shipping angle – two hundred and eight vessels were within a hundred miles of the *Marisa* when she was hit. We've cleared a hundred and ninety so far. The rest are still being followed up, but we think a large ship was close to the *Marisa* when it happened – possibly within twenty miles. Identifi-

110

cation's difficult but we've narrowed it down to three possibles: a Dutch freighter, a British cruise ship and a Libyan tanker."

"Go on."

"Well, we've had some radio contact with the British and Dutch ships. Enough to be reasonably satisfied they're in the clear. We're still checking of course – our people meet the liner at Oslo this afternoon and the freighter at Rotterdam tomorrow."

"And the tanker?"

"Not much really. We think she's the *Fadayeen* and if she *is* there's a bit of mystery about her," he frowned. "Well, not exactly *mystery*, but –"

"I'll evaluate."

Dorfman blushed. "A week ago she was in Copenhagen. She stayed overnight, carried out some repair to her electrics, then moved on." He consulted his notes. "Supposedly headed for Aberdeen, but she never made it. We checked with the Port Authorities there. But she *was* seen in Scottish waters."

Ross scowled. "So where is she now?"

"Tripoli. She docked last night."

"And?"

"Apparently her electrics blew up again while at sea. She stood by for about twenty-four hours to fix them, then put back to Tripoli for an overhaul." Dorfman shook his head. "And according to her log she never went near Scotland."

"But you believe otherwise," Ross watched him closely.

"We're double-checking the reports now, but we think she was sighted off the Orkneys." Dorfman returned to his notes, "By a Scottish trawler and a Norwegian tanker."

Ross pulled a face. "It's not much." He looked at LeClerc, "Any comment?"

The Frenchman shrugged and shook his head, but next to him the neat little man cleared his throat. When he spoke he sounded almost apologetic. "We did pick up *another* story from Copenhagen. I've told Archie about it and there's probably no connection, but Passport Control at Copenhagen reported two known I.R.A. men there last week." He searched half a dozen pages of his notes before he found the correct reference. "Purpose of visit, holiday, according to the immigration cards. The Danes noted which boarding house they were staying at and put them under loose surveillance," he giggled. "Well, it appears that it was a bit *too* loose – because they vanished."

"Vanished?" Ross echoed in disbelief.

The little man nodded. "The Danes are hopping mad about it. The boarding house were supposed to notify the police if the Irishmen checked out early, but they went out Saturday night and the boarding house forgot about it until Monday morning. Meanwhile, the Irishmen dropped out of sight. Passport control say they haven't left Denmark, but the police can't find them in Copenhagen."

Ross swore softly. "Who were they?"

"Not big wheels. I can show them to you if you like?"

Ross nodded. The little man extracted two cards like library tickets from an index box, while Elizabeth closed the shutters against the morning sun. The temperature dropped, Elizabeth clicked back across the marble floor and the little man punched buttons on a pocket calculator. One of the television screens lit up with a larger than life colour shot of a man in blue duffel coat. C.I.A. computer banks hold millions of cards on suspected terrorists, supplied by half the security organisations in the world, yet it takes less than a second to retrieve one photograph and flash it onto a T.V. screen. I grappled with the Orwellian significance of it while the man in the duffel coat changed position until we had seen half a dozen shots of him.

"Liam Reilly," said the little man. "Age thirty-eight, married, two children, occupation fisherman. Suspected I.R.A. courier for twelve years, believed to have smuggled arms into Ireland from France. No convictions. Generally considered a quiet sort, not ambitious. Possibly because of his occupation, however, it's thought he might have been involved in the *Claudia* incident in seventy-four."

"Is it now," Ross said with sharpened interest. The *Claudia* incident was one of the few provable instances of Gaddafi sending arms to the I.R.A.

The little man tapped a new code into his *calculator* and a different photograph appeared. "Pat Brady. Same age as Reilly, went to school together and been friends ever since – always ready to follow where Reilly leads. They both work for a set-up called Inishmore Fishing. Nothing known about that, so it's probably all right." He lapsed into silence while we stared at the dark-haired Irishman. Eventually Ross asked, "Is that all?"

"All we've got at the moment," the little man said.

Elizabeth walked to the windows and we blinked at the sunlight while Ross turned to Dorfman. "You're suggesting those two hitched a ride on your tanker?"

Dorfman shrugged. "It seemed a possibility to begin with –"

"Are they in Tripoli?"

Dorfman shook his head. "No, we *think* they're in Ireland."

"Ireland?"

"It seems likely –"

Ross scowled. "You're saying this tanker went to Ireland? As well as Scotland?"

Dorfman tried to explain. "We've been monitoring coastguard reports from all round Europe. Everything filed last week. It takes time of course but –"

"If anyone says *that* again," Ross threatened.

"But we think we've found something," Dorfman protested. "A report filed Wednesday by the Shannon coastguard. Routine interception of a fishing boat, skippered by a man called Liam Reilly."

"The same Reilly?"

"We're awaiting more detail, but we think so."

"Why?"

"Because the mate's name was Brady."

Ross winced. "Never look for Jones and Evans in Cardiff. There's hundreds of them. Like Reillys and Bradys in Ireland."

"*Liam* Reilly, and *Pat* Brady?"

"Tom, Dick and Harry" Ross was determined not to be impressed. "And Liam means Bill."

"But the fishing boat they were in, the *Aileen Maloney*, belongs to the Inishmore Fishing company."

"Oh," Ross sounded disappointed. "You never told me that."

Dorfman opened his mouth for a quick answer, but thought better of it.

Ross stared into space, turning the idea over in his mind while we sat and watched him. Finally he said, "I can't see the I.R.A. in this. It's too big, too well organised." He gazed around the table, as if inviting contradiction, and when none came he made up his mind. "Don't waste time on it. Pass it to Dublin and forget about it. Concentrate on the Middle East."

I watched Dorfman's reaction. His mouth drooped at the corners and he looked a shade crestfallen, but for the determined glint in his eye. He was about to make an issue of it when Ross cut him off and turned to me. "You're going to the pictures, with Elizabeth."

"Anything good?"

"Mug shots. People who were in the Lebanon camp with Negib Katoul, others who had contact with your girl in Paris. Let me know if you recognise any of them – okay?"

"Okay."

I followed Elizabeth downstairs to the studio, thinking Ross was making slow progress and wondering if Nikki Orlov was coping any better.

It took rather longer than an hour to view fifty mug shots. Elizabeth flicked her way through an entire library of cards while I stared dutifully at the screen. Only once did I think I recognised a face.

"Who's she?" I asked, looking at a slim blonde in her middle twenties.

Elizabeth sat a yard away, separated by dust motes and cigarette smoke trapped in a beam of light. She shook her head. "Sorry, you tell me." She must have sensed my irritation because she added, "It's the procedure. It mustn't be said that I led you on."

I gave her a few choice words about salacious gossip and turned back to the blonde on the screen. Something about her seemed familiar. Elizabeth tapped buttons and the blonde changed her position. And her clothes. Where she had been kitted out in an ankle-length leather coat, now she was dressed for tennis. Whoever she was she had a good figure and money enough to show it off. A third shot showed her at the races, complete with an Ascot-type hat and a man in a grey topper.

"What's a nice girl like that doing in a place like this?"

"Do you *know* her?"

"I could try. She's a lot prettier than Arafat."

Elizabeth sighed, then the girl changed into a bikini and sat on the edge of a swimming pool while I sighed and watched her.

"That's all we've got," Elizabeth said.

"Don't apologise. I'll take her."

We went through the sequence again. Leather coat, tennis gear, a day at the races and the bikini. "Go back to the race track," I said.

"My," Elizabeth purred, "the iron self control of the man." Obediently she changed the picture and the blonde and I stared at each other.

She might have been a model. Pleated silk skirt, full with a swirl to it, tight-waisted below a modest but well-shaped bust, with a haze of chiffon at her throat. The photographer had focused on her, catching her with compelling clarity although the man on her arm was blurred and indistinct. My eyes stayed on the girl. A snub nose with a hint of freckles, wide generous lips and deep blue eyes. I *did* know her.

"She's French," I said.

"Did you meet her in Paris?"

"No, not Paris." I was certain of that. It was the dress which reminded me. Put a dress on some women and it might be a shroud, it fulfilled a function, preserved their modesty, kept out the draught. Put a dress on this girl and she made you look at it – and what was inside it. It had something to do with the way she carried herself, the walk, the confident tilt of her chin – everything about her was captured in that one photograph.

"A friend of Suzy's?" Elizabeth prompted.

I hesitated. *Friend* was wrong. At least I had thought so at the time. I had distrusted her. Suzy had introduced us in her usual smooth way. " 'Harry, I'd like you to meet –?' Like you to meet? What the devil *was* the girl's name?"

It had been warm. An English summer's day. The girls had worn silk or cotton. Cool, formal, smelling of money and privilege. The accents were mainly English too, loud voices with all that haw-hawing which passes for upper-class conversation. Suddenly I remembered.

"It was Henley, two summers ago. We met quite by chance." I laughed at the memory. "I avoid that sort of thing like the plague as a rule. But I was staying the weekend with a friend who was more or less obligated to put in an appearance and I got dragged along."

"Which friend Harry?" Elizabeth coaxed in her golden brown voice.

"Does it matter?"

"Harry," she scolded. "Everything matters. You *know* that."

Did I? I sat hunched up in my chair, staring at the larger than life blonde and thinking back to the summer of '76. Next to me Elizabeth moved. I took no real notice but registered that I could no longer see her from the corner of my eye.

Henley, '76. I had been staying with Tubby Hayes. Strange bloke Tubby. Used to be a war correspondent years ago, way back in Korea and the aftermath. Then he'd gone to Taiwan, discovered their infant electronics industry and turned capitalist. Imported all sorts of stuff into the U.K: cheap tape recorders, intercoms, even walkie-talkies until the G.P.O. stopped him. Later it was hi-fi and all that nonsense, and now it's video recorders and calculators and God knows what else. Lives in opulence in a Georgian pile on the Thames at Henley and goes in for country house parties with as many as a dozen people staying for the weekends. You meet all sorts at Tubby's. Cabinet ministers, journalists, businessmen; all mixed up and talking their heads off. As jaw shops go it beats the House of Commons. I stay perhaps three times a year and entertain him in

115

London sometimes, as a token return of his hospitality.

There was nothing unusual about that particular visit, apart from it being Regatta week, until late on Friday afternoon when Tubby mentioned the promise he had made to call on a neighbour.

"Just for an hour, Old Boy," he said. "Scoff some strawberries and chat up the pretty girls. Want to come?"

We walked across Tubby's manicured acre to the copse screening the gardens from the river, along the tow path to the next boathouse and then through a wicker gate leading to another garden. Lawns bereft of a single daisy swept down to meet us and we picked our way through a dozen trees heavy with apples. The house was a hundred yards away, high up and skirted by a wide terrace from which gracious stone steps descended to the garden.

There must have been at least fifty people there, more women than men, their summer dresses catching the sunlight like butterfly wings and the sound of their laughter tinkling down to us on the soft summer breeze. White-coated waiters served golden drinks from silver trays to old men who looked faintly ridiculous in striped blazers and yellowed straw hats, and the air was heavy with the scent of honeysuckle and Chanel number five.

We had been on the terrace half an hour before I saw Suzy. I was astonished. We had met in Paris the week before and she'd said nothing then about visiting England. But there she was, at the far end of the terrace, flanked by two other girls and absorbed in conversation with a very tall man who stood partly in shadow. I excused myself from the people I was with and started across to her. She saw me when I was still six or seven yards away, our eyes meeting across the heads and hats of others. Her face froze with surprise, surprise and something else? I thought it was alarm for a moment, fear even, then I laughed at the absurdity of it as she turned to greet me with a radiant smile and elbowed her way through the crush.

"Harry! How marvellous. Oh, I wish I'd known you'd be here." She lowered her voice to a confidential whisper. "But – well, it's not really *your* scene is it?"

"Is it yours?" I was laughing, delighted to meet her. "What are you doing here anyway?"

"I'm here to meet –" she began, but she was interrupted by one of the girls she had been talking to.

"Suzy, darling, who's your good-looking friend?" The blonde with the blue eyes hurried to join us. People stepped aside to make a path for her so I got the full impact of the model's walk and the flashing confident smile. Even the tilt of the chin was exactly as in the image on the screen.

"Harry, I'd like you to meet Monique Debray," Suzy said, hugging my arm. "Monique, meet Harry Brand," she hesitated for the briefest second, then added, "my godfather."

The blonde engulfed me like a long lost cousin and gushed a lot of nonsense about how much she had heard about me. Then Suzy was tugging my sleeve again. "Harry, come and meet A–" she stopped abruptly, her gaze directed towards the end of the terrace where she had been a moment earlier. The man had vanished. He had been there seconds earlier, along with the third girl, now nothing, only empty space quickly filled by other people drifting across the terrace like leaves on the wind.

"He's making our goodbyes," Monique Debray explained. "Suzy, we're late already."

"Late?" Suzy's head snapped round, surprise all over her face.

Monique said, "I'm awfully sorry, Mr Brand." She had a hand on my arm, blood red fingernails complementing a huge ruby ring. "But we should have left half an hour ago. As it is we'll have to drive like maniacs to catch our plane."

"Plane?" I said stupidly.

"We're due back in Paris this evening," she nodded. "The time's just flown – hasn't it Suzy?"

Something in her manner worried me, as if she was warning Suzy about something, and Suzy was just about to speak when Tubby Hayes joined us. He looked strained and anxious which was unusual for him. Generally he's the most relaxed man I know. But he *too* was looking at his watch. I introduced him all round and Tubby flashed a perfunctory smile which barely concealed his agitation. "Rawlins has arrived, Old Boy," he said urgently. "Sorry to break the party up, but we really ought to get back."

Rawlins was a Parliamentary Under-Secretary who was driving over from Maidenhead or thereabouts for dinner. Tubby had mentioned something earlier about his coming especially to ask me about recent developments in Iran.

Monique Debray was talking into my other ear. "I'm so glad we met – and I'm sure we'll meet again." She transferred her hand to Suzy's elbow and was steering her away, edging her towards the French windows and the shade of the drawing-room. Suzy looked slightly dazed, but she leaned forward hurriedly and pecked my cheek. "It seems I have to go," she said. Behind me Tubby Hayes was saying goodbye in a loud voice and tugging my jacket at the same time. "I *say* Old Boy, I'm awfully sorry but we've *got* to dash. Old Rawlins will think it's no end bad form if I'm not there to greet him."

I turned to claim another minute to say goodbye to Suzy, but he was already shouldering his way through a group of people. "Tubby, hang on a sec." I swung back to ask when I would see her again, but she had gone. I caught the merest glimpse of her green dress next to the blue worn by the blonde as they hurried across the drawing room, and I was half prepared to chase after her when Tubby called, "I say Harry Old Boy, do get a move on! Rawlins will be absolutely furious!" So I went.

I watched the smoke from my cigarette curl up into the light, while above me Monique Debray smiled her confident smile and behind me Elizabeth massaged my shoulders, her long fingers working rhythmically inside the open neck of my shirt. Funny, but I had been too tensed up even to notice when she started.

"And *did* you meet again?" she asked, still in her golden brown voice. "Monique Debray and you?"

"No," I nodded at the screen. "Not until now. Who is she anyway?"

"What about the man? The man with the girls at the end of the terrace? Did you see him. Could you describe him? Or if you saw a photo would you recognise him?"

He had been standing almost in the drawing-room, cloaked in shade. I only saw him for a split second. Tall, at least a foot taller than Suzy, dressed in a pale-grey suit, holding a glass in his hand.

"Try," Elizabeth purred in my ear. "What colour was his hair for example?"

"God knows. It looked dark from where I was standing, black almost, but that could have been shadow. Close up he could have been fair. I'm sorry, but –"

"A beard? Moustache? *Try* Harry, it could be important."

"Dammit, it *was* two years ago!" Two years is just too long to recall something which seemed quite unimportant at the time. "Clean shaven I think, but don't rely on it."

"And his name – Suzy started to tell you?"

"Started is right. Then the other girl interrupted her. But I'm sure it began with an A – that's all I can remember."

"How unfortunate," Elizabeth said as crisp as dry toast. "Or fortunate. Depending on whose side you're on."

There seemed no answer to that, so I just sat back and enjoyed the massage.

"And this man Rawlins?" she asked quietly. "The Parliamentary Under-Secretary. Did he provide you with an interesting evening?" "That's just it," I laughed. "The message Tubby got was all cock. Rawlins couldn't make it. Tubby got a call saying Rawlins was at the house which he took to mean *his* house. Instead it meant Rawlins had been detained at *the* house – the House of Commons."

10.35 Friday

It had been a risk, but one worth taking Abou decided as he sat next to Big Reilly in the back of the old Ford. In front of him the driver edged the car into Gresham Street's heavy morning traffic and began the journey back to Conlaragh.

Reilly too was relieved to be leaving Dublin. Not that he was a wanted man, but he was certainly a watched one and with the new emergency regulations a tap on the shoulder was never more than a pace away. Especially in Dublin. But he was pleased with the outcome of the morning's work. "You'll have earned Mick's thanks for the way you've handled things," he said.

Abou nodded. He had spent most of the night thinking about Mick Malone. Malone and the gamble of changing the driver at this late hour. But without Cassidy what choice did they have? Cassidy? Now *there* was a worry. Cassidy in custody, being questioned, cross-examined by sharp-witted men, who spent their lives matching the pieces of one story to those of another until they had a tale worth telling. But he would deal with Cassidy later. The problem of Mick Malone had been the most urgent and now arrangements had been made strong enough to satisfy even Reilly's suspicions.

Reilly watched a truck pull out in front of them. "The police are looking for Suzy Katoul. Did you know that?"

"How did *you* know it?"

Reilly gave a sly grin. "Not every policeman is opposed to the unification of Ireland, you know. No matter what the Government says about it."

Abou knew better than to question that, but it was no surprise to learn that the I.R.A.–police relationship was not always the one read about in the newspapers. Just as it was no surprise to learn that the Irish police had been alerted about Suzy Katoul. Every police force in Europe would be looking for her by now, come to that every police force linked to Interpol.

"It was expected," he said.

"It makes our job harder," Reilly grumbled.

119

"Nothing changes," Abou said firmly. "She stays out of sight at Conlaragh until tomorrow. Then you give her a car and that's the last you'll see of her."

"And of you?"

Abou's dark eyes flickered. "Tomorrow will be the last you see of any of us." He closed his eyes to discourage further conversation and hoped Reilly had not read too much into his words. The drone of the engine and the motion of the car soothed him and made him determined to finish the journey in silence. Talk was dangerous, especially when he was tired.

Images glowed in his mind like a flickering fire in a darkened room. The darkened room at Conlaragh, the room shared with Suzy Katoul. Tonight would be their last night together – the last for a week was what she thought. But he knew better. It would be their *last* night. One last night spent enjoying the sight and the smell and the feel of her body, one last night witnessing her pathetic eagerness as he pumped a syringe into a vein in her arm. One last night with Suzy Katoul.

He squeezed his eyelids until the images changed. Paris, the school in the mountains, his feelings when he first saw his new face. Memories of his homeland, of growing up as the only son in the house of a powerful man. Visits abroad with his father, trips to Washington to meet the leaders of that colossal nation. Men they once had trusted. He remembered the promises over the years.

"America honours your valiant fight and is proud to recognise you as an illustrious ally."

"Your continued struggle is a glowing example to the rest of the democratic world."

"Our frontiers are your frontiers. Our enemies your enemies. Our *two* countries are as *one* nation."

He remembered the men. General Douglas MacArthur – President Harry Truman – President Dwight D. Eisenhower – President John F. Kennedy. So many men and so many promises. All had said the same thing: "The greatness of your task is exceeded only by the greatness of your determination. America will *never* desert you."

But America was planning to do just that. Three years ago their spies in Washington had sensed a chill wind and within twelve months Abou's father and the other family heads who ruled from behind the scenes had formed the Plan. Just in case, they said, just in case the unthinkable happened and their powerful ally chose to betray them. And now the spies had sent the proof. The unthink-

able was about to happen – America would betray them in 1978.
And the Plan was about to be put into operation.

We were still in the Studio when the buzzers sounded. They blared
like fog horns and with exactly that note of panic in them. The door
opened and the doctor poked his face in and then withdrew hurriedly. Elizabeth said "Come on" to me and scuttled to the door in a
walk fast enough to be a trot. I thought the Martians had landed.

Spitari's place was like an iceberg, only the tip was visible. We
headed to the mail room which was second level basement. Without
Elizabeth, I would have needed a map to find it and a ball of string to
get back again. Even finding it depressed me – it was like a German
bunker, massive steel girders supported the roof and the walls were
of reinforced concrete instead of the limestone blocks used for the
upper stories. A bench ran the length of one wall, not housing scales
and wrapping paper but x-ray equipment and electronic scanners.
And it was run by the demon driver from Luqa. Thirty years with
the Sappers had left Smithers as upright as a beanpole and about as
talkative. But he had his good points – like being an armourer and
explosives expert of no mean standing.

"Bit elaborate for a mail room, isn't it?"

Elizabeth gave me her sour look to shut me up. "Not when you've
seen someone maimed and blinded by a letter bomb." Her face
sweetened as she turned to Smithers. "Have you processed the mail
yet?"

"The old man collected it half an hour ago." Smithers had a jumpy
look in his eye and I got the strongest feeling he would have added
something had I not been there. So did Elizabeth because she
switched her eyes on full power until they jolted him like laser
beams.

Back in the corridor we bumped into Dorfman, halfway through a
door marked "Signals." He was sweating again, but this time *really*
sweating. A man could get less wet under a shower. "Ross wants
you," he told Elizabeth and then shut the door in her face.

Elizabeth shoved me into a little two-man lift and pulled the gate
closed behind us. She was worried sick and I began to wonder when
they would let me in on the secret. Something was going on and I
seemed to be the only person in the building not in on it. The doors
opened and we hurried down the corridor to Ross's office. LeClerc

was there already, with two other men I had never seen before. Ross looked shaken. "She's made contact. She's in Scotland." Which made even less sense than Libya until he elaborated. "Or she was, look at *that!*"

That was a page torn from an atlas. It showed Scotland from about Stirling upwards with an enlarged insert depicting the Orkneys and the Shetlands. North of the Butt of Lewis in the Outer Hebrides lies a tiny island – Rona Island – and half an inch or so to the left of that a dot said "read text" in green ink. The "text" was on a sheet of cheap notepaper taped to the edge of the map and Suzy had written: "Nuclear test to be carried out by the Deir Yassin Memorial – 02.00 hours Saturday. Estimated strength – one kiliton. Suzy Katoul."

"A *test* explosion?"

"It's a demonstration," Ross snapped. "One kiliton's nothing. They've got enough plutonium for a bomb a hundred times as big. They're proving they can deliver that's all."

The two new men were clearly as agitated as Ross. One said, "They haven't had enough time. I *still* say it. Even with access to the most advanced reactors – they haven't had enough *time!*" His partner couldn't agree fast enough. "Given the material they had, it would take at least a month to convert to fissionable material – *at least* a month."

The glare Ross gave him would have blistered paintwork. "So we all sit on our butts while this bitch lights a fire-cracker loud enough to deafen the Pentagon."

The first man snorted. "Oh really! A one kiliton explosion won't be heard in Edinburgh, let alone –"

"Ever heard of Polaris submarines?" Ross jabbed a finger at him. "Ever heard of an anchorage on the West Coast of Scotland? If you think a paper bag can burst within fifty miles of that without the Pentagon knowing, then you need your tiny scientific brain rebored right down to your ass!" He caught sight of Dorfman entering the room. "For Chrissakes Archie – you took your time."

"The R.A.F. can fly you out within half an hour," Dorfman panted to prove he'd been hurrying. "There's a chopper on its way over now. The Sixth Fleet have despatched *Nautilus* to rendezvous this side of Cyprus. They'll fly us Phantom direct to Scotland."

"Any word from Zebra?"

"Not yet. We're on standby now."

Ross turned to Elizabeth. "Get Control relayed to *Nautilus* – we'll pick it up there. You'll co-ordinate from here – usual procedures – London will be through within the hour. Key them into Langley."

He looked at LeClerc. "Has that other signal been sent to Twomey?"

"Half an hour ago."

"Jesus, can you imagine *his* reaction?" Ross pulled a face and then suddenly remembered something. "Oh shit!" he turned to Elizabeth. "Nikki Orlov is coming through tonight. Buy whatever he's selling but that's all, understand?" He ran the splayed fingers of his right hand through his hair. "Not that the bastard won't know all about it by now, anyway. Jesus Christ, what else?"

Dorfman said, "The British are making plans to clear the area of shipping now. The story is a N.A.T.O. exercise involving nuclear sub –"

"The *story*? You mean they've put out to the Press?"

"Not yet," Dorfman shook his head. "But if we're going to clear almost a hundred square miles of the Atlantic –"

"Okay, okay, who's handling it?"

"Murison – he's already on his way up from London. N.A.T.O. Brussels are standing by to confirm any story he puts out and –"

"N.A.T.O. *Brussels*!" Ross howled. "How many people are in the act already?"

Dorfman shook his head.

Ross glared. "Well at least Twomey told you which level of command this has gone out to?"

"He said he'd tell *you*. When he sees you."

Ross shook his head in apparent disbelief. "Meanwhile, the bastard keeps me in the dark and shovels shit over me – what's he think I am – a goddammed mushroom or something?"

"Coded instructions will be waiting for you on the *Nautilus*," Dorfman said apologetically.

"Well," Ross growled, "isn't that dandy."

The white telephone shrilled and LeClerc answered it. He said "yes" and "no" half a dozen times, then handed it to Dorfman. Ross seethed as he waited for the call to finish.

"Those Irishmen," Dorfman said when he put the phone down. "You remember the ones who –"

Ross purpled. "You really pick your moments, don't you?"

"Disappeared in Copenhagen," Dorfman said in a rush. "Well they've vanished again. Dublin sent a routine request to –"

"Can it, will you!" Ross was hunting through the papers on his desk, anxiously performing some last-minute check list. Preoccupied, he said, "Ireland's not Scotland and it's certainly not Suzy Katoul. I told you to forget it." He turned back to Elizabeth. "Anderson's going up from London. *Nautilus* will give you our E.T.A.

Scotland – make sure Anderson gets it and is there in time to meet us."

She nodded, white-faced and thin-lipped. Their eyes met in some private goodbye, then Ross was scooping papers into a briefcase and heading for the door, LeClerc and Dorfman a pace behind. Halfway there he remembered me. "Thank Christ you're not there! At least *your* typewriter won't be shooting its mouth off."

"I'll save it for my memoirs."

"You save *this* and it'll be on your fucking epitaph!"

The helicopter arrived a minute later. It clattered over the ridge behind the Health Farm and dropped into the courtyard like some demented dragonfly seeking a final resting place. It was a big Wessex 250 on which the R.A.F. had painted roundels in case they lost it. Yellow-clad arms pulled Ross aboard, others reached for LeClerc and Dorfman and the rotor blades never even stopped spinning. Elizabeth and I watched the machine rise and I caught a quick glimpse of Ross peering down at us – then it banked high over the ridge and into the sun.

Ross's office was empty when we returned to it. Elizabeth told me to wait there and I stood looking out at the view, nursing my thoughts until she returned fifteen minutes later.

"Tubby Hayes," she said crisply. "And the man in the pale-grey suit. London are interested in them."

I was still thinking about Scotland. After all, *that's* what all the flap was about. "Then tell London to talk to Tubby. He only lives at Henley."

"They tried that an hour ago. He's gone. And his house has been ransacked."

"Gone? Gone where? Tubby's big business. He's got an office in town, staff, employees, some sort of factory just outside Paris. Men like Tubby don't just *go*. He'll be around somewhere – wheeling and dealing."

"And his house?"

"How the hell do I know? Burgled – done over? Tell the police and the insurance boys, don't tell me."

She poured coffee for us both. "Listen Harry, it's not that simple. London think there's a line connecting Hayes to Monique Debray. And the same line links your girl Suzy to the man in the pale-grey suit." She sat in the chair opposite, her knees pressed tightly together, nursing her cup in her hands and leaning forward slightly to peer at my face. "And London are beginning to think very hard about *you*."

124

Once I got through shock it was funny. But I lost my temper first.
"I don't give a damn what London think! In fact I doubt they think at
all – not rationally anyway. Who the hell are *London* anyway? Some
faceless civil servants tucked away in a Whitehall cubby hole –"

"Harry!" She had the trick of shouting quietly better than anyone
I know. "We haven't got time for your outraged citizen act. Put it up
against the lives of half a million people and what's it worth anyway? Okay – yell to your M.P., scream your head off in print, do
what you damn well like *afterwards*! But right now you're going to
help, and if London want to know about Tubby Hayes or you, or
anybody else, so help me God you're going to tell them!"

"Or out come the rubber truncheons?" I asked quietly, but I was
shaken for all that.

She put her cup on the floor and ran a hand through her hair. "It's
just that we haven't got *time*," she said.

"Time? If anything's a *waste* of time this is. I should know – I
introduced Tubby to Suzy and that girl in the first place. They never
said more than hello and goodbye to each other. And as for the man
in the pale-grey suit, he'd gone by then anyway."

"All right, Harry," she sighed, "have it your way."

In a curious way she sounded almost resigned to it. But it was an
act. I was beginning to know Elizabeth. *My way* would count as
much as the doctor's when he stepped out of line in the studio
downstairs. Elizabeth's way was what counted. She was a damn
sight easier to look at than Ross, but under the skin they were two of
a kind. There was even the same note of determination in her voice
when she said, "You'd better start by telling me *everything* you know
about Tubby Hayes."

"I've told you. He's just an acquaintance, someone I meet now
and then."

"Someone you've known *twenty years*! Come on Harry – what
kind of man is he? You've stayed at his house. Does he like little
girls, big girls, little boys or what? What do you *do* on those long
weekends?"

"Christ, they're not *orgies*, if that's what you think?"

"Oh, for God's sake! That house at Henley is a honey-pot!"

My astonishment merely fuelled her temper, because she kicked
her cup over as she stood up. She reached for the internal telephone
and when someone answered she snapped. "Put the Willows film
on two. Yes that's right, the new one." Then she slammed the
phone back on its rest and said to me, "Close the shutters – you'll see
better. I'll be back in a few minutes." And before I had chance to

125

answer she left, slamming the door behind her.

The film lasted five minutes. I've never gone in much for blue movies, not even full colour ones. Sex makes a bad spectator sport if you ask me, copulation is faintly comic when it's happening to other people. I recognised Tubby straight away – even with his clothes off. Then I picked out a junior cabinet minister *and* the city editor of a rival paper. Life in the raw I suppose you'd call it, about twenty of them, all heaving away in Tubby's drawing room at "The Willows". There was even a shot of the garden through the French windows when someone jogged the cameraman's elbow. I said, "I bet they chewed his balls for that," without even realising it. Still they were *all* at it, lesbians and homo's doing their stuff alongside dull old heterosexuals performing the missionary shuffle. Pity there was no sound track. It would have benefited from the grunts and groans, and a wrestling style voice-over.

Elizabeth came back at the end of the last reel, just as all the upside down numbers were flashing past. She had the doctor with her in case I got over-excited. "Funny," I said as she opened the shutter, "there wasn't a pale-grey suit in the lot of them."

15.00 Friday

"You're out of your mind," Reilly said flatly. "Spring Steve Cassidy? From the Holy Cross Jail? It's the maximum security prison for all Ireland, you know that, don't you?"

"So much the better," Abou said quietly. "They'll never expect it."

"You're mad. I'll have nothing to do with it. It wasn't part of the deal we made and –"

"Nobody's asking for your help," Abou said coldly. "Except in the planning stage."

"Planning to get yourself killed," Reilly said hotly. "Leave Cassidy be. It's next to nothing he knows and –"

"No!" Abou shook his head. "It's not our way."

"And what'll you do if you get him out? There'll be a man hunt the length and breadth of Ireland."

"Cassidy won't be in Ireland," Abou said, coolly playing his trump card.

"So where will he be then?"

The three of them were in the cottage at Conlaragh and Suzy sat on the bed listening to the two men argue.

"In the States," Abou said and waited for a reaction.

126

Reilly was astonished. "You'll *still* send him? Even though he's not done the job?"

"We look after our own," Abou said softly.

Grudging admiration showed in Reilly's face, and it was a moment or two before he said anything. "It'll need more money. We used all we had for Mick this morning."

Abou smiled, "I'll find more money."

Impressed despite himself, Reilly fell silent and thought about it. Whatever he said wouldn't change the man's mind, that much was obvious. But the Holy Cross Jail? The place was built like a fortress. Mary Mother of Christ, didn't it used to *be* a fortress? But even after thinking about it for five minutes Reilly was still sceptical. "I still say it's impossible," he said darkly.

"Prisons the world over have one thing in common," Abou said quietly. "They're built to stop people getting *out*, not to stop people getting in."

Suzy spoke for the first time. "Ulrike Meinhoff got Baader out of jail in Germany. And Baader was a big fish. Whoever heard of Cassidy?"

"Things are different here," Reilly sighed and then he shrugged. "Anyway, so what are you wanting from me?"

Abou replied in a reasonable voice, "A floor plan of the prison. Showing where they're holding Cassidy."

"Is that *all*?" Reilly asked sarcastically.

"He's *your* man," Abou's voice hardened. "And *we're* getting him out. The least you can do is provide some information. Find someone who's served time there and knows the place well enough to draw a diagram. That should be easy enough – you've got the contacts and we haven't."

Reilly nodded slowly. He could do that without even leaving Conlaragh. But the other part was more difficult, finding out exactly where Cassidy was being held. He said as much, but Abou shook his head.

"Think about it. Cassidy's not been charged yet, so he won't be in the main part of the prison. He'll be in some sort of interrogation centre, I imagine. Isn't that right?"

Reilly's face brightened. Of course it was right! And the interrogation block was just inside the main gates. Why the devil didn't he think of that himself? "That's right," he said with rising excitement. "And the cells are above ground there. It's a single-storey block with about ten or twelve cells and a few offices for the C.I.D. and what have you." He pictured the place and his voice fell to an awed whisper. "You know something, Mister, it *might* just be possible at that."

"It is possible," Abou said grimly. "How quickly can you get the information together?"

"I'll get the plan of the place today." Reilly's enthusiasm grew as the prospect of success loomed in his mind. "And I'll be on to Dublin. There's a man out yesterday who's as like as not to know where Cassidy is."

Abou's interest sharpened. "Can you reach him today?"

"I'll try. Tonight more like it though."

Abou nodded. "So we'll have everything we need by tomorrow when we go to Pallas Glean?"

Reilly nodded. "When are you planning the raid?"

"Tomorrow night."

"As soon as that?" Reilly grinned. "I'll need to make myself scarce then – or find myself a good alibi."

"Tomorrow night might be a good time to go travelling," Abou said softly. "You know, I wouldn't be surprised if you went for a trip on that new fishing boat of yours."

Reilly looked astonished. A trip on the *Aileen Maloney* was the last thing on his mind. But when he said so Abou just grinned. "I think you'll change your mind," he said mysteriously, "after tomorrow."

23.20 Friday

We chewed Tubby Hayes to death all afternoon, Elizabeth and I, with the doctor adding his two cents' worth. Everything from when Tubby and I first met to what I knew about his early deals in Taiwan, and how the money had never stopped rolling in for him once he had started. Not that I liked doing it, after all Tubby had never done me any harm that I knew of, but Elizabeth kept on about how little *time* was left and if I *really* wanted to help Suzy. So we sat around in Ross's office and boozed a bit and jawed the hind leg off a donkey. Neither of them took notes, so I guessed Ross's place was wired for sound too – hell, maybe the whole building was. I swore blind I had never attended an orgy at "The Willows" which was the truth, but I doubt they believed me – especially Elizabeth who fixed me with her cold-eyed look for most of the afternoon. Then we had more of the picture shows – people I *had* met at Tubby's place, people I *might* have met, people who *should* have been there on the same dates as me. At one point I said it was a pity that we were not back at my flat

128

in London, because some old diaries might help jog my memory. Whereupon Elizabeth used the internal phone to summon dog-faced Smithers from his mailroom, complete with a pile of my personal papers thoughtfully forwarded by Special Branch. There wasn't even any point in getting mad about it – it had happened and damn all I said would change it. By five o'clock I had told them everything I could about Tubby and they still seemed a million miles away from the man in the pale-grey suit. I felt drained and edgy – and refused to believe it had anything to do with finding Suzy.

"That's enough for now," Elizabeth announced with surprising suddenness. "Why don't you relax and unwind a bit? Go for a swim or take a steam bath?"

I wondered what prompted the sudden concern, but like the obedient boy I was turning into I went on cue. I skulked in the steam room for an hour, my mind full of Suzy and Tubby Hayes and that little French girl, Monique Debray, until the thought of an atomic explosion made me shiver enough to turn the heat up. When Elizabeth joined me I was on the slab and Max was beating a military tattoo down the middle of my back. She had on the same playsuit as she had worn for Nikki Orlov's visit, and as she placed my scotch and water within arm's length I got the strong impression that I was supposed to react as he had. She stood very close, her black bikini briefs six inches from my eye level as she massaged my back while Max made a meal of my leg.

"Hey, big spender," she purred. "You're taking me out tonight."

"Out? You mean out of here? Out of Sing-Sing? What did you do – sleep with the guards?"

"Silly!" The bikini moved an inch closer and gyrated in time with her hands. "You know you're our guest. There's *nothing* we wouldn't do for you."

"Except let me go." I shut my eyes and cursed as my body hardened under me. The bitch must have been brought up in a shower – hot and cold moods at the push of a button. I began to remind her about Nikki Orlov, but the words drowned as the nicely upholstered black silk brushed across my mouth.

"You're taking me out to dinner," she repeated, "and then we're going gambling at the casino." Her fingers did some very sensuous things to my spine before she backed off and made for the door. "Better wear a dinner jacket," she called over her shoulder. "I'll meet you in an hour's time. Don't be late."

I sighed aloud and rolled over. "My, my, my!" Max looked bug-eyed at my body. "Go anywhere like *that* and you'll fall over and break your neck. Better take a cold shower man – or think of cricket or whatever you limeys do at a time like this."

I was on time. Seven-thirty in the hall, dressed up like a dog's breakfast in the dinner-jacket which had been delivered to my room. Elizabeth made her entrance ten minutes later, sweeping down the marble staircase flanked by old Smithers and a younger version who might have been his son. The men wore penguin suits and Elizabeth was wrapped in an off-the-shoulder length of yellow silk under a lace shawl. Her hair shone, her smile dimpled and she smelled delicious. We sat close together in the back of the two-year-old Mercedes and Smithers bumped us down to Marsaxlokk and then along the coast road. Outside an orange sun sank low in a deep-blue sky, while on the road ahead Son of Smithers drove a tatty Triumph Herald which clashed with his dinner-jacket.

Dinner at the Baracuda turned out to be a family affair. As soon as I set foot in the place I saw Max dining with the man who had carried my bag into the Health Farm. Max sat opposite the kitchen and stared at the kitchen door all through his meal. Maybe he was in love with the chef. Elizabeth and I took a table overlooking the bay and as I turned from tucking a chair beneath her bottom, I saw Smithers and Son accept a table just inside the entrance. I don't know who else was expected, but nobody could enter that restaurant without the boys from the Health Farm looking them over.

"Very cosy," I said. "And I suppose our waitress is the doctor in drag?"

Despite everything, however, we passed the next hour or so pleasantly enough. Dinner with a pretty woman has never been my idea of hard work, and the lobster was delicious and the wine cold enough to take the fur off my tongue. Years spent searching for stories has made me a pretty good listener, and usually I can find out what I want to know from people when I apply myself. And I applied myself with Elizabeth as if my life depended on it. But some Mata Hari spook school had taught her that the only thing to keep buttoned was her lip, so it was hard work – until we made a game of it, a battle of wits which amused both of us right through to the coffee and brandy. Then I paid the bill and dog-face Smithers was kind enough to drive us to Sliema Strand.

"The Casino is the other way," I said ungratefully when he stopped. "At Dragonora Point."

He ignored me and spoke to Elizabeth. "You're to take a karrozin from here. Don't worry, Max will be in the one in front and I'll follow by car."

Karrozins are the horse-drawn Victorias that the Maltese still run to please the tourists and enrich themselves. One jingled its way up from the Libyan Embassy, and I helped Elizabeth up and then climbed in beside her. The pony responded to the driver's whip and we moved off at a brisk trot.

"What next?" I grumbled. "Charades at the catacombs."

She squeezed my arm. "It's Orlov playing games with us," she said calmly. "He'll contact us when he's ready. Meanwhile *enjoy* yourself. It's not difficult." Her smile dazzled me. "Just lie back and think of England."

I wondered if that's what she did, but mainly I thought we made a hell of a good target, stuck five feet up in the air in an open carriage and moving along at eight miles an hour. It was feast day in one of the villages and fireworks crackled in the distance like gunfire, plucking my nerves to shreds in the process. We drove past the Exiles, around Balluta Bay and on up Grenfell Street. It was dark by now, but I could see the floodlit Corinthian pillars of the casino beyond Spinola Point. Through Paceville, full of Libyans, most in European dress but some in *djellabas*. Not long now – even by pony and trap. Around the corner and then up the long sweep of drive-way to the casino itself. We made it. I steered Elizabeth to the bar and watched the other drinkers get tennis neck as they followed her progress.

The Casino was crowded. We table-hopped for a while, though for the life of me I couldn't see why. Pink-skinned English tourists with north country accents played blackjack, while at the next table some prosperous Germans lost heavily at baccarat. Two Frenchmen hoarded their chips and gambled like misers, whilst a queer pouted prettily at a croupier. Elizabeth took the scene in at a glance, but kept moving purposely forward and it was ten minutes before I realised that she was looking for somebody.

"By the way," I patted my pocket to make sure that the two hundred pounds worth of gambling chips were still there, "thanks for the stake. Compliments of Joe Spitari?"

"Compliments of H.M. Treasury." She nestled into my side as we squeezed past a table. "And the Chancellor would like it back at the end of the evening." Which seemed unreasonable until she added, "But you're allowed to keep the winnings."

Orlov was at the roulette table, the big one, minimum bets five pounds Maltese. Elizabeth nuzzled his left cheek and I just beat an elderly Japanese into the chair on the other side. "You *are* playing?" the Japanese demanded, polite as ever but a bit cross for all that. I smiled and fished the gold and black plastic discs out of my pocket.

Elizabeth said, "Hello, Nicki," in her golden brown voice and up the table Max watched me with unsmiling eyes above a ruffled shirt. *"Numero quatre, Noir,"* said the croupier and raked in just about everything on the table.

Orlov scowled and made a mark with a gold pencil in a little black book. Funny how card-carrying commies never tire of capitalist games. He pushed some chips forward from the pile in front of him, placing bets on two blocks of six and taking a flier on the fifteen. The gold pencil recorded the move in the little black book. "Ross is away?" his question was barely audible above the murmur of voices around the table. In the ballroom next door the band knocked out a version of "Brown Girl in the Ring" bad enough to offend even the most insensitive ears.

"Yes," Elizabeth passed a single one hundred pound chip up the table for the croupier to change into tens, "but Harry's with me."

That seemed like telling Big Ben the time, but Orlov acknowledged my presence by turning his head and blowing cigar smoke into my eyes. "So," he said, "while the hunter seeks the tigress, the trainer gets into the cage."

I spread some chips around while I thought about that one. Finally I guessed: "Old Russian proverb?" His smile was straight from Siberia. "No, Mr Brand, but there's one I would commend to you. 'He who digs a hole for another may fall in himself'."

I nodded wisely and watched the croupier rake in fifty pounds of H.M. Treasury's Money. Orlov added a hundred to the winnings in front of him and we all tried again.

Elizabeth murmured, "Have you any news of the tigress – of where we might find her?"

Orlov updated his book. "Only of where you *won't* find her," he said, covering another six numbers and doubling up on the fifteen. "Which is in the Middle East. But I'll tell you something else – she's not being run by any friends of ours."

I concentrated on winning the fifty pounds back and behind me the Japanese gentleman calculated the square root of the winning number on a pocket calculator. Meanwhile, the band struck up *Rasputin* to make Orlov feel at home.

"But there is something of interest," Orlov leaned backwards, so that both Elizabeth and I could hear him, "which is that the senders of that parcel *expected* it to be interfered with. Didn't they, Mr Brand?"

Elizabeth's eyes froze into green pebbles as she looked at me. I was too confused to answer. What the hell did Orlov *mean*? And what was he trying to do with a remark like that? At the other end of the table the ball-bearing weaved around the wheel until it exhausted itself and fell into a receptive bay. *"Numero quinze,"* shouted the croupier. *"Rouge."* An excited buzz hummed around the table as Orlov recovered his money plus another thirty-five hundred pounds.

"We call it the Big Game, Mr Brand." He left a hundred pounds worth of gratuities. "And if you're going to play it properly, I'll give you a tip." He stood up, smiling broadly. "Always back the reds – they invariably win, in the end." He bowed to Elizabeth and then turned to go.

I tapped his chest. "Mind the hole Nikki – it's been freshly dug." Still smiling he nodded and then stepped past me to make his way to the door. Behind me the Japanese had taken Orlov's place and Elizabeth was rising to go. Max and Smithers appeared on my shoulders like process-servers.

"I've lost fifty pounds," I said.

Max smiled. "It's the diet at the Health Farm, Mr Brand. Some of our guests have been known to fade right away."

Midnight Friday

Elizabeth lived under the roof at Spitari's place – two rooms with a bathroom and a view of the sea. The connecting door from the sitting-room was open just wide enough to see an olympic size bed beneath a ceiling fan big enough to lift a helicopter. Landing pad took on a whole new meaning.

I asked, "Is this where I mix the drinks while you slip into something comfortable?"

"If you like." She kicked gold sandals from her feet and tucked her legs under her on the sofa. "Fixing a drink sounds a good starting point."

Driving back from the casino had been as nerve-racking as the ride out. Max must have lip read Orlov's implications about me, because he was distinctly hostile. And dog-face Smithers was hardly a barrel of fun. Whereas Elizabeth had gone all broody, as if decoding Orlov's meaning while deciding on her next move. Which – to my surprise – turned out to be to squeeze my hand and invite me to join her for a nightcap. What the hell – I had nothing else to do.

"Harry, just who do you work for?" She accepted a drink and patted the place next to her.

"Crusader Press. I thought you knew that?"

"Mmmm," Those green eyes were watching me again. "But I mean as well. Who do you *really* work for?"

The message sank home. "You mean like Kim Philby writing for *The Observer* while collecting royalties from the K.G.B.?" I humoured her. "Okay, I'll come clean – I'm working the same racket."

She shook her head, "Nikki Orlov doesn't think so."

"That's where we were clever. He and I staged that act back there to throw you off the scent."

"It doesn't work like that, Harry."

"You would know."

"You wouldn't be the first newspaperman moonlighting for somebody's security service."

At least I knew that was true. There had been a time in the sixties when so many American journalists in Egypt were working for C.I.A. that the papers thought they had a strike on their hands.

"Okay, what gave me away?" I shrugged, still humouring her and not believing for a moment that she was serious.

"There are too many co-incidences. You're Suzy Katoul's godfather. You know Tubby Hayes. You were introduced to Monique Debray. You even met Philby for God's sake!" She looked puzzled. "And in the background is this tall dark stranger."

"It's not much of a case."

"*You* are tall and dark, Harry."

I patted her hand. "But hardly a stranger."

She frowned. "You see, I've got this little idea nagging at the back of my mind, and it won't go away."

"Until you tell me about it." Nothing would stop her, I could see that.

"We get glimpses of meetings from you. Not many and nothing very substantial – but enough to send us back to the archives, burrowing away like mad, questioning, interviewing, searching. *That* kind of thing." She smiled an apology. "You *know*, the terribly boring things we go in for. And from time to time your little glimpses co-incide with those of other people. They *too* remember a tall, dark man – and they describe you. Of course we say 'not him – *the other one*.' And they frown and scratch their heads and scowl furiously – but you're the only one they remember."

I stared at her. She was deadly serious.

She smiled again and cocked her head to one side. "Well, this little idea of mine says perhaps there isn't another man at all. Perhaps we're all looking for someone who doesn't exist? Silly, isn't it – but it won't go away."

I sipped my drink. "And what are the implications of this little idea?"

"Tubby Hayes was an agent. We know that much. And we think the tall dark man was running him – *and* Suzy Katoul."

"Tubby Hayes must know hundreds of people – thousands probably. Why me?"

"Because Nikki Orlov thinks so."

"And you'll take *his* word – against mine?"

She pouted. "I told you it was just a little idea."

"Yeah? Well kill it before it grows up into a big mistake."

"I will – if you'll help me."

"And how do I do that?"

"By telling me *everything*." A faint smile touched the corners of her mouth. "You see, as Ross says, what you've told us so far is fine. I mean it all checks out *beautifully*. But are you sure you're not holding some little piece back? Some *vital* little piece?"

I glared furiously and said nothing at all.

"You see, Harry," she said thoughtfully. "What worries me is *time*. We're getting frightfully short of it."

I remained silent even at that. The big green eyes blinked and then she said, "Did you ever wonder what happened to Rossi's hand?"

I busied myself re-filling the glasses, feeling in sudden need of yet another scotch.

"It was in Vietnam," she said. "He was up behind the lines somewhere and they caught him. Time was short and they wanted answers quickly. So they staked him out and rolled a ten ton truck over his hand – an inch or so every ten minutes. They promised to do his arms first and then his legs, so as not to kill him. And all the time he lay there with the truck's engine blasting hot air into his face, expecting it to crush him to death at any second."

"So he talked?" I tried not to let her see how shaken I was.

She shrugged, and sculptured bronzed shoulders moved inwards in a way which accentuated the cleavage of her breasts. "He says his own kooks counter-attacked and got him out in time. Perhaps they did – perhaps they didn't – who knows?"

"And something like that is going to happen to me?"

"Oh, Harry, I *do* hope not." Her concern was touching. "It's just

135

that I'm *so* worried about you."

I waited for her to make the point she was leading up to.

She smiled the kind of shy, hesitant smile people give you with bad news. "For instance, something you don't know is that Rossi got you out of your London flat just in time. Six hours later the place was raided. Luckily Special Branch had called back and the men were chased off." Her eyes clouded with concern as she shook her head in bewilderment. "But you do see what I mean?"

"No." I had an idea but she was going to have to spell it out for me.

"Of course you do, Harry," she corrected gently, still in the seductive feline voice. "It means other people are afraid you'll tell us what you know. Afraid enough to *kill* you to stop that happening."

I tried to make it into a joke. "Perhaps it's as well I came along with Ross."

"That's what I thought," she nodded as her eyes locked on mine and her mouth dimpled into a smile of perfect innocence. "But well, you can't stay here forever, can you?"

5

THE FIFTH DAY

"I asked Tom if countries always apologized
when they had done wrong, and he says:
'Yes; the little one does'."

Mark Twain – *Tom Sawyer Abroad* (1894)

01.45 Saturday

Ross chewed the end of a cigar and thought about the message he
had just decoded. It had taken three years to infiltrate the P.L.O.
Three years and the loss of eighteen men and one brave woman – all
of whom had died violently when their real loyalties had been
discovered. But now they had one man in a key position, one man
who had risked everything to meet the deadline Ross had handed
him. *No evidence monkey loves candy*, the message read, repeat, no
evidence monkey loves candy. *Monkey* Arafat and *Candy* Katoul
were *not* in bed together. But Ross had long ceased to suspect they
were – even if confirmation had been needed for the meeting with
Twomey. But if not Arafat, who? Someone was running Katoul. The
Khomeini, who sat in his French villa and meddled in the politics of
Iran? Hardly, if he had the bomb he was unlikely to waste any part of
its destructive power in a demonstration off the coast of Scotland.
Why Scotland anyway? What for? To pressurise the British? Into
what, for Chrissakes? What was the next move? There *had* to be one.

"Fifteen minutes to go," LeClerc said. "Shall we go up to the
bridge?"

Ross made him repeat the question before it registered. Dorfman
was already climbing into a borrowed Navy anorak. The three of
them were alone in the wardroom of *HMS London*, the R.N. destroyer which had been designated control ship for "Operation
Flashpoint" as some humorist had named it.

"You mean there's still room up there?" Ross asked drily.

The destroyer was crawling with top brass – not just British either.
Somebody had pushed a panic button and word had gone out to

half of N.A.T.O. Ross had been furious. And he was still crusty with temper as he followed LeClerc up to the bridge, with Dorfman bringing up the rear to close the hatches which LeClerc opened, while Ross clambered through with both hands thrust deep in his pockets.

"One of your naughty boys got a bit out of hand, what?" an English voice greeted him. He recognised a junior S.I.S. courier. "Shove it! And I'll report your breach of security to James when I see him." The Englishman backed away, blushing as he realised that the reason why Ross and his party were simply designated "observers" on ship's orders was because few men there knew the exact nature of their function.

Ross looked about the bridge. There must have been thirty men crowded into the confined space, most of them Admirals if the gold braid was anything to go by. He chewed a bit more on his cigar and nursed bitter thoughts about the potential security leak until Dorfman caught his eye and they squeezed through to a space on the far side.

"We're on station ten miles from where we expect 'Flashpoint'," another youngish English voice explained to a Rear Admiral standing next to Ross. "It's as near as Admiralty permit."

Ross wondered how near the bloody fool wanted to get to a one kiliton bomb, but he said nothing. He was under *orders* to say nothing. "Simply observe and report to Command in the morning," Twomey had told him. Very well, that's what he would do – but he needn't like it. And he damn well didn't.

"There're a hundred weather balloons in ahead of us," the English voice continued. "The R.A.F. have been at it for hours – purpose being to measure radiation of course, sir."

The Rear Admiral nodded.

"The R.A.F. are upstairs now, sir. Vulcans I think at about seventy thousand feet. And above them's a couple of Yank spy planes," the Englishman chuckled. "Trust the Yanks, eh, sir? Always that bit further away from the real action."

Ross glowered and the Rear Admiral answered in a chilling voice. "You were much too young for the war Lieutenant, but the Yanks I fought with then weren't afraid of getting close to – what did you call it – the *real* action."

"No sir," the Lieutenant was properly contrite. "Of course not. Er, I didn't mean to imply. . . ." The sentence remained unfinished as he squirmed with embarrassment. Listening, Ross warmed to the

Admiral and wished he had been allowed to wear uniform instead of a nondescript suit.

"All shipping been cleared?" asked the Rear Admiral.

"Hours ago, sir. Bit of trouble with some Russian trawlers, but they moved off in the end – though I daresay they're only a few miles adrift of us now."

You bet your sweet ass, Ross thought. He edged past LeClerc and peered down to the forward decks. A mass of scientific equipment had been bolted into position and men in spacesuits hovered behind lead screens to monitor the readings. Ross wondered what the Admiral made of it. Bit different from the last war, eh Admiral? When the biggest bomb dropped on Germany was a ten ton block-buster. Ten tons of T.N.T.! Four years of bombing to kill 400,000 people. Suzy Katoul could kill more in half an hour. Oh Sweet Jesus Christ, don't let it happen!

"Five minutes to go," a voice crackled. "Glasses everybody please."

Ross fumbled into infra-red goggles and listened to others fidget as they did the same. One kiliton, Ross thought. Why *one* kiliton? One kiliton was nothing – a kid's sparkler at a fireworks party. A thousand tons of T.N.T., that's all. Even the Hiroshima weapon was twenty times that big. One kiliton today and *ten megatons* tomorrow – was that the plan? Ten megatons! Jesus Christ, even the crater would be seven miles across. Seven miles in which all construction would be pulverised and all living matter vaporised. There would be no fires in the crater because there would be nothing left to burn, but fires would blaze for twenty miles around it – and catastrophic damage would occur for another twenty miles beyond that.

"Four minutes."

Ross calculated the fall-out from a ten megaton bomb. The lethal area alone would extend to *two thousand square miles*. The radiation fall-out would kill even more people than the initial heat blast! Even those who found a deep shelter fast would have to stay there for two whole days – and then get out afterwards like bats out of hell.

"Three minutes."

Hell, it had to happen. Sooner or later. The Pugwash Conference was up in arms about the risk factor years ago, but no-one had listened. What's a ten megaton bomb anyway – compared to the stocks held around the world? The States was sitting on at least 50,000 megatons, and the Russians had about 40,000. Add the British and the French and the Chinese and what have you got? At least 150,000 megatons. The governments of the world had bequeathed more than a hundred tons of T.N.T. to every man, woman and child on the planet. Manufactured it, stockpiled it, hoarded it – and then told everybody "hands off." But Suzy Katoul had turned a deaf ear. Like Eve in the Garden of Eden.

"Two minutes."

But Suzy Katoul had just stolen the *raw materials*. She needed more *time* to make a bomb, or so the scientists said. They said it couldn't happen, not *this* fast. But nobody would pull a stunt like this without being *sure* of being able to deliver. They would lose all credibility for the next round. And there *had* to be a next round. Didn't there?

"One minute."

Who's running you, Katoul? Who's pulling the strings? What are you anyway? Some screwed-up bitch with an Arab militant for a mother and a Jewist terrorist for a father? What does that make *you* – daughter of Dracula or something? And what's bugging you so much that you're playing God on a scale this size?

"Thirty seconds. Quiet please everyone."

Ross felt the palm of his right hand turn to grease. He hoped that the sweat didn't show on his face. He always sweated. Once a man had mistaken it for fear until Ross had loosened a few teeth for him. Please God – don't let it happen. We need more time! Three days gone and we're nowhere. But more time could make all the difference. We might get lucky, strike a new trail, find a clue, something, anything! But give us more *time*.

"Fifteen seconds!"

Oh, God in Heaven, I know I'm a miserable bastard but you've got to help me this time. Just this *once*. If this thing goes off this screwed-up bitch can make all the demands she likes and get away with it. You see *that* don't you? We need time, some more *time!*

"Ten seconds."

Look, if you *are* God, be on the side of the good guys just for once, eh? This bitch is *evil*! Dammit, there's not another word for her. So just let the scientists be right for once – let nothing happen. Let it fail to go off. That's all I'm asking for Chrissakes! Let it be that way and we get more time.

"Four – three – two – one."

Silence. No flash in the night sky, no noise, nothing. Nothing! Just beautiful, blissful silence. The sea glittered under a yellow moon and rain clouds hung low in the sky, and not a bloody thing had happened! Oh God, *thank you*. Most of the time you're a miserable stubborn unyielding bastard, but for once you've delivered. Baby, you're beautiful. Nothing damned well happened! Hear that Katoul – nothing! Screw you to hell baby – you gambled and lost.

Then the sky lit up. For two whole seconds it was daylight again. Brighter than daylight. A blaze of white lit the sea and sky like the floodlights of hell. And a second later the heat wave sighed through the night like a soft summer wind. Then came the noise. Men forward on the *London* crouched behind lead screens and played with their dangerous toys for all they were worth; on the bridge Ross closed his eyes. One kiliton, that's all *that* was. One kiliton exploded three hundred feet down on the sea bed. One kiliton seen from ten miles away. And Suzy Katoul could deliver ten megatons!

Without a word to Dorfman or LeClerc he turned and walked slowly back to the wardroom, clambering through hatches and passing along passageways as if in a dream. Then he went to the heads and was violently sick.

06.30 Saturday

They really liked their early mornings at the Health Farm. Mostly I'm never out of bed before eight in the morning and not even then unless it's a work day, but Max woke me at six and insisted I join Elizabeth for breakfast. I dressed and followed him downstairs, wondering what had happened in Scotland and guessing that Elizabeth would know the outcome by now. Max probably knew too, but he was doing his coloured-butler-been-in-service-for-years bit, grave and dignified with downcast eyes and a buttoned lip.

"The scientists made it one kiliton exactly," Elizabeth said over orange juice. "It's all the proof we needed. We're convinced she's got the bomb."

I don't think I said much. Something like that is a real conversation stopper anyway. Especially first thing in the morning. Muzzy-headed, I listened while she told me that nobody had been hurt and that the explosion had barely been heard in the Orkneys. And after coffee we went down to the studio.

"Harry, I want to wire you up to the lie detector," she said, as she closed the door behind us. "It's not painful and it just might help."

The doctor stood one side of her and Max towered behind like a cardboard cut-out of Othello. Except there was nothing cardboard about Max's biceps.

"And if I refuse?"

"Drugs," Elizabeth said briskly. "Pentothal if it takes with you.

141

If not, sodium amytal and L.S.D. The amytal is painful and combined with L.S.D. it takes a long time to wear off." She shrugged. "But if we've no choice?"

She sounded as efficient as a hospital matron and the white sweater and slacks she wore even lent colour to the part. I remembered the sexy looks of last night – all the come-on signs she had put out – the hand squeezes and the act with the bikini in the steam room. *Act* was right.

"You bitch," I said.

"Open your shirt, man," Max said. "And come and sit down. It won't hurt none, believe me."

I was still looking at Elizabeth. "What *don't* you believe?"

"Oh, I don't think you've lied to us. It's more that you haven't told us everything." She dimpled her smile, just to prove she was the same sweet girl – deep down. "But you will tell us – eventually."

"Harry, baby," Max coaxed. "Come and sit in the chair, man. We don't want no foolishness now, do we?"

The door opened and Smithers and Son arrived to make sure.

I'm fifty-three years old. I know I *look* younger and most of the time I *feel* younger, and even fifty-three isn't really *old*. But my kind of life hasn't equipped me to take on the likes of Max, let alone son of Smithers who was less than half my age. Especially when the doctor and old dog face looked set to lend a hand if need be. For a moment I stood my ground, trying to think of someone who could help me, then realising that not a single friend as much as knew where I was. Max led me to the chair and after that I let them wire me up. He was right, having electrodes fastened to your head and chest and wrists isn't painful – but it's damn worrying.

Max flicked a few switches on the machine, while Elizabeth made herself comfortable in the chair opposite. Then she began by saying: "The doctor's theory is that you've only loved one woman in your life. And that was Haleem Katoul."

I shrugged until the electrodes pulled the skin on my chest. "Psychologists talk a lot of cock."

The doctor beamed his plastic smile. "Freud was obsessed with it, Mr Brand."

"What went wrong with your marriage, Harry?" Elizabeth asked.

"What the hell's that to do with finding Suzy?"

Her face creased in a tiny gesture of irritation. "Your ex-wife says you wanted children and she didn't."

"You've *seen* Elaine?" I said in astonishment.

142

"She was interviewed yesterday," Elizabeth smiled. "She sends her regards."

"She knows where I am?"

"Of course not. Very few people know that." She paused to let the point sink home. "Did you quarrel with your wife about –"

"It's none of your damn business!"

"Everything's our damn business. Get used to that and you won't get hurt," she said sharply. "Now – did you and your wife quarrel about children?"

I remained silent for a moment. Max looked up from his machine and the doctor licked his lips at the prospect of topping my blood stream up with sodium amytal. Elizabeth tapped her foot and waited until finally I said, "We didn't really quarrel. Not that much anyway. I don't think we cared enough for each other to argue. The marriage was a mistake, that's all."

"You never loved your wife?"

"What does it matter? I *liked* her – to begin with. Isn't that enough?"

"It wasn't for you, apparently."

I glowered, tight-lipped and determined they could make whatever they liked of my silence. Eventually Elizabeth said, "The doctor was right wasn't he? Elaine *was* a substitute for Haleem Katoul."

"It wasn't a bloody football match. I don't understand the language. Anyway, leave Haleem out of this – it's nothing to do with her."

"She *was* Suzy Katoul's mother," Elizabeth said. She stared at me for a while and then spoke in a lighter tone of voice. "Very well, have it your way. Let's talk about Suzy. When you met her again, in '76, she was very affluent. Mink coats, works of art, chauffeur-driven car – what was the car by the way, can you remember?"

"Mercedes, I think."

"There you are then – chauffer-driven Mercedes and an apartment in one of the most expensive areas in Paris. Where did all the money come from, Harry?"

"I told you, she was a purchasing agent for –"

"And she was involved in politics. Don't forget the politics, Harry."

That seemed not to require an answer so I remained silent, like a fighter pacing himself in a slow round.

"What about her *other* income? You mentioned an allowance for instance."

"That was paid to Farida."

She raised one eyebrow. "Oh, I didn't realise that. Did Farida need the money? Wasn't she working as an interpreter or something?"

"I got a lot back when she died. It was in a separate account."

"Which bank?"

"Bank Commercial Francais, Rue de Lyons, Paris."

She nodded and stored the information away to check later. I was sweating slightly, but apart from that I had adjusted to the electrodes quite well. Max sat hunched over the machine watching wavy lines trace themselves across graph paper while the doctor stared hard at me from the chair next to Elizabeth. Dog Face and Son had withdrawn once I had taken the stand.

Elizabeth resumed. "So Suzy's new-found wealth didn't come from you?"

"Obviously not."

"And you're saying some money was from business and the rest was from politics?"

"I'm saying I don't know."

"But you *think* some was political?"

"If I *don't know*, what's the point in guessing?"

"Try."

I shrugged. "Well, the P.L.O. have never been short of funds. They had more than fifty million invested in London alone last year. I suppose they might have had cash in Paris and perhaps the Marxist Front did too. Maybe Suzy handled some of that – I just don't know."

"You just *don't know*." Her sarcasm was scathing enough to open my sweat glands another millimetre. "Whatever happened to Negib Katoul, by the way?"

"I've no idea."

"You never saw him again? After that last meeting at the camp in Lebanon?"

"I never saw Negib Katoul again," I said carefully.

"But you asked Suzy about him – when you met her again?"

"No, I don't think so."

"And she never *mentioned* him?"

"I don't think so. I really can't remember."

"You *really can't remember*," she mimicked. "You never discussed politics – you a political journalist and she a political activist. You never enquired where her money came from – you, a newspaper-

144

man with a renowned sense of curiosity. You never asked about the uncle who changed the course of her life? Don't you find all that a bit *odd* Harry?"

"You obviously do."

"Who are you working for, Harry?"

"Crusader Press."

"What are you trying to hide?"

"Why should I *hide* anything? I'm as anxious to find Suzy as you are."

"Did you know she was on drugs?"

"I – I think she *was* – used to be I mean – she isn't anymore –"

"How do you know?"

"I – I just *know*. She must have told me at some time."

"Who started her on drugs, Harry?"

"I – I don't know."

"It was Negib Katoul, wasn't it?"

"I tell you – *I don't know*."

"But you know damn well Negib Katoul was mixed up in the drug business in Lebanon, don't you?"

"I didn't know – not for sure – I wasn't there and –"

"But you found out about it, didn't you? You knew he'd disappeared from Beirut."

"I may have heard something. I'm not sure – it was a long time ago, and –"

"What did you hear?"

"Good God, if I told you all the bar room gossip I've heard over the years –"

"Just the gossip about Negib Katoul."

"He got involved in a drug racket. Beirut was full of them. I think the P.L.O. raised some funds that way and –"

"And Negib got ambitious, didn't he? Went into business for himself."

"That's what I heard. How true it was –"

"And he skipped Beirut?"

"Yes."

She sighed. "Harry, I'll ask you again. What happened to Negib Katoul?"

"I don't know."

The questions were coming thick and fast now, too fast to draw a breath between them, too fast to work out the answers.

"Harry, I *know* you met him again."

"You're wrong. You can't *know* – nobody can –"

"He changed his name, didn't he? And the Swiss Clinic changed his face."

"I never saw Negib Katoul again."

"Why do you phrase it that way, Harry? You've said it twice in the last three minutes."

"Said what? I don't know –"

"You never saw *Negib Katoul* again. But you met him under another name, didn't you? Technically you're telling the truth, but you're trying to beat the machine, aren't you?"

"Rubbish, why should –"

"Harry, all over Europe people like me are asking people like you questions. There's a massive search going on. And as time gets shorter we become more desperate. You do understand that, don't you?"

"Of course I understand, but –"

"Then *what* the devil are you hiding?" She lashed out in sudden temper.

"I'm not –"

"Harry, you're *forcing* our hands," she almost cried with frustration. "For God's sake, *tell us*! Tell us before we all do things we'll be ashamed of afterwards!"

"I've answered every one of your bloody questions –"

"But not explicitly!" she whirled round in her chair, trembling with exasperation. "What's the machine say, Max?"

Max tapped a switch and studied his graph paper. It took him a long time to answer, and when he did my blood ran cold. "Says he's lying his head off."

Her hands bunched into tight fists and her knuckles showed white through her tanned skin. For a moment she looked at the floor, and when she looked up her green eyes were wet with tears. "You damn fool, Harry," she whispered. "You *can't* hold out. Don't make us do it for God's sake!"

"I'm not responsible for your actions," I said coldly, "so don't pretend I am."

"You're leaving us no choice," her voice broke in a husky sob.

"So what choice have I got?" I asked angrily.

Nobody answered that. Elizabeth sat bolt upright in her chair, all colour drained from her face and her lips so tight they might have been stitched together. Then she released a long suppressed sigh of tension. "Very well, doctor, we'll do it your way."

146

It was dawn over England. Ross opened one eye and watched the fields below turn to a faded watercolour. They were losing height and the pilot was discussing his descent pattern with the tower ahead, using English place names like Hereford and Worcester and R.A.F. Fairford. Christ, will you listen to the way that kid says *Fairford*? Like he was reading Shakespeare or something. Ross closed his eyes and cursed all Englishmen. Either they were cynical bastards like that clown Brand or damn fool anachronisms like Elizabeth's father. Now he really was a cold-eyed s.o.b. – all stiff upper lip and dry as old bones. Brigadier Sir Maurice Twomey, D.S.M. and Bar and Christ knows that else. Forever spouting crap about duty and discipline and love of one's country, and Britain's role in the world as if she still had an empire or even counted anymore. For a boy, a man, okay – a *man* should be a patriot. But when a man like Twomey puts his only daughter into *this* business – Christ, how cold-blooded can you get? Ross mumbled a few obscenities and twisted in his seat. It bugged him – to run an outfit like Spitari's and then be answerable to Twomey. Brigadier Twomey, whose one human act had been to take part in the conception of Elizabeth in the firm expectation of a son. But spawning a daughter was one thing, raising her another, and Twomey had made a thoroughgoing mess of that. It had taken Ross two years to straighten her out – and even now there were times when she chilled him to the bone.

The lush Gloucestershire countryside rose to meet them, and Ross abandoned his last chance of rest, opening both eyes to look down one of the longest runways in Britain – two and a half miles of smooth concrete which could take the SR–17 Black Bird or even the Lockheed A–11 spy planes when need be. Not that the local farming folk were told much about *that*. For the most part only Hercules transporters flying training exercises disturbed the West Country skies, though why R.A.F. pilots should train to fly those old crates was thankfully a question only asked by a few.

The car met them on the tarmac. A plainclothes sergeant from Special Branch with a uniformed driver, who kept the engine running. Ross flicked his I.D. card and waited while Dorfman and LeClerc submitted their papers for inspection. Then they were on their way, past the sentries at the gate and out onto the lane which led to Cirencester. Suddenly something caught Ross's attention with almost physical force. He jerked round to stare back through the rear window. Something had changed since his last visit. Something was different. An inner *and* an outer gate! Last time a simple barrier like a railway crossing had been sufficient. And look at the sentries! The sentries were armed for Chrissakes!

"Bit of a flap on this morning, sir," the sergeant apologised. "Training exercise I shouldn't wonder." His quizzical look sought confirmation, but Ross's snort was non-committal as he slumped back into his corner.

A mile or so after Cirencester the road forked and the police driver took the secondary lane to the left-hand side. Trees lined the verge – elms mainly, but with a sufficient scattering of beech and silver birch to make an impenetrable thicket when seen from the road. And the driver hurried, rarely dropping below sixty, so casual sight-seeing was in any case difficult. But not so impossible that Ross missed sight of the marked police car half hidden in the bushes of a small clearing. Nor did he miss the police motor-cyclist parked alongside. For a split second he felt the scrutiny of hard eyes, then the lane twisted and they were gone. He scanned the road ahead, thinking "bit of a flap" typical British understatement, then gritting his teeth as, with no lessening of speed, the driver swung the wheel and shot the car between the grey stone pillars marked Bampton House.

Ross jerked upright. He was no stranger to Bampton – all told he had been there a dozen times. But never to a reception like this. The driver braked hard and the car slewed broadside on the gravel drive, spraying grit in all directions and coming to a halt ten yards from the men with the guns. They stood in a semi-circle – grim-faced and steady-eyed as they looked down the sights of Remington pump action shotguns aimed at the car.

"What the hell?" Ross demanded.

A police inspector hurried forward, an *armed* police inspector, whose Smith and Wesson swung from an open holster at his waist. For the second time in fifteen minutes their credentials were examined down to the smallest detail. Ross seethed with irritation, then the car was waved forward to crunch its way up the drive. Armed sentries were posted at twenty yard intervals and LeClerc pointed to a half-track bristling with radio antennae half concealed by the rhododendron bushes. Dorfman hissed "some training exercise" and then fell silent as the car swept round the final curve and Bampton House was revealed in front of them.

It was an impressive building – a Cotswold manor house of mellowed stone under slate, with its own preservation order to prove its four-hundred-year pedigree. The locals knew it as the residence of Brigadier (Retired) Sir Maurice Twomey, while the department referred to it simply as "the Country House" or, less reverently, "Twomey's Sweat Shop". Ross knew it as "Command".

An armed guard snapped to attention on the steps and a uniformed marine stepped forward to open the door. "The Brigadier would like you to join him in the breakfast room, sir." Ross nodded, muttered encouragement to LeClerc and Dorfman, and allowed himself to be led down a flagged hall to the corridor which ran to the back of the house. Dorfman and LeClerc were intercepted by other men, who led them away separately for individual debriefing sessions with trained interrogators. "Twomey's Sweat Shop" lived up to its reputation.

The Brigadier was alone. He sat at a table covered with a yellow checked cloth and a clutter of dishes, a buff folder next to his coffee cup. Ross turned from closing the door to face green-flecked eyes set deep in an emaciated face. Twomey had nicked himself shaving and a tiny spot of dried blood showed on skin drawn so tight that his chin looked like a polished bone.

"Ah, Ross," Twomey said in his clipped fashion. His head bobbed on a scrawny neck which sprouted from the khaki sweater worn beneath a grey flannel jacket. "Sit down. There's coffee there – and toast if you want some."

It was four months since last they met. Another man would have enquired about the health of his daughter – or even asked what sort of flight Ross had had. But not Twomey, and Ross had long ceased to expect it. He took the chair opposite and reached for the coffee pot. "Thank you, Brigadier." It was a point of honour never to call the other man "sir".

"The real thing this time, eh?" Twomey spoke through the pipe clamped hard in his teeth. "Up in Scotland."

"Scared the living shit out of everyone up there." Ross poured the coffee.

"And down here – that's what all the commotion is about – bloody performance I can tell you – conference in an hour's time – everyone's coming, Home Office, War House, the lot."

Ross nodded and sipped the coffee.

"Hell of a puzzle," Twomey said. "Wasn't our stuff, don't you know."

"No, Brigadier, I *don't* know."

"The cargo on the *Marisa* – so much sand – no plutonium at all – we changed the route at the last minute. Only three people knew about it."

If Twomey had hit him, Ross would have been less surprised.

149

"But for Chrissakes?" he checked himself. *Not* plutonium? Sand? What kind of sense was that? He *had* seen the explosion – hadn't he?

"And yet they explode a nuclear device." Twomey emptied the dregs of the pot into his cup. "What do you make of that?"

Ross stared, bewildered, not making anything of it and being unprepared to guess.

"Means they already had one." Twomey removed his pipe and showed his teeth in a superior smile.

Ross had anticipated a difficult meeting, but nothing could have prepared him for this. "So why hit the *Marisa*?" he said with unconcealed astonishment.

"Simple. To make it *look* like our stuff." Twomey scraped his pipe into the ash tray. "They'll leak the story now. Oh, not British press of course – we'll make damn sure of that. Splash it in the *Singapore Herald* or some foreign rag. Atomic explosion off British coast. Then it will *all* come out. Bound to, no way of stopping it. Plutonium shipments, risk of accidents, all the very nonsense we've tried so hard to avoid."

"But if that's *all*?" Ross struggled to understand. "That could be denied, surely?"

"Of course it can't be denied! Explosion that size – seismographs all over Europe will have picked it up – let alone the bloody Russian spy ships."

"The *source* of the plutonium could be denied," Ross persisted. "If your people shipped sand –"

"Don't be a bloody fool." Twomey stuffed his pipe with fresh tobacco. "We've denied transporting the stuff for years. To admit any part of the story is tantamount to admitting we've misled the public for God knows how long. We'll be discredited either way. Which is what *they* want."

Ross blinked and wondered if the Brigadier had the faintest idea of who *they* were. He remembered Gaddafi's boast. "Tomorrow we'll be able to buy an atomic bomb – the nuclear monopoly is about to be broken." Had tomorrow arrived?

Still struggling to understand Twomey's reasoning, he asked, "So the story gets leaked – in the *Singapore Herald* or wherever – what then?"

"Public Outcry – hell to pay for your people I daresay – sneers from the French – N.A.T.O. enquiry – general bloody panic." Twomey picked at the blood spot on his chin. "Then they'll deliver the blackmail note."

"On the end of a nuclear warhead?"

150

"When they've scared people witless," Twomey guessed. "Which gives us time – find this Katoul woman and see what she wants – meanwhile play the whole thing down."

"And that's playing it down?" Ross jerked his head at the window.

Twomey bristled. "None of my doing – took me an hour this morning to stop the War House cancelling all leave passes. Even so they'll try to force my hand later." He shook his head. "Your people are as bad – they'll bay for my hide along with the rest when it comes to it."

Ross kept his face expressionless. Sooner or later he would be asked how close he was to finding this "Katoul woman" and then the sparks would fly.

But Twomey surprised him. "We've found the link," he said softly. "Or, to be more precise, we've found *a* link."

Ross managed to stop his relief from showing and said nothing.

"Starts with this fellow Hayes." Twomey puffed on his pipe. "*Tubby* Hayes to your guest at the Health Farm. Hayes and a fool of a parliamentary secretary, who'd better remain nameless – though God knows for how long – be the very devil to hush this up. Hayes has been big in electronics for years, not just domestic stuff, but things for the military too – security devices mainly. Started making sneakies for the French years ago – showed his stuff to our people, but there was nothing new to it and we had our own sources – so we told him nothing doing. But Hayes was persistent, made a few friends, did some favours – catered to all tastes, if you know what I mean." He leered at Ross to make sure. "Anyway, he picked up a few contacts – not difficult when you're throwing cash and crumpet around – and amongst them was this parliamentary secretary whom he set out to impress. Stressed how much business he was doing with the Frogs – how much they trusted him – even mentioned the *Marisa* shipments, dates, consignments, the whole damn shooting match – all classified. Then he asked for a list of *our* agencies – not for the first time you understand – but this time he more than just asked, follow? Went on about past indiscretions, the rising cost of London tarts – enough to push the point home before coming right out with it – bold as brass – film of some damn debauchery in exchange for active help in securing contracts."

Ross wondered which French agency had leaked information to Hayes and felt glad not to be running it. Someone's head would roll – if it hadn't already.

"Thank God this bloody fool secretary panicked," Twomey said.

"Made a clean breast of the whole thing to his Minister the next morning. I got called in and decided to give Hayes enough rope to hang himself." Twomey bobbed with a small nod of self-approval. "Gave him an enquiry big enough to get this damn fool's film – and then passed your name and Spitari's address down the line."

"You *blew* us?" Astonishment gave way to anger as Ross realised the implications.

Twomey shrugged. "You only had another few months there anyway. We all know that, don't we? And I had to see what would happen. Couldn't give him anyone else – nothing personal – you do see that, don't you?"

Ross burned. Six months earlier a German newspaper had published a certain address in Milan and twenty-four hours later the house had been bombed and two operatives killed. Even now the sole survivor was fighting for his sight and learning to live with a face that would be forever disfigured. No, Twomey, *nothing personal* – not with your own daughter there. That proves it, doesn't it? Like hell it does. Red-faced with temper he asked, "What happened then?"

"We switched the *Marisa* consignment and put Hayes under surveillance," Twomey hesitated. "The *Marisa* end went all right – more or less – but Hayes must have got wind of us – because he skipped two days ago."

Ross bit his tongue. Brilliant, he thought – Hayes slips out from under and the *Marisa* gets hit. Absolutely brilliant!

Twomey read his mind. "Hayes getting away was a bad show, but the *Marisa* thing was something else. Half Lowestoft was wired up when that container went on board –"

"But not the high seas!" Ross erupted, tormented by the thought of Spitari's being blown sky high at any moment.

"They stole some *sand!*" Twomey snapped back, "*Not* plutonium."

That seemed so unimportant to Ross right then that it took him a minute to get his temper under control. When he calmed down he asked, "So Hayes is the link with Katoul?"

"We think so. We raided his businesses last night. LeClerc is being briefed about the Paris factory now – I think he ought to get over there to handle it."

Ross was about to comment on that when a knock at the door revealed the marine sergeant. "I'm sorry to interrupt, sir," he said to Twomey. "But I thought you'd want to see this straightaway."

Twomey read the telex placed in front of him and swore violently.

Then he read it again carefully and signed one corner as proof of having seen it. He let the door close on the departing marine before confiding in Ross. "Report from the Berkshire Constabulary. Hayes has been found – dead – picked out of the Thames at Maidenhead." Ross groaned. Another door closed – another lead snuffed out before they even got to it. Thought of Hayes prompted a memory, it was vague at first but when it crystallised in his mind he said, "According to Brand, Hayes and Katoul were strangers to each other."

"According to Brand," Twomey said drily.

"You think he's lying?"

"Someone is. Brand's a man of some reputation, but he's not renowned for his sympathy towards the establishment. If this story ever leaks out I'm damn sure whose side Brand will be on."

"So squeeze him harder?"

"I've sent the film and a few other bits and pieces on Hayes to the Health Farm already." Twomey began to scrape his pipe into the ashtray for the second time that morning. "So I don't doubt the process has already started."

08.00 Saturday

Elizabeth's eyes were growing. They were green lakes, shimmering emerald flecked with gold in fields of snow. White snow – smooth *cold* snow surrounding *cool* green water – water so still that ice frosted the surface like glass. Yet sweat poured down my face, soaked my shirt and trickled into the waistband of my trousers. Someone was hurting my arm. It ached, throbbed, trembled with pain. Then the golden brown voice told me to relax and I forgot about it. All pain fell away. I was floating – relaxed and floating – looking down on my body strapped to the chair, watching the ebony that was Max and the grey that was the doctor and the beauty that was Elizabeth. But the lakes had gone and the curious cat-like eyes watched me without blinking, while all the time the golden brown voice coaxed and soothed and pleaded.

Then the grey voice said, "Block the vein again. And have the megimide ready."

"It's ready," Max said. He sounded a long way away. Perhaps he was in the other room or out in the courtyard. Or even back in the steam room. Good old Max. Atta boy Max – don't you have anything to do with it.

"For God's sake," said the golden brown voice angrily. "Can he *stand* that much? He's not a bull like Max –"

"Time," said the grey voice. "We're running short of *time*. I want him responding for at least half an hour."

But she still scolded. She held me in her arms, wiping the sweat from my face. Oh Elizabeth, I can smell your skin, feel the plump curve of your breast, enjoy your body under my hands.

"Negib Katoul," the golden brown voice whispered in my ear. "Changed his name, didn't he Harry?"

"Yes."

"What was his new name?"

"Khouli – Yassif Khouli."

"And they changed his face too – didn't they?"

"Yes. They changed him altogether – he was a different man."

"Different? How *different*?"

"Rich – assured – worldly. Yassif Khouli as opposed to Negib Katoul. He was an animal Elizabeth – an *animal*. Negib should have died in the camps – perhaps he really died when he found Haleem with me – perhaps the boy I knew died then. Yassif Khouli was –"

"The man in the pale grey suit, wasn't he? The man you glimpsed with Tubby Hayes on the river that day."

I giggled. How silly to get it wrong. How stupid. Oh Elizabeth, how could you be so lovely and yet be so blind? *Blind!* You with your big green eyes which see nothing.

"How did Negib become rich, Harry? Where did all the money come from?"

I was laughing and feeling randy at the same time. Oh Elizabeth, you're *beautiful*. How many men have told you that? My lush voluptuous Mata Hari.

"Where did the money come from, Harry?"

"Money? He was so *rich*. It was really so simple – so simple to become so incredibly rich. Opium from the Turkish poppy fields – smuggled through Lebanon into France – converted to heroin and exported to the States."

"It was big business in the sixties, wasn't it?"

"Big! Big, big, big!" I was laughing helplessly, clinging to her body, pulling her into the chair with me, fondling her, kissing her. "It *was* big! It *is* big!" Her hand was in mine and I was pushing it under the sweat-soaked waistband of my trousers. "Elizabeth – you can *feel* how big, *feel* –"

"Soon Harry, soon," said the golden brown voice. "Later – in bed – not here –"

"Why not? *Here* is where I want you. Here and now, my beautiful

154

green-eyed goddess – my white-faced spook –"

"Soon Harry, I promise." Cool hands wiped my face and unbuttoned my soaking wet shirt, caressing hands which saved me from drowning in the sea of my own sweat. "When did you meet Negib again? Was it with Suzy?"

"He was an animal I tell you. A *dangerous* animal. More dangerous than you – you're just a cat – a wonderful, purring cat – with the loveliest eyes in the world."

"What made him an animal? Why Harry, tell me – please tell me."

"An animal," I giggled and clung to the lush fullness of her body. "But I beat him in the end. He was *bad* for Suzy. Bad for *my daughter*. I *had* to do something." The golden body twisted in my arms and the golden voice kept saying soon. But soon wasn't enough. "Now Elizabeth, *now!*"

"Will you tell me in bed? Will you? Harry, darling, tell me everything?"

"Everything, I promise. Come on, I'll carry you. Look, I'm so strong, so very strong." Then I was falling and hands were holding me upright, hands which slipped and skidded over my wet body – until we were in her room – beneath the fan – in the huge, soft bed with her golden brown body.

I never visited Suzy unexpectedly. Except that once. It was last year and about eight months after I had seen her with Tubby Hayes. I was in Paris and the chap from *L'Express* who was supposed to have dinner with me couldn't make it. He was stuck out at Lyons or somewhere, covering a story which had dragged out for an extra day so, unexpectedly, I had time on my hands. I phoned Suzy from the hotel and when her number was engaged I thought what the hell – her place was only a few minutes' walk away, why not go round to see her?

It took her a long time to answer the door. So long in fact that had it not been for the engaged telephone only five minutes earlier I would have given up and tried again in the morning. Even the boy from the Sûreté was missing from the parked cars opposite. But just as I was writing a note to stick through the letterbox, the door opened.

She was surprised. I remembered the look on her face at Henley that time, and it was the same expression, surprise, tinged with apprehension and mingled with fear. She said my name in a very loud voice and seemed unsure about inviting me in, so that we stood awkwardly on the threshold for at least a couple of minutes. Then she stepped aside and waved me across the entrance lobby.

I smoke too many cigarettes to have a good sense of smell, but some scents register instantly. And by then I had visited too many American camps in Vietnam to be mistaken about *that* smell. The thought of her being into the habit had never occurred to me, but it hit me then like a sledgehammer, and I was about to say something about it as we entered the drawing-room.

A man sat on the sofa. He was in his forties, I guessed, well-dressed, smooth black hair, prosperous looking – looked like the son of an Italian industrialist if you know the type. He seemed startled to see me, but I put that down to the unexpectedness of my visit. Until he spoke.

"Hello Harry, it's been a long time again, hasn't it?"

It was Negib. His nose had been shortened and the angle of his ears to his head altered somehow. His hair was smooth and uncrinkled and even his teeth were different – but it was Negib all right. He and Suzy were amused by my astonishment and giggled about it for minutes afterwards, the smug "aren't we clever" type of giggle that got on my nerves eventually.

"Meet my business partner," Suzy waved a hand at Negib. "Yassif Khouli."

"Khouli?" The name struck a chord immediately and suddenly all of my doubts crystallised. For months I had pondered on her affluence, telling myself that she was involved in legitimate business, and comparing her with others I knew who were making fortunes from the newly-rich in the Middle East. But her involvement with Negib – *Yassif Khouli* – changed all that.

"Everything you see," Suzy indicated the apartment. "Negib made possible."

Negib sensed my concern. "I'm sure Harry doesn't want to hear –"

"Oh, but I *do*," I insisted, staring at him. Trying to match *that* face to the voice was like watching a badly dubbed film. "I'm *very* interested, Negib. What business are you involved in these days?"

He tried to dismiss it. "Oh you know, Harry, this and that."

"This and that must be pretty dangerous – for you to alter your appearance and change your name."

His false teeth showed in a false smile. "When I left the P.L.O. I just wanted to make a new start, that's all. Politics is a dangerous game. Mossad had a hit team looking for me, and I'd grown tired of Arafat's tantrums. And Habbash is no better – wasting time bomb-

156

ing London supermarkets when he should be cultivating allies strong enough to stand up to the Jews."

"And that's what you're doing – making friends and influencing people? Funny, but I never pegged you for a Dale Carnegie type."

"A political movement needs funds, Harry, and it's not compulsory for its leaders to starve in a garret."

I waved Suzy's glance to the paintings on the wall. "And how you came by all of this doesn't worry you?"

She must have detected a note of censure, because she answered coldly: "Our business interests subsidise our political activities."

There was still a *chance* I thought – still a chance that she didn't know – a chance that Negib was using her and had never told her what his business interests were. But I *had* to find out.

"So you're in business with *him*," I began, but she put a hand to her temple as if nursing a headache. "Harry, I've had a rotten day and I can do without any sermonising from you."

She *did* know. Sick with anger I looked back at Negib. Negib who brought nothing but trouble whenever he turned up. He sat with a sneer on his face, watching my humiliation and enjoying it.

"I was in the Normandy in Beirut the other day," I said as steadily as possible. "Someone was telling me all about Yassif Khouli and his *business* interests."

He shrugged. "People get envious –"

"Or revolted!"

Suzy sprang to his defence. "All right, Harry, so now you know where the money comes from. I've told you before – it's none of your damn business."

"But Suzy, you'll destroy *yourself*. Don't you see that? It's a vicious racket –"

"It's America's biggest consumer import," Negib laughed. "Worth four billion dollars a year."

"Don't come the business analyst with me, Negib. It won't work."

"Oh, but it does," he contradicted. "It works very well. Buy a kilo of raw opium for thirty-five dollars, convert it to heroin and sell it for two thousand."

"Ruining thousands of lives in the process!"

Suzy went white with temper. "And saving thousands of others. Palestinian lives!"

"Yeah? How? How many Palestinians have you helped? I don't see any signs –"

"You will," she blazed. "Alliances are being formed now –"

"What bloody alliances? Alliances with half a million addicts in New York."

"That's *their* business! The legacy from Vietnam." Her laugh was a sneering bitter sound in the elegance of that room. "Oh, the States might leave Nam but the Vietnam war will never leave the States."

"Damn right it won't! So long as people like you feed the habit."

"Oh, will you *shut up!*" she screamed, ugly with temper. "You're no better than a filthy voyeur anyway, rushing from place to place watching the world squirm in its misery. What do you ever *do* about it? Write about it, turn it into some grisly fairy story, then run away from it. And all the time you're putting money in the bank and living in the best hotels. That's how *concerned* you are about the misery in the world."

"I don't contribute to it."

"That's right, Harry, *you don't.* You don't do anything! Just write your pious bullshit about the state of the world. Did you ever try to change it? Did you? Did you ever say this is a monstrous injustice and I'll fight and fight until it's put right? Did you hell! Well, that's what we're doing and if life becomes hell on earth for a few American pigs in the process that's a bonus not a drawback."

"The ends justify the means?"

"Of course they do! They always have, but your kind never admit it."

"You're wrong Suzy. Nothing worthwhile was ever built –"

She spat with temper. "Will you stop being so bloody sanctimonious! Do you think I even want to *listen*? Isn't it enough that I put up with your bloody claptrap whenever we meet–"

"I never realised it was such a hardship."

"You never *realised* anything," she shouted furiously. "You never even realised that we didn't meet again by accident. You never realised we *planned* it, did you?"

The silence which followed deafened me. My ears buzzed in a noiseless vacuum, broken finally by my shocked voice saying, "Planned? I don't understand. It was –"

"You're a contact, Harry," Negib interrupted smoothly. "That's all, a contact. You're less committed than some – you don't take Israel's side on every issue. Sometimes we can feed you an angle for your column – that's all."

I was still looking at Suzy. "And that's *all* I am?"

"What the hell d'you want to be?" she sneered. "My sugar daddy?" She giggled hysterically. "My sugar *god* daddy? Come off it, I've seen the looks you give me, the way you take my elbow –"

158

"That's ridiculous."

"Is it? Well, if you don't want *that* what the hell do you want? To claim me as your daughter? Is that it? Don't look so bloody shocked. Did you think I didn't know? Never knew you took a little Arab whore in her own bed –"

"Shut up! Don't call her –"

"She went with *you*, didn't she? What kind of Arab –"

"I said shut up! I don't know what Negib's been telling you, but –"

"Enough to give me a gutful of you," she screamed. I took a step towards her, but she backed away. "Get away from me will you – I never want to see you again – understand! Never! Never, never, never!" For an instant she stood there, white-faced and trembling like a leaf, then she put her hands to her face and ran from the room.

I sat down heavily in the nearest chair – trembling myself and feeling sick and bewildered – and *hating* Negib. It was *his* fault. He contaminated everything he came into contact with. If only he had stayed away from her. If only he had remained away, had never come to Paris in the first place. If only Suzy had been left alone, to grow up with Farida. If, if, if.

"You've had your answer, Harry," he said in that deadly quiet voice of his. "I think you'd better go."

"You're destroying her. You're evil, Negib, and somehow I'll fight you. I'll expose this racket in the French press –"

"Don't make me laugh. We've got protection now. Why do you think the guards have been pulled off? How do you think we operate? Half the French Cabinet know we exist and they turn a blind eye to it. Know why Harry?" He was laughing, "because most of their kids are customers of ours."

"I'll still expose you," I said defiantly.

"Not in France, you won't." He was so damn *certain*. That's what made me so mad. He stood up to show me to the door. "Goodbye Harry Brand."

Then I had an idea. "I'll turn your new identity over to Mossad."

The flash of fear in his eyes filled me with a surge of sadistic pleasure. I had got back at him and it showed. We stood facing each other, both trembling – me shaking with hate and him with sudden fear. I tried to brush past him to the door, but he stopped me. "You try that, Harry, and I'll kill you."

I laughed. I was just so damn *pleased* with myself. I had found a way of hurting him for a change. "You'd better be quick about it, Negib, that's all I can say – because Mossad will have your name and description in the morning."

159

I was still jeering at him and turning away to the door when I heard the click of the switch-blade. I jumped to one side as he lunged with the knife. It was sheer instinct and good luck that I avoided it. So was bringing my knee up. If I tried to do it that quickly again I would fail every time. But I think my knee caught his thigh muscle and the force of his rush jarred him off balance. And he fell on the knife. It all happened in less than a second. He was writhing on the floor, gurgling blood, the knife deeply embedded in his throat and his hands clutching air. A moment before I had hated him, yet all I could think of then was that I was killing Nadi's son. Then the door opened and Nadi's grandchild stared at me with eyes full of horror. Negib was making awful noises. The knife had slashed an artery I think, because blood was shooting up like a fountain. I *had* to help him. Get a doctor, an ambulance, anything. But Suzy had a man with her. I was in too much of a state then to realise, but he must have been there when I arrived, perhaps hiding in a bedroom and waiting for me to go. He was past me in a flash and bending over Negib while I searched the room for a telephone. I heard the sound of someone vomiting followed by a sigh like air escaping from a tyre. Then, as my hand closed over the telephone, the man behind me said, "He's dead, Mr Brand."

I spun around in horrified amazement. Negib was *dead*! I had *killed* Nadi's only surviving son. And I was grappling with the terrible significance of that when Suzy sprang at me.

"Murderer! Fucking British murderer!"

She tore at me like a wild animal and spat in my face as I tried to hold her at arm's length. Her nails raked my face, trying to gouge my eyes, and I was ducking away from her when the man pulled her off. He smacked her twice across the face, very hard, so that the imprint of his hand stood out on her skin. Her face was wet more with her own spit than with tears. She moaned, then turned and stumbled from the room.

"The police," I said. "A doctor. We'd better call them –"

"You'll be charged with murder," the man said. He was so *cool*, whereas I was trembling and on the verge of being sick. Then he added: "Which wouldn't suit my plans. Just go Mr Brand and keep quiet about this. I'll attend to everything."

"Go?" I said stupidly.

"Yes *go*." He began to get angry. "Get out of here." He was alongside me then, his hand on my arm, propelling me towards the door. "And Mr Brand – you'd better keep *very* quiet – understand?"

I wasn't thinking straight. Fear I suppose, fear and horror at having killed a man. But a moment later I was outside the apartment and looking at the closed door. I can't remember the journey back to the hotel. Once in my room I swallowed a tumbler of whisky and then was as sick as a dog. Of course, I *should* have called the police. But would they have believed it was an accident? Especially with Suzy screaming "murderer" at the top of her voice. And how did I explain running away to begin with? In the end I did nothing – at least not until the morning.

I went back to Suzy's place at eight o'clock, but no one answered the doorbell. I returned to my hotel and tried again later on, just before noon and again in the evening, but all to no avail. I was as jumpy as a tick all day long, expecting to hear the wail of sirens as a squad of policemen arrived to arrest me. But nothing happened, until that night.

My contact on *L'Express* had shaken free of his Lyons assignment and had arrived in Paris to have dinner with me. Afterwards we had a drink together, but I was nervy and irritable and very poor company, so he shoved off before eleven and I went to my room, seeking the solace of sleep after the nightmares of the night before.

A note had been pushed under my door. "Palestine has lost one of her bravest sons," she had written in the green ink she always uses, "but soon the day will dawn when his name will be honoured everywhere. Please make no effort to contact me ever again. Suzy Katoul."

The golden voice purred from the golden body which lay in the crook of my arm. "And did you ever see Suzy again?" I muttered "no" and kissed her breasts. She stretched one long leg over mine in a graceful feline movement, and her hands busied themselves wiping my sweat away. Above us, the giant fan revolved slowly and beneath us the soft white bed cushioned our naked bodies.

The green eyes stared into mine. "Was she such a great loss, Harry?"

Nadi was answering for me. I could see his face and hear his voice.

"They are *still* my children – even if they treat me like – like a United Nations." Oh Nadi, the promise I made you – to cherish your daughter and look after your son. And I *killed* him. I killed Nadi's youngest son.

Her golden body was wet with my sweat and still her hands wiped my brow.

"You killed a murderer, Harry – in self-defence – an accident –

don't be so hard on yourself."

Would Nadi understand that? Would you, Nadi? Do you? Does Haleem understand the daughter we made on the bed in your house the night you were killed? Suzy is *our* child, I'm sure of it, ours, mine and Haleem's. We saved her once – Farida and I – and then we lost her again.

"Tell me about the man," said the golden brown voice. "The man who hid in the bedroom."

"Tall – as tall as me, maybe slightly taller – dark, another cat, like you."

"How?" purred the voice "How like me?"

"The eyes I think – something about the eyes."

"Green?"

"No, not green. Black, but as still as yours can be. Dark eyes with a slight almond shape to them – shaped like a cat's – a siamese cat – a chinese cat."

"Was he the man in the pale grey suit?"

"I don't know – not for sure."

"But you think so?"

"Yes."

"Why didn't you tell me before?"

"All this? Confess you mean? Confess to murder. Tell you my only child was mixed up in a drug racket. Tell you she *hates* me. Confess to being ashamed."

"We're all ashamed at times, Harry, about some of the things we do."

"But the ends justify the means?"

"Sometimes."

09.00 Saturday

From the shed which served as his office, Mick Malone watched the men load the lorries in the yard outside. The excise officer stood in the doorway, drinking tea while his mate sheltered in the lee side of the big truck and counted the batteries on board.

"Not much of a day for travelling," the excise man sniffed as he emptied the dregs of his tin mug over the asphalt.

Mick joined him in the doorway, twisting his neck upwards and screwing his eyes into slits against the drizzle of rain. "Sure now, and the farmers will be pleased to see it – and like as not it'll stop by dinner time."

"That when you take off?"

162

Mick grinned. "I'll be long gone by then. A man likes time on his side. Especially when he's dealing with officials." His grin widened. "Now aren't they a blight on humanity? Forever holding a man up and making easy things difficult."

"We'll not take much longer," the excise man grumbled. "And after us there's not a custom's man who'll bother you this side of Cologne."

Mick clapped an arm around his shoulder. "And isn't that the freedom of the road for you?" He chuckled and walked away, into the main building and up to the office to collect his travelling money and passage documents. When he returned, the T.I.R. plates were already in place, the doors at the back of the lorry were locked and bolted, the padlocks were being sealed over with the lead imprint of the excise seal. Mick went into his office for the very last time in his life. From now on he would do so many things – *for the very last time in his life*. His face twisted into a wry smile at the thought of it. Was that such a bad thing? Was life so good that he wanted to hang onto every last minute of it? He had answered that already – two days ago.

It took him half an hour to check the other lorries out of the yard, shouting back to the drivers and promising to bring a buxom fraulein back for each of them, or a bottle of schnaps for old Tim Corrigan who claimed the pleasures of the bottle outlasted those of the body any night of the week. Tim was taking over from him, just until he returned of course, so another half hour was spent in explaining company procedures for the fourth time. And then, quite suddenly it seemed, Mick was free! He had never felt so *free*. Hugely triumphant – as if he had achieved something, won something, like a medal or scored the winning goal in the cup final. It was as much as he could do not to *run* to the cab. He left the shed for the wagon, catching his breath as excitement brought a stab of pain to his chest, talking to himself like a man to a horse – steady Mick, steady – you've a way to go yet. He sat behind the wheel, getting his breath back, calming himself, using the time to check his instruments like a pilot before take-off. Then he was turning the ignition key and the huge diesel engine was roaring into life beneath him, vibrating the cab as he left the factory yard – *for the very last time in his life*.

He had time enough, he knew that, but there were things still to do. And the next two would be the hardest. The next two would hurt more than the pain in his guts and the ache in his back put together. And as he turned into the narrow street of terraced houses he found himself wishing it was all over – once and for all.

163

The kitchen had never looked cleaner. The plates shone on the dresser and the saucepans gleamed on their shelf like a display at the corner shop. A fresh tablecloth graced the old deal table, and above the spluttering fire even the mantelshelf had been dusted and tidied for the first time in years.

"The kettle's on," Molly called from upstairs. "Tea won't be a minute. Sit yourself down and let the fire warm your bones for a while."

She was wearing her best dress and when she smiled twenty years fell away. He remembered courting her, taking her to Bantry fair, him tall and proud and her hanging on his arm and looking up to him with laughing eyes. He had wanted to fight the world then, fight it and beat it and change it all for a better place. Sweet Jesus Christ – where had all the time gone?

"I've packed your bag." She poured hot water over the leaves in the pot. "And the paper's by your elbow. So rest a while, Mick Malone – it's a long journey you've got – bonus or no bonus."

He rested. He even closed his eyes. Not to sleep but to save himself from her conversation, from things he didn't trust himself to say. An incautious word now and she would guess everything – and if she ever did that she'd never touch a penny of the money afterwards.

At the door he kissed her, clumsily, like the very first time, so that she looked up at him with startled eyes. "Mick, you're not to be worrying about *us* now. We'll be all right." She kissed him again quickly and smiled. "It's not like the old days, when I never knew where you were or what you were doing." She squeezed his arm. "At least this time I'll not need to be worrying about *that* now, will I?"

He kissed her one last time and swung the canvas grip over his shoulder, then he left. He never looked back – there was no point – not even when he drove down the mean little street *for the very last time in his life*.

He took the top road out of Cork, away towards Mallow and Tipperary beyond. Even were it not part of his route he would have gone that way, to look at the school from the top of the hill. The ground fell away on his left-hand side, dipping down across the new housing estate while the road continued upwards, curving past the houses with gardens like pocket handkerchiefs. Men in shirt-sleeves cultivating vegetables, bonfires spiralling smoke into the grey sky. Then the school itself, a new two-storey building of yellow brick, flanked by an asphalt playground and a patch of green where the boys played football. They were playing now and he stopped the truck to watch them, twenty-two lads of all shapes and sizes chasing a ball like dogs at a rabbit, pushing and shoving and shouting for the sheer fun of it.

He switched the engine off and clambered down from the cab, lighting a cigarette as he sheltered from the wind. Below, a mighty shout signalled a goal and the two sides reformed into patterns on either side of the halfway line. One boy peered up towards the road, cupping his hands like binoculars as he walked to the edge of the pitch to get a better view. Then he was waving wildly, and Mick recognised him for his very own son. He waved in return and cocked his head to catch the boy's shout, but the wind caught the unbroken voice and carried it away.

The man climbed back into the cab and started the engine. The boy waved again and the man answered before turning his eyes to the road ahead. He never looked back – there was no point – not even when he knew he'd seen his own son *for the very last time in his life*.

Up through Mallow, down through Killmallock, familiar buildings, churches and houses, pubs and shops, passing the lot of them *for the very last time in his life*. But no longer with sadness. Instead he felt a huge sense of triumph which grew with every passing mile. He no longer cared that his back ached. He swore at it, sang at it, gloated and sneered at it. Ache you bastard – ache! His back was the whole rotten system and he was beating it to hell. Molly would have her little shop and the boy his university. Molly would have a life worth living and the boy a future worth having. And all because Mick had beaten the system. And he drove into Tipperary and out again – *for the very last time in his life*.

10.00 Saturday

Ross followed the Brigadier into the conference room. Formerly the billiards room, it was well proportioned and of a good size, but was now sparsely furnished with a number of chairs grouped around a big table. Eight tall windows overlooked the front drive and another door led off to a small room in which Twomey's secretary worked. Ross counted the chairs; eighteen, arranged in two ranks which meant nine participants, each with an advisor seated behind to guard his back and prompt when necessary. Some were there already – separate knots or three of four people, all men, talking in low voices like guests at a funeral. Ross hoped it wouldn't be his. The department had its enemies and some would gather here this morning – ready to pounce on his lack of progress, concealing their triumph behind snide remarks and worried expressions. Twomey would have the thankless task of papering over the cracks, of course – though Christ knows how he would explain Hayes skipping like that. And now Hayes was dead!

"Davies has arrived," Twomey said at his elbow. They looked down to the gravel drive and watched the black Humber roll to a halt. The chauffeur opened the door before the marine corporal reached it and Davies bounded up the steps and into the front doors. Years ago Davies had played prop forward for Wales and it still showed in his broad shoulders, even when they were covered with a black melton coat worth at least three hundred pounds in Savile Row. Guineas, Ross corrected himself, three hundred *guineas*. Wasn't that how upper-class English shopkeepers made enough to buy racehorses? Davies was followed by *two* assistants and Ross heard the scrape of furniture as somebody hastily re-arranged the chairs behind him. He stayed at the window for a moment longer, making a game of counting the soldiers hidden in the shrubbery before glancing up at the same Hercules as it circled its tight pattern against a grey sky.

There were no introductions. Those who knew each other exchanged sly smiles of recognition, but mostly people nodded or said "Good morning" in a manner which suggested it was anything but. Ross knew the C.I.A. boy and Thompson from S.I.S., but nobody else – except Davies of course, and *everybody* knew Davies. Just as they all knew that Davies had opposed the formation of the department from the start. "Job for the police," he had argued. "And Scotland Yard already has an anti-terrorist squad." But Davies had been over-ruled and had crept back to the Home Office like a whipped dog, whereas Twomey had gone on to raid every security organisation in the Western world to recruit the members of his team. But even whipped dogs have their day – and Davies had chosen this as his.

"I am led to understand, Brigadier," he said after opening the meeting in that soft Welsh lilt he could adopt or abandon as the mood took him, "that the United Kingdom is under nuclear attack."

Ross winced. The department's role would come to an end if Davies made it a *national* issue. The department's field of operation was *international*. If Twomey lost the argument Ross would be compelled to hand everything over to British security and take a back seat.

"Whereas the facts are," Twomey answered mildly, smoke billowing from the bowl of his pipe. "That an *international* terrorist group with bases in Tripoli and Paris has exploded a small nuclear device –"

"On *our* bloody beaches!" Davies roared.

"In point of fact twelve and a half miles outside British territorial waters," said the Brigadier gently.

"After attacking a *British* merchant ship," Davies snapped back.

Twomey remained unperturbed. If he was worried sick about the whole situation nobody would have guessed. Everything about him suggested calm confidence. He accepted that the *Marisa* was a British registered ship, but pointed out that it had been nearer France than Britain when it was boarded. He spoke of the man, Hayes, certainly a British subject, but one whose business interests included making electronic devices for *French* security forces, and whose knowledge of the *Marisa's* cargo had been gained undoubtedly not in England but in *Marseilles*. He drew attention to the fact that Suzy Katoul was a *French* citizen of an *Arab* mother and that her first communication had been postmarked *Tripoli* and sent to the department's cover in *Malta*. And Katoul purported to represent something called the Deir Yassin Memorial, and whatever *that* was Deir Yassin was certainly not within the United Kingdom, but within the borders of modern-day *Israel*. Like a skilful boxer taking a back street slugger apart, Twomey piled up the points until the *international* ramifications of the affair were endless.

Davies's scowl deepened. "We might be a good deal wiser now if Hayes had been called in for questioning at the outset."

Ross bit his lip, waiting for Twomey to answer, but surprisingly the Brigadier conceded the point. "I quite agree," he said.

"The *key* witness." Davies warmed to his theme with Welsh fervour, like a barrister at a murder trial. "A man *known* to possess classified information. A man *known* to be running prostitutes – *known* to be a blackmailer –"

"Suspected certainly," Twomey interjected mildly. "But *known*?"

"*Known* to threaten the very existence of the United Kingdom," Davies thundered. "Allowed to go free! It's positively criminal. Criminal irresponsibility of the kind –"

"Oh, I say," Twomey protested. "For any security department to –"

"Mr Chairman, may I be permitted a question?"

Ross craned his neck. The man who had spoken was dressed in civilian clothes as was everyone else, but his manner marked him for a soldier. A *British* soldier, Ross noted from his clipped speech as the

167

man took advantage of Davies's hesitation to put a question to Twomey. "Once you suspected Hayes, Brigadier – what steps did you take?"

Twomey looked surprised. "Why, the only ones open to me, of course. My department has no independent authority within the United Kingdom. I passed a request to Scotland Yard for them to place this man under surveillance."

"And when did you do that?" asked the soldier.

"On Wednesday morning."

"And where was Hayes at that time? Do you know?"

"In his London office," Twomey replied without hesitation. "Two of our people were maintaining temporary observation – quite unofficial you understand – and they handed over to Scotland Yard officers at 11.42 am. I believe I have a copy of their report if anyone would –"

"Thank you Brigadier," the soldier's face was expressionless. "I don't think we'll need that for the moment." He turned back to Davies, "Thank you, Mr Chairman."

Ross hid a grin behind his hand as he watched the flush creep across Davies's face. It was a put-up job. Anticipating Davies's attack, Twomey had ambushed him.

"Bound to happen," Davies recovered with a politician's skill. "Whenever the interests of two departments overlap it creates confusion." He glared balefully around the table before launching his own counter-attack. "What I want to know is what the hell you're *doing* about it, Brigadier?"

Twomey puffed his pipe. "With due respect, Mr Chairman, a good deal of that must remain secret. Even from this committee." He smiled thinly, as if goading Davies to challenge his right to withhold information. Only when no such challenge came did he continue: "But certain conclusions are inescapable. Obviously the first is that a political organisation purporting to be something other than a national entity has possession of a nuclear device. I say purporting because although a number of organisations operating outside of international law have considerable *financial* resources, none as yet has the scientific know-how necessary to produce an atomic bomb, or so our combined intelligence reports tell us. Assuming that to be so, we can only conclude that a foreign government has sold a bomb or bombs to Katoul, *or* is, in fact, controlling the operation for its own purposes."

Smothered gasps of astonishment swelled to mutters of speculation, all of which Twomey ignored as he scraped his pipe into the nearest ashtray. When all comment had subsided he said, "I'm rather inclined to dismiss the idea of a government selling a nuclear device. Any State with the resources to develop its own nuclear weaponry is unlikely to be so hard up financially that it has to sell those weapons for cash. Thus my suggestion is that Katoul is merely the front for some nation hostile to the West."

"Jesus Christ!" the C.I.A. man broke in. "You mean this is a Russian attack?"

"I didn't say that," Twomey corrected smoothly. "All I'm doing – at this juncture – is to ask you to accept a certain line of argument."

"Pointing to the Russians," the C.I.A. man said.

Davies coughed importantly. "If we accept the intelligence reports, Brigadier, we have little choice, but to agree with your conclusions."

"You doubt the intelligence reports?" Twomey's apparent surprise cloaked another trap.

"I only see the yellows," Davies backed off. "Not individual reports. That being so –"

"Then you *doubt* the digests?" Twomey's voice hardened as he jerked the hook.

Davies abandoned a lost cause and blustered back to attack. "What we all want to know, Brigadier, is what in hell's name you're *doing* about this. The P.M. will want to know –"

"The P.M. had my report an hour ago," Twomey said coldly. "I am instructed to discuss only certain of my conclusions with this committee along with an outline of some of the defensive measures taken."

Davies's face burned and the Welsh lilt vanished entirely. "Then get on with it, will you. I'm due back in London for lunch and I imagine you've other things to do apart from talk to us."

Ross watched Davies wilt under Twomey's glacial stare and felt his admiration swell to unqualified proportions. Yes, he conceded, there were times when having a cold-eyed s.o.b. for a boss paid dividends.

Twomey turned back to the meeting. "Eight countries are known to have the bomb, and at least four more are suspected of having it. Not one of them is Arab, yet whoever we're up against has chosen Katoul – a known supporter of the Palestinian cause – to be the front runner. What promises have been made to her – or whether she even knows that she is being used – are things we can only guess at. But that she is *not* our *real* enemy I for one have no doubt." He sucked on his empty pipe as if waiting for a question. When none came he said, "A test explosion can mean only one thing. Blackmail. They've demonstrated that they've got the bomb and will no doubt go on to claim to have produced it with *our* plutonium – thus still further disguising their real identity. The problem is that so long as the identity of the blackmailer eludes us, so does the identity of the victim."

It was left to Thompson to break the silence. "Surely, Brigadier," he demurred, "the very name of Katoul's outfit suggests the victim will be Israel."

Twomey raised his eyebrows. "If *you* wished to threaten Israel, would you choose to demonstrate your strength a thousand miles away from her borders?"

"Is distance important in this context?"

"Perhaps not – but if your intention was to blackmail Israel, surely you'd make your intention known to your victim, not to a member of a European security organisation."

"You're suggesting that the victim will be a European country?"

"I think it's more than a possibility."

Davies snorted. "And I think you're like a little lost sheep, Brigadier. With no idea who we're up against or what they want. Or even of what their next move will be."

"On the contrary," Twomey replied quickly. "Their next move is entirely predictable. Like any other blackmailer, they'll make their demands known to us."

"While we're dazzled by the glare of annihilation," snapped Davies, trying to win back lost ground, "like frightened rabbits."

"Blackmailers never *kill* their victims, Mr Davies," Twomey's smile was like the onset of winter. "They merely *try* to frighten them."

Davies snorted. "It would be less frightening if we heard what defensive measures you've taken."

"The P.M. will be discussing the matter fully at the Bonn summit tomorrow – or even tonight, since I believe all of the participants arrive there this evening. My recommendations include putting all N.A.T.O. forces on standby prior to Red Alert and that extra security precautions be taken at all ports of entry throughout Europe. All cargo in transit will be subjected to geiger counter tests for radiation and –"

"You think they'll *move* the bomb by car?" Davies was astonished.

"Why not? Three years ago Russian agents did just that. They stole a Nike missile from the U.S.A.F. base at Karlsruhr and drove three hundred miles across Germany with the tip of the missile sticking through the back window."

"But a nuclear bomb?"

Twomey shrugged. "Nike missiles are fitted with nuclear warheads."

Davies was still incredulous. "They're going to move a nuclear bomb *around* Europe?"

"They already have done. And to demonstrate off Scotland can only mean one thing in my mind," Twomey paused. "That the victim will be a European city."

"You think they're going to *position* it?" Davies persisted. "Like leaving a bomb in a supermarket?"

"It would be the most effective way."

"Why not simply fire a missile?"

"Many reasons, but perhaps the most obvious is the most important. The countries of Western Europe have lived under the missile threat for twenty years. The source of any missile launched against Western Europe would be identified within seconds. Retaliation would be almost instantaneous." Twomey fumbled with his tobacco pouch. "Whereas if the blackmailers were to claim the bomb is *already* in position?"

"You mean it could be in position *now*?"

"The one off Scotland was."

"But – but do we have any *proof* that they've *got* another bomb?"

"What would be the point of demonstrating the first one if they hadn't?"

Davies struggled for an answer, then ventured, "To make us *believe* they've got another one."

"Bluff you mean? Are you prepared to call their hand, Mr Davies?" Twomey spoke with less personal antagonism than before. The mood of the meeting had changed, even Davies sensed that. The personal feud between the two men was now of no consequence. The appalling prospect of Twomey's theory swamped the mind of every man there, but only the soldier wanted to spell out the details.

"Let's get this straight, Brigadier," he said. "You're suggesting that Katoul's organisation will place the bomb and make certain demands on a Western government. Then if those demands are not met, they will explode the bomb."

Twomey nodded. "Something like that."

"Holy shit," said the C.I.A. man. "And you're going to comb *all* Europe for a bomb the size of a suitcase?"

"A ten megaton bomb would be something larger than that,"

Twomey corrected. "But still highly transportable."

"And it could be *anywhere?*" The C.I.A. man shook his head.

"Why ten megaton?" somebody else asked.

"An assumption of course," Twomey admitted. "But it equates to the kind of material which should have been on the *Marisa*, and if that's the story –"

"What other defensive measures have been taken?" Davies butted in.

"Customs and excise teams all over Europe have been strengthened with men drafted in from other security organisations. Border checks on travellers and cargo will be carried out with unprecedented thoroughness. Internally each country will be mounting vigorous campaigns against all people suspected of being connected with terrorist or dissident groups. An entire programme of activity is being co-ordinated to come into effect at midnight tonight. Every police force in Europe will be engaged in the biggest man hunt ever carried out –"

"The biggest bloody cock-up," Davies said. "Geiger counters at ports of entry –"

"Are being rushed into position now," Twomey barely paused. "As from midnight, all freight moving across Europe will be subjected to tests for radiation at every national frontier."

"There'll be uproar from the Press," somebody remarked.

Twomey shook his head. "The geiger counters will be designated x-ray devices similar to those already in use at airports."

"But is there to be a statement to the Press?" the questioner persisted.

Twomey frowned. "I hope not. On the face of it nothing unusual will be happening – there's no need for the public at large to know –"

"They'll *know* all right," Davies barked. "Can you imagine the slowdown this will cause at ports and border crossings?"

"With *three* times the number of men handling the traffic?" Twomey countered. "Granted there'll be some delays, but hopefully none that will become noticeable for at least the next few days."

"Is that how long we've got?" someone asked.

"God alone knows," Twomey sighed. "God and Suzy Katoul – and whoever's running her. But if you ask me to guess, I'd say there's one person in this room who will know the answer to that quite soon."

They looked at him curiously, half expecting him to claim that distinction for himself. But he turned to the man behind his right shoulder. "Major Ross appears to be at one end of the channel along which Katoul has chosen to communicate."

Ross remained impassive in the face of the scrutiny accorded to him. Someone asked, "And you expect the Major to hear within the next few days?"

"Perhaps even within the next few hours," Twomey said wearily, and for the first time that morning some of the strain showed in his tired expression.

"Hours?" the C.I.A. man was badly shaken. "That makes the problem more than European. I'm sure I don't need to remind you gentlemen, but the President of the United States arrives in Bonn this evening for the summit conference."

Twomey nodded. "As well as the political heads of Britain and France, and Japan and Canada."

The information was digested in silence for a minute, then Thompson said quietly, "Suddenly, Brigadier, your theory about the bomb being in Europe makes a hell of a lot more sense."

11.00 Saturday

Mick Malone's back hurt. "My bloody back's killing me," he complained to the empty cab and then laughed aloud at the truth of it. But the *whole* truth was that after driving for almost two hours his back ached more than he had anticipated. He squirmed in the seat to allow the pillow to slide an inch lower, telling himself that for twenty thousand pounds a man should be ready to drive to hell and back. He chuckled. "Or at least half way."

He checked his watch. He was on time. The wipers flicked back and forth across the windscreen while beneath him the huge wheels rolled relentlessly onwards. Reilly would make contact soon. Mick smiled at the thought. Now *there* was a cautious man. Somewhere between the factory and Limerick Reilly would make contact, and that was all Mick knew. But wasn't that Reilly all over? Never tell a man more than he needs to know – *just in case*. Just in case the poor bastard ends up in Holy Cross like Steve Cassidy.

Left at Limerick Junction, twenty miles to go. Through the lush green hills of the Golden Vale where grazed the fattest cows in all the world. Nineteen miles to go. Eighteen. The road filled up with traffic delayed by roadworks and thinned out again on the other side. Mick checked his wing mirror and watched the old Ford ease out into the traffic flow three cars back. Wasn't that the same car he had seen in Mallow? Perhaps and perhaps not, but it was the same shade of blue with a dent in the offside wing. Seventeen miles to go and a signpost told him it was another mile to Pallas Glean. The Ford pulled out, passing the other cars and then Mick's truck with a quick burst of speed. It tucked in in front of him and Mick touched his brakes lightly as he gauged the gap between them. A cut-out board was slotted into the Ford's rear window to conceal any view of the interior. A cut-out board which suddenly said "Follow me" in thin strips of red neon. The message blinked on and off three times and then stayed off for good. Mick chuckled – Reilly had made contact.

Through Pallas Glean, left off the main road, right and then left again. Country lanes, an old tractor straddling the road until the Ford's horn blared to make it pull over. A bend, a turning, a gap in the hedge, a farmyard and two enormous barns with the doors gaping open. The Ford drove into the first barn and Mick followed, the gloom of the place engulfing him as the doors quickly closed behind.

Reilly climbed out of the Ford's passenger seat and walked back to the truck, grinning hugely. "All right, Mick? Time for a bit of a blow before the run down to Limerick."

They crossed the concrete floor, stepping around an oil drum and some coiled ropes, and skirting an old horse box sitting lopsided on a broken axle. It was gloomy in the barn, a dozen bare bulbs strung so high in the roof that their light barely reached the floor. Gloomy and cold, Mick thought, missing the warmth of the cab. He followed Reilly towards an office at the back which was no more than a cube of cement blocks done over with a coat of whitewash. But the light was better in there, it splashed out through the window and threw a long yellow finger across the concrete from the open door. Reilly entered and Mick followed.

The man startled him. Ay-rabs Reilly had said, and if Mick had found a dozen squatting on the floor smoking a hookah he wouldn't have been more surprised. But this man wore a well-cut suit and looked like a prosperous businessman. Tall and dark-haired, with sharp watchful eyes in a face that looked more tanned than brown. Mick shook his hand and sensed the piercing scrutiny of those clever eyes. The man never introduced himself, but then Mick had not expected he would. Reilly's friends rarely did.

"Your condition has been explained to me," the man said quietly.

"Condition?" Mick warmed his backside over the paraffin stove and turned the word over in his mind. He misunderstood it to begin with, but then as the man's meaning dawned on him it amused him. "Condition is it?" he grinned. "If the doctor says I'm pregnant then

I'm having it, and we'll have no wicked talk of abortions."

Nobody smiled, not even Reilly. The tall man eyed Mick's sallow complexion and yellow-tinged eyes with obvious misgivings. "Your substitution has caused us to alter our plans," he said. "To allow for your – illness."

Suddenly Mick was afraid the deal was being called off. Reilly proffered a pack of cigarettes and he took one gratefully, straightening his back in a determined manner. He met the man's dark eyes without blinking and searched his mind for something to say which might convince him. But after a moment or two the man nodded and Mick knew it was all right.

"We'll talk money first," the man said. "Twenty thousand pounds, payable in instalments."

"Instalments? You'd better not make them too far apart," Mick said uneasily.

"Five thousand today. Another five in Cologne. And ten when you reach your destination."

Mick nodded his acceptance. The truth was that he was more worried about how the cash would be explained to Molly – afterwards. "And how do I get the cash?" he asked.

"You don't," the man said. "Payment will be made by insurance endowment policies. Three policies – made out in your name with your wife as beneficiary."

"Insurance policies?" Mick's brow crinkled. "That'll take some thinking about." He turned to Reilly. "You never said anything about –"

"Think about it Mick. How else can twenty thousand pounds be explained to Molly? Come to that, how else could *she* explain it, if the police ever checked. It makes sense –"

"I don't like it," Mick shook his head. "Cash is best. With this there's no –"

"Security?" the tall man interrupted. "Oh, but there is. We were very busy yesterday – and all for your benefit."

"Listen to him, Mick," Reilly urged. "I'd never have gone along with it unless it made sense."

The man said, "We went to the bank yesterday and deposited twenty thousand pounds. Bank of Ireland, Gresham Street, Dublin. Mr Reilly has the paying in slip if you wish to inspect it." He paused long enough for Mick to see the answering nod from Big Reilly. "The Bank have been instructed to make payment against three policies, all of which mature within the next seven days. They receive the policy document and then they pay out – it's as simple as that."

Mick scratched his head. "And just how would these *policy* documents get to them?"

Reilly grinned. "Simple. I've got them." He reached into an inside pocket and withdrew a bundle of papers. "Or at least I've got two of them. The bank's already got the first one."

The man smiled thinly. "And one matures today. For five thousand pounds."

Reilly was still grinning. "The bank wrote to Molly last night. Just a short letter saying a policy has matured, and enclosing a nice fat cheque. She'll have it Monday morning."

Mick began to feel a lot better. Getting the cash to Molly had been worrying him. This way was as foolproof as any he had thought of. *More* foolproof if he was honest about it. And this way it was only Big Reilly that he had to trust – not the dark-haired man who watched him so closely.

The man read his mind. "Mr Reilly sends the second policy when you've passed Cologne and the final one when you reach your destination. The bank can only cancel the arrangements if they fail to receive all policies by the end of a month."

Mick was about to query that when the sound of his truck distracted him. He took a step to the door, but Big Reilly stopped him. "It's okay Mick, they're just moving it out the way, that's all."

The dark-haired man smiled. "For the next month the bank can only pay out against the policies. Nobody can withdraw the money in the meantime – if *that's* what you were thinking."

Mick grinned as if such a thought had never entered his head, but secretly he was pleased – very pleased.

Big Reilly beamed at him. "The bank's already sent five thousand Mick. And don't worry about the rest, Molly will get every penny of it, I'll make sure of that."

Mick was nodding his acceptance of the arrangement and grinning foolishly. There wasn't a man living he'd trust more than Big Reilly, wasn't that the truth of it? And now it was just up to the two of them – Mick to drive the truck and Reilly to make sure the bank paid Molly afterwards. It was a marvellous arrangement – far better than any he had dared hope for.

"There is another matter," the dark-haired man said, "I understand that you were planning to stay in Germany after finishing the job?"

Mick was caught halfway between surprise and amusement. "In a

176

manner of speaking," he said carefully, straightfaced but with a glint in his eye.

The man shook his head. "I'm sorry, but that won't suit us at all. If they identify you, it's but a short step to Reilly here – and from him perhaps to us. By then it might be unimportant, but loose ends like that are – unprofessional."

And whatever else you are, Mick thought, it's for sure you're not that. He wondered what Reilly had said about his *condition* and was surprised as the man apparently read his mind again.

"Severely damaged kidneys are not unique," he said. "I'm not a doctor, of course, but –" he shrugged, watching the effect of his words on Mick's expression. "Arrangements can be made. So, after the job you'll be taken to Switzerland, to the Arab clinic at Lucerne, where you will undergo an operation."

"An operation?" Mick was dazed.

"I can't *guarantee* the outcome," the man said. "But some of the most skilful surgeons in the world reside at that clinic. The best doctors money can buy. I'm giving you the chance of life – a good chance – a sight better chance than you've got now."

Mick sat down beside the stove. A chance of *life*! Just when he'd made his mind up to end it. Did he want that? It changed everything. A chance of *life* the man said. A chance to see Molly and the boy again! Not soon perhaps but someday. To see Molly again.

"I – I don't know," Mick groped for the right words. How could he explain that he had settled his mind to it. A man should settle his affairs and this was his way of doing it. But a chance to see Molly again?

"It's not an *offer* Mr Malone," the man said. "It's part of our agreement."

It changed *everything*. A chance of *life*. A proper life, a whole man again, without this constant ache in the back and cramp in his guts that creased him at times. And with Molly with money in the bank and the boy with the best schooling money could buy. And himself with a chance of seeing them again.

A minute passed before he trusted himself to speak. Even then the words fell short of what he wanted to say, of what he really *felt*. Words could never explain his gratitude. Words might explain what he felt for his family but they were private words, not for the ears of a stranger. So he would express himself not with words but actions he thought, as the determination welled up inside him. Nothing would stop him from finishing this job, *nothing*! Never in his life had he felt so certain, so determined. Never before had he experienced such singlemindedness of purpose. If the job *could* be done, then Mick Malone was the man to do it, he'd see to that.

He glanced across to where Big Reilly stood grinning at the door, and then turned to the tall dark man. In a thick gruff voice, almost unrecognisable as his own, he said: "It's a condition I accept – and thanks."

Reilly came over and slapped an arm round his shoulder, while the tall man thrust out a hand to shake his own. They were both *so* pleased, it could have been their own lives they were saving. After a minute or two Reilly brewed tea on the stove and they talked of the route Mick would take to Germany. Once there, someone would contact him with his final instructions – and that was all he knew. Then he heard the engine of his truck outside and it was time to go.

"Big Reilly was right," the man said at the door. "I am proud to know you, Mr Malone."

They shook hands and Mick straightened his broken body until he felt ten feet tall. Then the man said, "But from now on you make contact with *nobody* – that's another condition, understand? Whatever happens – even if something goes wrong – you'll make no attempt to contact anyone, not the factory, not Big Reilly here, not a single living soul. Just wait for us to contact you. It's a dangerous journey you're going on, but do it my way and we'll all come through it."

Again Mick struggled for the right words. And again he was unable to find any strong enough to express his determination. In the end he simply shook hands and said: "Don't worry – we'll do it your way all right." And then he left.

It was not until half an hour later, as he approached the outskirts of Limerick, that Mick realised his truck was in some way different. The clutch pressure was maybe an ounce stronger and the load behind him felt strange, as if the cargo had been restacked or had transferred its weight slightly. But that was impossible. He had supervised the loading himself, all of the restraining ties had been checked and double-checked. But something was different. He looked around the cab, concentrating on his immediate surroundings. Everything *looked* the same, the same St. Christopher swung on the key ring, the same map folder was lodged in its place, the same cushion pressed into the small of his back. The same tax discs, the same spare pack of cigarettes. Yet the upholstery had an odd smell to it and although the dashboard was scratched in a similar way, similar was not identical.

. At the first lay-by he stopped and clambered down from the cab. At the back the same T.I.R. plates adorned the doors above the same licence plate, and the bodywork looked as it usually did. He slid beneath the vehicle to examine the chassis number and found it as shown in the log book. But something was *different*, he was convinced of that. He reached back into the cab to release the catch which held the engine cover in place – and there he found it. Six months ago the cab had been sprayed with a paint batch that had differed from the original. Not much, but a tone darker than the company's usual green livery. He had been called across to the paint-shop to give his opinion. Some paint had been sprayed on the underside of the bonnet to demonstrate the difference. Mick had told them to go ahead – saying a blind man would be pleased to spot it – and the next day the lorry had been on the road again, looking like new. But the painters had forgotten the underside of the bonnet and the two shades of green had remained ever since. Except that now, as Mick stared at it, all of the paintwork was the very same shade of green.

He ran his hand over it, feeling for a difference in the thickness of paint, knowing there would be none, but needing to check just the same. After that he searched the cab, remembering having dropped a lighted cigarette between the seats which had burned a hole in the fabric. Now there was *no* hole. He examined the offside mirror, remembering a hairline crack caused by a bump in the yard. There was *no* crack. And all this despite the chassis and engine numbers being correct. But all doubt vanished from his mind. It was *not* his lorry. His had been swapped while he had talked to the others in the office at the barn.

He smoked a cigarette, feeling confused and more than a little angry. Big Reilly *must* have known, yet he hadn't said a word. But then, wasn't that Reilly's way all over – never tell a man more than he needs to know. And did it make the slightest difference? To the twenty thousand pounds to Molly and a future for the boy? Or the chance of an operation and the gift of life itself? He was dealing with a very clever man, that was for sure. A very *thorough* man. A man who thought of everything. And now it was up to Mick himself, hadn't the man said as much, and hadn't Mick given his word?

He switched the engine on and checked his mirror before pulling away from the lay-by. Without Mick knowing his jaw had thrust forward and the determined glint was back in his eye. Hell could freeze over before Mick Malone let that man down. Dammit, hell *would* freeze over – nothing would stop him from taking this load to wherever they wanted it – whatever it was. And he still felt that way an hour later – when he rolled down the ramp and onto the ferry bound for France.

Noon Saturday

Ross sat alone in the small room that had once been the butler's pantry, thinking about the meeting which had just ended. Twomey had made it look like a walk in the park, but that did not prevent Ross sharing some of the doubts which had been expressed around the table. He shovelled sugar into a cup of appalling coffee and gloomily waited for the others to join him. Hell, if they only had *one* worthwhile lead! Something tangible for a change – something to work on.

The door opened and LeClerc walked in. "Is that coffee?" he nodded at the pot.

"Skimmed mud. What happened?"

"We spent the first two hours analysing data from the *London*. Waste of time for the non-scientists." LeClerc chanced the coffee. "Then I had a separate meeting with Harrison. You heard about this factory belonging to Hayes? Well they want me to go to Paris at once – if it's all right with you?"

Ross nodded gloomily.

"How did your end go?" LeClerc asked.

Ross shrugged. "Twomey thinks Katoul will contact us. With a blackmail note."

"And you disagree?"

"I don't know. Hope to Christ he's right, that's all. Meanwhile, I just wish we could do something positive."

LeClerc nodded. "They're all convinced the bomb's in Europe. Ugh, it's undrinkable." He pulled a face and emptied his cup over the rubber plant. "What do you think?"

"About Europe? It's possible. The C.I.A. is having a fit about the summit conference, and Twomey's issued every cop in Europe with a geiger counter."

LeClerc smiled. "You're tired. It's a bit more positive than that. The Dutch police have already hit six Red Brigade cells and from what I hear the German GX9 squad are planning more than a hundred raids for tonight."

Ross held up his hands. "Yeah, I know. The biggest man-hunt in Europe. Twomey told me. I'm impressed."

"But you think we should be doing something else?"

"Damn right I do, but don't ask me what." He was interrupted by the arrival of Dorfman. "You get lost on the way, Archie?"

"Just staying in touch with the Irish situation." He felt the coffeepot. "Still no trace of the boys who went to Copenhagen."

"That Copenhagen thing is the only thing keeping that theory alive." Ross sounded bored, he shook his head. "I still don't think it means anything."

Dorfman poured himself some coffee and changed the subject. "I understand Paul's going to Paris?"

A knock at the door revealed the sergeant from Special Branch enquiring about their travel arrangements. "One flight to Paris immediately," Ross said. "And I want a car to take Mr Dorfman and me to the Hayes house at Henley. And I want someone maintaining round-the-clock radio contact with the Health Farm. We'll stay here tonight and return to Malta as early as possible in the morning – okay?" The sergeant nodded and withdrew.

Dorfman seemed surprised. "Special Branch have been in residence at 'The Willows' for forty-eight hours. Every floorboard in the house will have been taken up by now."

"Well, we'll take them up again. Then we'll take every tile off the roof. If those dummies had done their job right to begin with we'd be talking to Hayes now instead of looking at his corpse."

Dorfman scowled at his coffee. "You think Katoul was running Hayes?"

"I think the guy running *Katoul* was running Hayes. And he thinks people are more disposable than Kleenex."

Dorfman stuck his neck out. "I think Reilly and Brady have been disposed off as well."

Ross sighed. "You won't be satisfied until you go over to Ireland to look for yourself, will you?"

Dorfman maintained an attentive silence.

"Tell you what we'll do," Ross decided. "We'll try this place on the Thames first, and in the morning you can look over the Hayes London office. Then if we're still scoring zero you get over to Ireland while I get back to the Health Farm."

Dorfman tried to conceal his satisfaction by pouring his coffee over the rubber plant. Ross watched him for a moment, then closed his eyes and tried to imagine the whereabouts of Suzy Katoul.

13.30 Saturday

Suzy Katoul was still in the cottage at Conlaragh. Big Reilly had

181

spread a map of Dublin across the bed and was explaining the exact location of the Holy Cross Prison for the sixth time since he and Abou had returned from Pallas Glean. Enlarged photographs of the approach roads to the prison had been pinned to the whitewashed walls and every so often Abou would stare at one as if committing it to memory.

"Steve Cassidy is in the detention block here," Reilly pointed to the rough sketch map. "It used to be the prison hospital until a few years ago."

Abou nodded, no more than faintly amused at the prospect of inflicting casualties in a building once a hospital. He pointed. "How high are the walls here?"

"Twelve feet."

"And the hoist?"

"Has a maximum upward reach of fifteen," Reilly said with satisfaction.

Abou examined another photograph. It showed a hydraulic hoist mounted on the back of a lorry, like a gigantic pair of dividers, with a platform set at one end. In Dublin such vehicles are used by Corporation electricians when maintaining overhead street lighting, and indeed the City's crest of arms was painted on the driver's cab of the one shown in the photograph.

"And it raises at a foot a second," Abou murmured, rehearsing the details of the operation in his mind's eye. "Very well, let's go through it once again."

Reilly curbed his impatience. If they had been over the plan once they had been over it a dozen times, but something told him that the man opposite would examine it a dozen times more if he felt unhappy about the slightest detail.

Suzy smoked another cigarette and tried to concentrate. Not that the plan to release Cassidy was of any direct concern to her. She would have left Ireland by then anyway. Left Ireland and left Abou. But now that it had come to it, the prospect of being alone frightened her. Not just the prospect of being away from Abou's protection, but the thought of what she had to do. It had made sense originally, when Abou had first told her. There had been something intensely dramatic about it. "A uniquely historic mission" he had called it and she had succumbed to the glamour of it. But now that it was only hours away the dangers terrified her, even though Abou promised it would only last twenty-four hours at the most. Then they would be re-united, re-united in triumph, their photographs on every front page in the world and their names on everybody's lips. And in one audacious move she would have liberated Palestine! The very prospect made her tremble.

"Good enough," Abou frowned with final approval. He picked up the map and folded it into squares. "Now let's hear your plans."

Reilly sat back in his chair. "We're going fishing, just like we said." He smiled, pleased to be finished with the planning session and pleased that the job was almost over. Circumstances had forced him to work with the tall dark stranger, but nothing about the man's personality appealed to him. And every time he thought of Liam, suspicions crept out from the dark recesses of his mind.

"You're to be at sea when we do this job," Abou nodded at the photographs.

"That's what we agreed."

"And you'll warn all other I.R.A. men to have a good alibi for tonight."

Reilly nodded. "None of our people will be within five miles of Holy Cross. That's already been taken care of." It still surprised him that the man was going to such trouble to spring Cassidy, but he was glad the Movement was to be kept out of it.

Abou nodded his satisfaction. He had his own reasons for wanting the I.R.A. well clear of the Holy Cross Prison tonight.

Reilly said, "So if we could talk about the ammunition, I'll be making the rest of the arrangements."

Abou smiled thinly and reached to an inside pocket, withdrawing the chart he had brought with him from the *Aileen Maloney*. "It's about five miles out from Conlaragh Creek. The spot's marked on the chart here."

Reilly was astonished. "The ammo was aboard the *Aileen Maloney* all the time?" For days he had wondered how the promise would be kept.

Still smiling Abou said, "When you get there, you'll find a yellow marker buoy. You'll need a winch – it'll be a heavy business lifting it."

Reilly studied the chart and wondered what it was about the arrangement which troubled him. Something did. Was it a trick? Were they to be sent on a wild goose chase – hunting for something that wasn't there? Yet there seemed no point to it. The man had kept his word on everything else – the *Aileen Maloney*, the Kalashnikovs, the money, all had been delivered as promised. And look at the trouble he had taken to see Mick all right, and the efforts he was making for Steve Cassidy. Yet something nagged at the back of Reilly's mind.

"You'll be gone when we get back, of course?"

Abou smiled. "Don't worry, you'll find what you're looking for. I guarantee it."

He had no choice but to accept it, Reilly knew that. And hadn't that been the way of things all along? He folded the chart into his pocket and stood up. "I'll be making arrangements for the motor cars then?" He looked at Suzy. "Yours will be ready inside the hour. Is that when you're leaving?"

"Yes," Abou said in a determined voice before Suzy could answer. "An hour will be plenty."

Suzy closed the door behind Reilly. "Abou – do I *have* to go?" she pleaded in a desperate rush of words. "Surely there's another way. Perhaps if we sent –"

"Suzy." He drew her into his arms, hiding his face in her hair to conceal the contempt in his eyes. Another hour and he would be rid of her. It would be a relief. To be free of the strain of forever encouraging her, supporting her needs, feeding her ego, pretending to care for her when all he cared about was the Plan. He would miss her body, but there would be other women. Others he could train to perform those very special duties. Training them was part of the enjoyment, watching their initial revulsion become an urgent need in a matter of weeks.

He comforted her for a few minutes and then went to the briefcase to collect the leather-covered box which contained the syringe. Her eyes widened as she watched him and her face lit up with pathetic gratitude.

"One shot now," he said, "and the others will give you another one in Rome."

She bared her arm hurriedly and sucked her breath in sharply as the needle found a vein. A shot now was a bonus, she knew that, a present, a parting gift. Oh Abou, you're so kind and wonderful and . . . her breathing came in huge panting gasps and all she could think about was the exquisite pleasure which engulfed her. He drew her back into his arms and could feel her wanting him. He smiled. Instant gratification, like a child or an animal. He would deny her now, but the two commandos travelling with her to Rome would give her a shot tonight and then she would take both of them. Both of them tonight and both of them tomorrow morning when they gave her the booster shot. His smile broadened. Perhaps the man with the broken hand would at least feel compensated.

"Enough," he pushed her away. "It's time to get ready."

It took them most of the hour. Abou applied make-up to her face

184

like an artist putting paint on canvas. From time to time he glanced at the photograph of the other girl he had propped up next to the briefcase, working continuously to achieve a good likeness. But not until the specially made blue contact lenses were put on her eyes and the blonde wig arranged on her head was the transformation complete.

She giggled at her reflection in the mirror. "I get to look more like Monique every time you do it," she said.

16.00 Saturday

A gremlin was trapped in my head and was using a pickaxe to get out. Even that would have been bearable if I could see straight, but every now and then my vision distorted and the room closed in on me. One minute I was in the middle of Carnegie Hall and the next suffocating in a space no bigger than a coffin. I was on a bed in a room with whitewashed walls – *my* bed in *my* room at the Health Farm. God, had I reached that stage, so institutionalised that I thought of it as my room, possessively, like a child clinging to an old blanket. If only I could stop shivering it would help. And the sheets beneath me were wet with sweat. The room opened out again to a hundred feet long, and in the far distance a tiny door opened and Elizabeth entered like Alice coming through the looking glass.

"You've got your clothes on," I said when she was near enough to hear me.

She wore the same white sweater and slacks she had started out in – before we went to bed.

"I've never taken them off." She offered me a glass of something, but my hands were shaking too much to hold it. "The doctor will be in to see you soon."

"I'll kill that bastard if he comes in here."

She sat me upright and held the glass so that I could drink. I was thirsty enough to empty the swimming pool. Something was wrong with her eyes – they were as green as ever, but one was twice the size of the other. "You're still hallucinating," was her excuse when I told her, but I knew she was wrong.

"What happened in Scotland?" I asked, knowing something was supposed to happen without being sure of what.

"They exploded the bomb."

"Did they kill Ross?" I panicked. Ross was the only friend I had. If Ross had been killed . . . ?

"No, he'll be back here in the morning."

185

"I want to see him. Understand that? As soon as he gets here."

"I understand."

God I was tired, so bloody desperately *tired*. I could hardly keep my eyes open.

"Harry, I want to talk to you. Don't go to sleep. I want you to remember something for me."

"Oh no! Not more bloody questions." I closed my eyes and clung to her.

"Remember the blonde you met at Henley with Suzy?"

"I'm tired, just let me sleep –"

"You said she was French. Why did you tell me that, Harry?"

"Oh my God! Why would I say De Gaulle was French? Why would I say Maurice Chevalier was French? Because they are – were – French."

"Harry, we know that she *wasn't* French."

I nestled my head into the soft yielding mounds of her bosom and kept my eyes tightly closed.

"Please Elizabeth – let's talk about it tomorrow. I'm tired, just so bloody tired –"

"Why did you say she was French?"

"For Christ's sake! She had a French accent and was called Monique Debray! The dress she wore looked like something by Nina Ricci and she reeked of Ma Griffe. What more do you want?"

The white sweater swelled against my mouth and her lips brushed my ear. What the hell did she mean about *not* taking her clothes off?

"Did you ever know her by another name?" a grey voice asked from nowhere.

I jerked upright. The doctor stood at the foot of the bed, and Max looked over his shoulder.

"Get out," I said coldly and then erupted in a fury of temper. For two or three minutes I laid my tongue to every swear word I could muster. But it made no difference.

"Monique Debray could be important," Elizabeth whispered in my ear. "Please, Harry – you've got to tell us everything you know about her."

"I have – I have – I have!"

But it was no good. The needle was going in just the same.

18.00 Saturday

LeClerc's home was in Paris. Not that he saw much of it these days.

Just every other weekend and the fourth week if he was lucky. But he had phoned Madelaine from Heathrow to let her know he would be home tonight – tonight or in the early hours of the morning – or, at the very least, in time for lunch tomorrow. He had phoned from Heathrow to avoid Ross knowing. Ross would expect him to catch the first flight back to Malta, without so much as letting Madelaine know he was in town, let alone see her. LeClerc sighed. It was all very well for Ross. He had *his* home comforts at the Health Farm. LeClerc disapproved, but not being able to do anything about it he rarely thought about it, and he bore Elizabeth no ill will because of it.

Jacques Bernier sent a car to meet him at Orly, an unmarked car driven by a plainclothes detective, who merely touched LeClerc's elbow as he came through customs. LeClerc approved. He had worked with Bernier before and had been impressed by the man's thoroughness. Not a flash of inspiration man, LeClerc judged, no genius, but the ideal type to go through a man's pockets – or his house – or indeed, his factory. Bernier could turn the President's Palace over and nobody would be the wiser afterwards – least of all the President himself. A good old-fashioned cop LeClerc thought, nodding with approval as he gazed out at the traffic on his way from the airport.

The factory was situated in the sixteenth *arondissement*. It was an appropriate place for it. Half the businesses in the area were into electronics. Plessey had a place there and Siemen's had covered sixteen square kilometers with an assembly plant – and the computer boys had bought up half the Rue de la Martin. The talk in the local cafés was of printed circuits and chip technology, of high rates of pay and scope for advancement. And, but only occasionally, of the women who worked there in their thousands. LeClerc knew all about it, his daughter was one of them.

There were no outward signs that the police had taken possession of the factory. A few cars stood in the car park – a blue Citroen next to a Renault with a bent nearside wing, a Mini Cooper and a Lancia – but they could have belonged to some of the company's managers sacrificing their Saturday evening to catch up on paperwork.

The detective led the way past another plainclothes man at the front door and along a corridor to a flight of steps at the far end. Upstairs the walls were wood-panelled and the carpeted floor muffled their footfalls, otherwise the corridor was the same – running in a straight line from the front to the back of the building. Bernier must have seen them arrive because he opened a door at the far end of the corridor and stepped out to greet them.

You can tell a lot about a man from his office. LeClerc was impressed as soon as he crossed the threshold. Louis XIV furniture and Persian rugs over oak strip floors, silk drapes at the windows and a chandelier big enough to grace the reading room at the Bibliothèque Sante-Genevieve. Paintings adorned the panelled walls and two pieces of sculpture were skilfully displayed in alcoves on either side of an ornate secretaire.

Bernier smiled. "The paintings alone are worth ten million francs – maybe more, I'm no expert."

LeClerc nodded. "The office of a successful man."

"A rich one, certainly," Bernier agreed.

LeClerc prowled around the room, peering at a charcoal sketch by Picasso and then stepping back to admire a bronze bust of a young girl. He took his time, soaking up the atmosphere of the room, his eyes registering as his mind catalogued like a connoisseur in an auction room. It was not what he had expected. LeClerc had imagined Knolle International, cantilevered chairs and plate-glass tables, and he was disappointed not to find them. It meant that his mental image of the man was wrong and that disturbed him. To catch a man you had first to understand him. To catch a *dead* man was the hardest thing of all. You could not interrogate or apply pressure, or watch for a reaction as you turned the screw, nor could you listen for the give-away lie – all you could do was imagine.

Two photographs stood on the desk, both in gilt frames. LeClerc recognised the girl immediately, he had seen enough shots of her at Bampton House. It was Monique Debray. But the other photograph was of a horse. True it was a racehorse and a handsome enough creature, but he was surprised to see it.

"I never knew Monsieur Hayes was into racing?"

"Not here, not in France," Bernier settled down to report on the results of fifteen hours work, "but he races in England."

"Raced," LeClerc corrected. "Monsieur Hayes is dead. Murdered."

Bernier's eyebrows may have risen a fraction and perhaps his eyes narrowed thoughtfully, but apart from that there was little change in his expression. Nothing surprised him, it was written in the lines on his face. Even in repose his face conveyed a look of sad acceptance. Thirty-five years as a policeman had taught him the inevitability of such things. If the nature of man was to lie and cheat, then murder was no more than the ultimate theft.

"So he raced in England?" LeClerc settled into the desk chair, stroking the wood of the desk as he looked about him, anxious to get the feel of the place and desperate to learn about the character of the man whose chair this once had been.

"And in Ireland. His horses were trained there – at a place called Limerick."

An Irish connection? LeClerc had doubted it before. He had been as sceptical as Ross about Dorfman's theories in that direction. But here it was again, and yet there had been no mention of it in the file he had studied during his flight. He marshalled everything he knew about Hayes. A busy man – a businessman, with interests in the Far East as well as Europe. A man with an eye for a pretty woman and with enough money to indulge his sexual fantasies at the house on the Thames. Rich, cultivated, a man whose wealth had secured contact with the power elite of England and France, and now it would seem, perhaps of Ireland too? But with no business connection which linked him to the Middle East. So why does a man like *that* get mixed up with a Palestinian terrorist organisation? Why? Where's the profit for a man who set such store on money? He cleared his throat. "What about the business here? Is it all right? Pay its bills, make a profit, declare a dividend, pay tax?"

Bernier nodded. "Yes to everything. The fraud squad have completed an initial examination of the company's books – everything's in order so far."

"*Too* in order?" LeClerc cocked his head. "Even the best-run businesses have discrepancies – queries – human errors. A perfect set of books screams fraud louder than anything I know."

Bernier shrugged. "I said as much myself. There were some *small* queries – a few loose ends, perhaps enough to account for human fallibility." His smile made him look ten years older. "The company's accountant was embarrassed enough when we pointed them out earlier."

"But eventually he found answers for them?"

"Enough to satisfy the fraud squad."

LeClerc detected a slight uncertainty. "But not *you*?"

Bernier pursed his lips and was about to say something when he stopped and changed his mind. He shook his head. "I know as much about a set of accounts as I do about painting."

"But you know men, Jacques," LeClerc persisted. "Something made your nose twitch, eh?"

Bernier was pleased. Even his face failed to conceal his sly look of gratitude. "He knew we were coming."

LeClerc was astonished. "He *said* as much?"

"On the contrary. He was surprised, shocked, argumentative.

189

Telling us his rights and demanding access to the company's lawyers. But he *knew* – he *expected* us."

LeClerc stared across the desk. It would be a mistake to press Bernier. Policemen cannot explain their hunches. A hunch is a feeling not a fact, a sixth sense developed from watching people under strain. Arrest enough people at two in the morning and you learn to expect a certain pattern of behaviour. You look for the pattern. When it varies, something is wrong. That it can vary in a million different ways is what makes pinpointing it so difficult. The nose can twitch as much about something not said as something said; days may pass before realisation dawns, but you never miss it.

"What about the other managers?" he asked. "Have you interviewed them?"

"But of course," Bernier said huffily. "There are six managers. They run the place really – Hayes only came over three or four times a month."

"And did your nose twitch with the others?"

"No, not in the slightest."

LeClerc frowned. Perhaps it made sense. If anything odd was happening in a business the money man would be the first to know about it. Except, on the face of things, nothing odd was happening.

For the next hour Bernier unfolded his report – details of the managers and employees, cross-referenced with police files, the normal detailed screening which men like Bernier excel at. But nothing dramatic was revealed. Even the business itself was straightforward to the point of being downright boring. It was little more than an assembly plant – nothing was made here – components were bought in from outside contractors; nothing was designed here – Hayes brought prototype products back from the Far East, so all the factory did was to assemble. And make money.

"Were any profits transferred overseas?" LeClerc asked at one stage.

"Overseas no – abroad yes. Monsieur Hayes had a partner – in Switzerland."

Another surprise. There was no mention of a partner in the reports. LeClerc said as much.

"I agree," Bernier nodded. "On paper the company is owned by Hayes alone. But large fees are paid to Switzerland on a regular basis. According to the accountant they are royalty payments to Hayes's partner. 'His partner in the Alps' – apparently that's how Hayes referred to him."

"Has he a name? Does he visit this place?"

190

"It's a Swiss company. No more than a bank account, I'd say."
Bernier shrugged. "Nobody knows much about it, but we're checking into it as far as we can." He consulted his notes. "We think the
man running it must be an invalid."

LeClerc waited for an explanation.

"Some of the royalty payments," Bernier murmured, "are sent
direct to a clinic in the Alps."

Like peeling an onion, LeClerc thought, remove one skin and you
find another, each so like the one before that it was hard to tell them
apart. But where did it get them?

They worked for another hour. Bernier produced a list of the
company's customers, amongst them the government departments
who had provided Hayes with so much of his business. And behind
that list was another – this time the names of the people who ran
those government departments. Slowly the files transferred from
Bernier's side of the desk to LeClerc's, file after file and list after list.
Occasionally the men would pause to discuss a point and back-track
to an earlier file – only then to start a new list of unanswered queries.
Nine o'clock became half past and that in turn became ten. Bernier
had worked for hours without rest and finally LeClerc took pity on
him. LeClerc was tired himself, tired and dispirited and, almost to
his surprise, hungry. He considered whether to phone Madelaine –
perhaps suggest they go out to supper, just the two of them – but he
dismissed the idea. His mood was wrong – he was too on edge to
enjoy it – dammit, soon he would even feel guilty, knowing that
Ross was in England eating his heart out for news. News? There was
no news, nothing worth reporting. Bernier had taken the company
apart and found nothing – just a well-run business with nothing to
hide.

At ten fifteen he sent Bernier home and had one of the detectives
drive him to the La Pactole, a little bistro on the left bank where he
resigned himself to the prospect of a solitary meal. It was the best
way – it gave him time to brood without needing to make conversation. He ordered *pastilla* and half a bottle of burgundy and settled
back in his chair to think about a man called Hayes. The character of
the man – that's what was important. What kind of man was he? A
man with a partner in the Swiss Alps and racehorses in Ireland and a
smart house in England. An international man with a business in
the Far East and a girlfriend in Paris. *A girlfriend in Paris!* Monique
Debray! Bernier had never mentioned her, not once had her name
cropped up or shown itself on a list or appeared on a file. Bernier had
interviewed all of the managers, but had never mentioned the girl.

Yet her photograph had stared at them all evening. Monique Debray who was on file at Bampton House. Yet nothing was known about her and the only reason she made the file at all was because she was listed as Hayes's constant companion, which certainly meant mistress. Hayes's *mistress*! LeClerc cursed himself for being a fool. Hadn't Brand claimed to have introduced them? With Katoul at Henley? As a friend of Katoul's, meeting Hayes for the first time and briefly at that.

He bolted his pigeon pie and finished the wine at a gulp, and hurried back to where the detective waited in the car. He took the Bampton House file from his locked briefcase. Somewhere was her address – somewhere – somewhere. At last he found it. An apartment in a fashionable part of the city. By the time they reached the factory LeClerc had dictated precise instructions to his driver. Go first to the home of Monsieur Bernier to confirm that no contact has been made with the girl Monique Debray. Then take a squad of four men to her apartment and bring her back to the factory for questioning. "And hurry man – hurry!"

21.00 Saturday

They had the nets out and lamps suspended over the side in the traditional manner of night fishermen everywhere. But it was not fish they sought. Big Reilly walked back to the deckhouse on the *Aileen Maloney* and cursed all Arabs to damnation. For the tenth time in an hour he checked their position against the spot marked on the chart and told himself that he had been tricked. There was *no* marker. Neither was there the five thousand rounds of ammunition which had been part of the deal. He swore bitterly and told the helmsman to go round again – to "give it one last try". Then he turned on his heel and rejoined the men in the bows as they stared down into the black water.

The *Aileen Maloney* swung slowly in an arc and retraced her passage through the choppy seas. Reilly had men fore and aft, keen-eyed men used to the ways of the sea, but after searching for the yellow marker buoy for more than an hour they were all tired and depressed. The prospect of turning for Conlaragh and a welcoming woman in a warm bed became more appealing by the minute. "One last time," Reilly encouraged and one last time they agreed it would be. A squall of rain beat down and seagulls screeched low over the water in search of fish drawn by the lights, as the wind howled and the men shivered with the raw cold of the night.

Reilly wondered whether the marker might have broken away from its anchorage and drifted away, dragging its precious consignment with it. But he calculated the weight of the ammunition and thought it unlikely, even though the sea had been running fast for the past few days. He laughed aloud, a bitter laugh, empty of humour. There was no buoy – didn't he know that in his heart? Hadn't he suspected the trick for long enough now? Once more he squinted into the black night and cursed all Arabs – and it was then that he saw it – bobbing aimlessly, barely on the surface, ten yards away and at the very edge of the light. "Stop engines," he roared.

They hooked the buoy with a line at the second attempt, and marker and boat drew alongside each other. The man aft started the motor for the winch and eager hands linked the line to the heavier lifting tackle. The cold was suddenly forgotten. Excited shouts rose to mingle with the screams of the gulls as ten feet of rope disappeared over the side and the winch started hauling back in. The men clustered at the boat's gunnels and willing hands lent power to the winch. Then the black surface of water broke – and Brady's body emerged, feet first. Big Reilly had six men on board – seven counting himself. They laid the bloated and mutilated body carefully out onto the deck. Sight of it made the younger men retch to the pits of their stomachs. Reilly turned the body over – to avoid looking at the decimated face where the fish had been – and then he found the knife wounds which removed any last doubt about how Brady had died. Murdered by the Arabs! Horror turned to burning temper which fused with a hatred so black that Reilly almost lost control of his limbs. He shook with anger and vowed to head straight back to Conlaragh. He would drive through the night to Dublin and pick up their trail from there.

But the winch still turned and another body broke the surface. Reilly knew it would be Liam's. Finding Brady had told him that Liam would follow. Rain and tears wet his cheeks as, with the gentleness typical of big men, Reilly laid his brother's body out on the deck. He forced himself to look into the face and groaned aloud. Oh Liam, did I do *that* to you? Was it me who sent you to Copenhagen to meet those murdering bastards? Oh Liam – forgive me, forgive me, even though I'll never be able to forgive myself.

But still the winch turned. The oilskin covered crate weighed half a ton it seemed, and all hands were needed to lift it inships. Reilly turned away – no longer concerned about the ammunition – sick with grief for his dead brother. Why, he asked himself, why? Why kill Liam and Brady in the first place? And why arrange for their murdered bodies to be found in so cruel a way as this? Didn't they realise he would come after them? Didn't they realise he would follow them to the ends of the earth to take his revenge? Were they that sure of themselves? *That sure*? The answer tore at his brain and he swung back to the men crouched round the crate – words of warning already springing to his lips. But he was too late. The oilskin cover had already been stripped away and one of the men already had the metal lid half open.

The explosion tore the *Aileen Maloney* apart. The deckhouse blew out like matchwood and the hole in the deck broke the back of the boat in two. Most of the men round the crate were killed instantly and part of the metal lid caught Reilly across the throat, severing his neck like a blow from a sword. He reeled drunkenly, the light fading from his eyes, blood covering his chest in gushes, pulsing between his clutching fingers until it reached his elbows. He felt weak, too weak to stand, pitching forward like a novice in a rowing boat. The gulls screeched and the wind roared in his ears, and water rushed into the boat as if through a sieve. Big Reilly lay next to his brother, one arm thrown across the younger man's shoulders as if in a final act of protection. All of the men were dead and a minute later the engines fell forward through the collapsing hull, and the *Aileen Maloney* died too.

LeClerc was a pacer. When something perplexed him he would clasp his hands behind his back and pace up and down, with his head inclined forward so that his chin rested on his chest and his gaze fixed just far enough ahead to ensure clear passage for his feet. Rooms were crossed and criss-crossed until he knew every thread of carpet, so that gradually the size of the office registered in his sub-conscious, the placement of the furniture, the distance from door to windows, the space between the alcoves and the length of each wall. He paced like a caged animal and all the time he thought of the man whose office it once had been and of a girl called Monique Debray.

After half an hour of such exercise the wine consumed earlier reached his bladder and he needed to relieve himself. The physical need annoyed him. Bodily functions were a nuisance, a distraction, they interrupted a line of thought, interfered with the careful piecing together of the jigsaw. The jigsaw of the character of this man Hayes. The man who had furnished this office with such taste – the elegant man who had been murdered in the muddy waters of the Thames – the man who . . . dammit! It was no good, LeClerc *had* to go in search of *le lavabo*.

Finding one was harder than anticipated. The office on the other side of the corridor quite clearly belonged to a secretary, and the one next to that was a general typing pool. LeClerc made his way down the corridor, his pace increasing as his need became more urgent. Beyond the typing pool two offices had a smaller room jammed between them in which a secretary would work to serve two masters. On the right-hand side was the boardroom, another lavish affair furnished much in the style of Hayes's own office, beyond that a supply closet and then a small office which was completely unfurnished. LeClerc hurried past two more offices, one on each side of the corridor, until, almost at the head of the stairs, he saw two doors marked *Dames* and *Messieurs*. He bolted in with a sigh of relief. After he had washed his hands and dried them on a crisply-starched roller towel, he stepped back into the corridor. Hayes's office was at the very far end. LeClerc sighed, dropped back into his pacing position and shambled back down the corridor – his mind already retracing his earlier thoughts like a finger finding a page in a book.

The character of the man. An international man. A rich man. A busy man – a man used to getting his own way – used to his comforts. LeClerc stopped. It seemed such a preposterous thought – but why would a busy man have the nearest *lavabo* thirty-five or forty metres away? A man who liked his comfort. A man with power to change such a simple but such a fundamental thing. Why walk forty metres to relieve yourself and stand in the next stall to the office boy? It was out of character.

At first he was disinclined to take his own thoughts seriously. Probably there was another washroom at this end of the corridor, one he had missed in his haste. But when he could find no trace of one – even after checking for a second time – he became increasingly curious. The thought tugged at his mind like a fretful child at a mother's sleeve. It was quite absurd of course . . . but all the same?

He retraced his steps to the washroom at the far end, counting as he went. Thirty-eight metres. Hayes would walk further than any employee. LeClerc began to pace out the other offices, the big one at the end, the empty one, even the stationery store which was no more than a very large cupboard; and with every step he told himself he was wasting his time. But in the boardroom he paused long enough to pick up a scrap of paper on which he jotted the measurements, roughing out a floor lay-out as he went. He concentrated entirely on the right hand side of the corridor, being the side which housed Hayes's office. And when he finished, the results astounded him. The figures were unbalanced. A corridor thirty-eight metres long and yet the sum total of the interiors of the offices measured only thirty. He calculated the width of the dividing walls – over-allowing just to make sure – just to throw the last bucket of cold water over his rising suspicions. But by no stretch of his imagination could five partitioning walls be eight metres thick. There had to be another room! A hidden room! His suspicions grew to convictions and convictions grew to certainty.

Back in Hayes's office he tapped the panelling like a doctor examining a patient's chest. He stood on a chair to reach the highest points and he sank to his knees to test the skirting-board. He removed the Guardi and examined its mountings, unscrewing the picture lights with his nailfile before probing the cornice at the ceiling and examining the floorboards at the bottom. He worked for half an hour – and found nothing.

Bleak with disappointment he fell into the chair behind the desk and thought about it. Hayes had been some kind of electronics genius, hadn't he? Whereas LeClerc himself knew next to nothing on the subject. But he was convinced that hidden behind the panelling lay another room. A room with a door which opened electronically? Could that be it? There were such devices – garage doors opened electronically and . . . LeClerc cursed himself for a fool. Electronic security systems accounted for half the factory's turnover. How else would a man like Hayes protect himself from prying eyes?

He began to search the desk – searching for what he couldn't have said. Some kind of switch, a button perhaps, a lever, a key, a laser beam? Something, anything with which to find and open that door. By now it was almost midnight, but he felt wide awake. Dammit – hadn't he *been* sleeping? Listening to old Bernier droning on about employee records and profit and loss accounts – as if Hayes had been some kind of petty crook.

He found it in the second drawer of the right-hand pedestal. It made sense for it to be in the desk. Hayes would want it close to hand. It was in *character*. Really it was quite simple. Open the drawer halfway and nothing happened – except that various papers were revealed and enough space was provided for things to be put in and taken out again. But LeClerc wanted more than that. He had already taken every drawer out of the left-hand pedestal to examine their undersides and their backs – just in case a key of some kind had been taped to the surface. But as he pulled this drawer to a point beyond that normally reached in everyday use – he felt and heard the click. He spun in the chair to look at the wall behind him. A gap in the panelling – a gap three metres wide. The door to the hidden room!

He was right, there was a lavatory. Six metres square makes quite a large room. Large enough for a lavatory and sink, and a shelf full of colognes and silver-backed hairbrushes. And large enough for the spiral staircase in the corner.

He sniffed as he climbed the wrought-iron stairs. It was a familiar smell. One he had met all too often in the course of his career. Even the air-conditioning which chilled the whole place to morgue temperature could not disguise the smell of death.

But there was no sign of death in the small sitting-room at the top of the stairs. Not amongst the Chinese newspapers on the coffee-table, or in the Chinese books on the shelves. Nor even in the picture of Chairman Mao smiling down from the wall – though he had been dead for at least two years.

In one corner was a radio transmitter which looked powerful enough to beam half way round the world, but apart from that there was nothing unusual about the furnishings. A couch, two armchairs, a coffeetable, bookshelves and bric-a-brac. All of which so lacked the elegance of the room downstairs that it might have belonged to another man.

As LeClerc turned for the door he caught sight of a framed photograph which had fallen to the floor behind a chair. It was face upwards and as he bent over it he was able to see it without picking it up. Monique Debray smiled back at him from beneath a floppy hat. Dressed in a pretty blue frock, she clung to the man beside her as if afraid of losing him. But Tubby Hayes wasn't going anywhere – at least not now. And on the other side of him stood Suzy Katoul, smiling in that half sneering way which characterised every picture he had seen of her. LeClerc stared for a moment before turning to examine the other man in the photograph. Tall and dark and dressed in a pale grey suit, good-looking in a taunting cruel way which some women found attractive. LeClerc had never seen him before – he was sure of that, but whoever he was he certainly was *not* Harry Brand.

The bathroom was empty. He pushed the door open with his foot and stood in the entrance, fixing the scene in his mind. A bath with a shower attachment, a matching hand basin, lavatory and bidet. So much pink enamel against so many black tiles. A glass-fronted wall cabinet with a razor socket. Black carpet, white ceiling.

He put a handkerchief to his nose and turned slowly to make his way to the bedroom. He was in no hurry and whoever it was in there had waited a few days already. The room was a mess. Discarded clothing lay everywhere on the floor. Mainly women's clothing, but he noticed a man's jacket thrown down beside the bed. Dressing-table drawers had been wrenched from the cabinet and their contents were littered beneath the mirror like a stall at a jumble sale. Something crunched under his foot and, looking down, he found that he had trodden on a woman's watch. Slowly he raised his eyes back to the bed.

Monique Debray was completely naked. She lay spreadeagled across the bed, her wrists tied to the headboard and her ankles secured to the bottom rail. Cigarette burns were still visible on her darkening skin – up the insides of her thighs, low on her stomach and in a blistered rash around her breasts. Her face was badly bruised and her lips were pulled back on her teeth in a grin of frightening viciousness. A syringe lay on the bedside table, next to an ashtray full of discarded cigarettes.

LeClerc studied the body for several minutes. It would have taken her a long time to die, a *very* long time. Death, when it came, must have been a merciful release. He wondered what secrets had been stored behind those pretty blue eyes that someone should have gone to such lengths to prise them from her. Then he turned and walked slowly back to the sittingroom, where he nodded thoughtfully to Chairman Mao and continued on down the spiral staircase – and back into the office that had once belonged to a man called Hayes.

23.55 Saturday

The car travelled slowly along a deserted O'Connell Street, then second right down Jacksons Lane, moving just quickly enough to avoid suspicion and just slowly enough to arrive at Holy Cross exactly on time. Raindrops the size of marbles battered the car roof and ran in rivers across the badly paved road, collecting in pot holes to glitter like black oil until the tyres hissed over them.

In the back seat Abou checked his watch. Five minutes to go. Five minutes before he claimed another life – perhaps more than one if others interfered, or had the misfortune to get in the way. The thought never worried him. How could it when the lives of a few were weighed against the future of fifteen million? How could it when the war was not of his making? It was the impending American betrayal which made it all necessary. Once Washington had taken that fateful decision – once Washington had decided to renege on a thirty-year-old alliance, what options were left?

At the corner of Fitzpatrick Street a lone street lamp cast a yellow glow over a billboard. A blonde in blue uniform smiled damply into the night on behalf of British Airlines. He looked into the larger than life blue eyes and remembered another blonde. The one they had known as Monique Debray. Just the thought of her made him curse so violently that the driver jumped with nervousness.

"It's all right – get on with it," Abou muttered, and the man's gaze swivelled back to the road.

But was it all right? How much had she found out and whom had she told? Even when tortured, she had revealed only a part of the story. She had resisted pain like a professional. But *whose* professional? It was a thought he preferred not to dwell on, knowing it could fester and weaken his confidence. After all, it had changed nothing. It had not changed the Plan. She was dead now, along with that fool Hayes – as dead as he had planned them to be once their part in the scheme came to an end.

He had found her quite by chance. Late at night, alone in the Hayes place in Paris. He had gone there just to make sure it was exactly as he wanted it to be – for when the police arrived. And she had been in the secret room.

"How did you get in here?" he had asked softly, standing at the top of the spiral staircase, blocking her only means of escape.

She had whirled round, a tiny Minox camera in her hand and the code books still open next to the transmitter. "Abou – I – Abou I thought you were in –"

He had hit her then. The factory was deserted and there was no chance of her screams being heard. She had run to the bedroom, trying to lock the door against him, but his strength had been too much for her. And after that . . . his nose crinkled as he remembered the animal smell of scorching flesh.

She had been the only member of the team he had not selected personally. All of the others he had chosen himself. Hayes years ago in the homeland, Negib Katoul after meeting him in the Clinic, and then, through him, Suzy Katoul herself. Even the Irish end he had personally vetted as far as he could. Only Monique Debray had been accepted on another man's word. Hayes had vouched for her and in the rush and flurry of events which followed the inception of the Plan, Hayes's recommendation had been good enough.

"Orlov," he said aloud. It was the one name wrung from her torment. It sounded Russian, certainly Slav. But then Eisenhower sounded German and Willy Brandt sounded like an American shoe salesman. Damn Hayes to hell and back for letting a girl like that get under his skin.

The car crept along Fitzpatrick Street until the bulky outline of the Holy Cross Prison loomed as a solid mass at the end of the road. The rain still lashed down in torrents, bouncing high on the pavements and hurling itself against the car in angry squalls driven by a gusting wind. The street was deserted except for a solitary car parked on the other side of the road. It blinked its lights in greeting before making a tight U turn to head them by about ten yards, leading the way across the junction with John Street before turning left by St Michael's Church.

The hoist was parked by the path leading to the old railway yard. Big Reilly had conveniently arranged for it to "break down" there late that afternoon, when the driver had locked it up and gone back to the depot, saying it was safely parked until the service crew came to fix it in the morning. But it was *fixed* now – fixed and waiting.

The car ahead slowed and two men sprinted into the rain, stumbling and sliding across the wet road until they hauled themselves up into the cab. A moment later the interior light flickered briefly, then one of the men left the cab for the platform of the hoist itself. All three vehicles moved off – past the church to the beginning of the long high wall which surrounded the prison. Fifty yards, that was as far as they needed to go – travelling in convoy at ten miles an hour, the hoist already raising its platform like a snake about to strike.

"Now," Abou snapped and his driver accelerated hard, pulling out to pass the hoist. Abou twisted in his seat and wiped the condensation from the rear window. The platform was already almost as high as the wall, with less than twenty yards left to go. He could see the commando bracing himself against the restraining rails as he pulled the pins from the grenades. Ten yards – five – the platform soared above the wall to give the commando clear sight of the detention centre. Then his arm jerked like a whip against the night sky and the grenades were flying through the air. By the time the explosions occurred, the platform had already dipped back below the wall. The air shook with noise as the commando leapt the last six feet to the ground. The driver of the hoist flung open his door and both men raced for the second car. Abou's driver had already gunned the engine and a gap of thirty yards had opened before the other car gathered speed, a back door swinging wildly like a broken wing until one of the commandos jerked it shut. Abou's car thundered past the prison's main gates and he watched the other car slide into a four wheel skid as it turned left. But it righted itself and disappeared from view to begin its race for the border.

"Shannon Airport – here we come," Abou's driver muttered and swung the car right into Jamestown Road.

Abou straightened in his seat, sighing with relief as he watched the road ahead and barely hearing the distant sound of an ambulance as it rushed through the night to the Holy Cross Prison.

The Irish connection was broken. Killing Cassidy had severed the last link. Now nobody was left who could tell of the tall dark stranger who had arrived with the others on the decks of the *Aileen Maloney*. Now it was up to a dying Irishman named Mick Malone and a half-breed Arab called Suzy Katoul.

6

THE SIXTH DAY

"Political power grows out of the barrel of a gun."
Mao Tse-Tung, *Quotations from Chairman Mao Tse-Tung* (1966)

10.40 Sunday

The R.A.F. Valiant touched down opposite the Civilian Air Terminal at Luqa and ran on for another mile before turning off the main runway to taxi the last eight hundred yards into the R.A.F. compound. But for the fact that whenever he closed his eyes he had a nightmare, Ross might have slept during the flight. The stump of his left arm ached abominably and he was dog-tired but despite that, rest was impossible. He yawned widely and then blinked out into the white glare of reflected sunlight where his tired eyes came to rest on Smithers waiting with the Mercedes next to the Officers' Mess.

LeClerc's signal had reached command at two in the morning and Twomey had called an immediate security conference. Even now Ross struggled to believe the events of the past eight hours. He would have dismissed the entire affair if LeClerc had not been involved. But LeClerc's evidence had been shattering. The corpse of Monique Debray. And the transmitter. And the code books. Together they would bring about the biggest confrontation with Red China since the Korean War. And for it to happen *now* for Chrissakes! That's what was so dammed puzzling. Five or six years ago maybe, but since the death of Chairman Mao relationships with China had improved so steadily that Twomey's conference had been stunned speechless by LeClerc's discoveries. Even now there were some who could not believe that Red China was running Katoul. Twomey's usual composure had shattered to a million splinters, especially when he had been summoned to Bonn to report to the Prime Minister personally, and no doubt through him to the Summit itself.

"Thanks, Charlie," Ross called to the pilot. He gathered his case, shook his head to clear the cobwebs, and rose to make his way back to the door. But Smithers blocked his way at the top of the steps.

"Excuse me, sir, but may I have a word first?"

"Hi, Smithers, everything all right at Spitari's?"

"Yes, sir."

Ross yawned again and promised himself an immediate visit to the steamroom for a work out with Max. "Jesus I'm tired." He looked at the other man's expression. "Nothing wrong is there Smithers?"

"Perhaps not, sir. There's a lady to see you. She's in the car now, but I thought I'd better warn you first."

"A lady?" Ross knew very few ladies in Malta. Apart from Elizabeth, of course, and clearly Smithers couldn't mean her. A suspicion formed in his mind. "If this is some personal problem you're handing me I warn you – I'm in no mood for –"

"Nothing like that, sir." Smithers sounded insulted at the very idea. "It's Suzy Katoul."

"What is?"

"She's here, sir – in the car."

"Jesus Christ – you're out of your mind!"

"No, sir. I'm quite certain it's her. In fact she admits it."

Ross sat down in the nearest seat. "Katoul *here*?"

"She arrived an hour ago – scheduled Alitalia from Rome – wearing a blonde wig and carrying a French passport in the name of Debray."

"Debray?" Ross repeated in complete astonishment.

"The lad's with her now, sir," Smithers said. "We searched her, she's not carrying –"

"Katoul *here*?" Ross scraped his brains in an effort to understand.

By way of further explanation Smithers added: "She asked for a cab to take her to the Health Farm."

Nobody asked for a cab to Spitari's Health Farm. Guests who were expected were collected from the airport by Smithers personally, so anyone asking for a cab clearly was not expected, and arrangements had been worked out long since to deal with them. Every cab driver on the island had his standing orders. Such guests were driven directly to the R.A.F. Guard Room and locked in until Smithers arrived.

"Anything else, Smithers? Did you find out anything?" Some of the colour had returned to Ross's face.

"No, sir. I arrived twenty-two minutes after the call from the Guard Room and by then she'd got rid of the wig, so I recognised her straightaway. I said, 'You're Suzy Katoul aren't you?' and she said 'Yes, I'm here to see Major Ross on a matter of great urgency'."

"The hell she did." Ross buried his head in his hands. "And that's *all*?"

Smithers wondered if he had neglected some part of his duty because he said: "Well, I thought that as you were due in within the hour it was best to keep her here, sir – pending your arrival."

Ross shook his head. "I mean did she say anything else?"

"No, sir," Smithers looked puzzled. "She's pretty jumpy though – on edge if you know what I mean."

"Her and me both," Ross mumbled. Twomey *had* to be right. It could only mean blackmail. But for her to deliver the blackmail note herself demonstrated some nerve. Christ, she had to be confident – confident that she'd get away with it – whatever *it* was. And for a moment or two Ross was too frightened to go and find out.

He stood up slowly, more in control of himself again. "Okay Smithers, you'd better show me our little wildcat."

She sat in the back of the car waiting for them. Wait was all she could do, since her right hand was handcuffed to the doorhandle and the door itself was locked. A lighted cigarette was held in her left hand and she blew smoke at him as he peered through the half open window.

"Major Ross, I presume?" she attempted a smile which didn't quite come off.

Ross clambered in next to her while Smithers joined his son in the front.

"Do you always chain your guests up as soon as they arrive?" she asked.

Ross turned to stare at the handcuffs as the car edged forward to begin its journey back to Delimara Point. Privately he regretted it. If she had taken this risk to visit him, she was hardly likely to run away now. But he managed a shaky smile and said, "Take it as a compliment, Miss Katoul – we'd just hate to lose you."

11.00 Sunday

Mick Malone was a good sailor and the long crossing to Boulogne had left him rested and anxious to get on his way. He had spent much of the previous evening playing cards with another long distance driver and two off duty crew men, and the five pounds it had cost him had been well spent in terms of occupying his mind. Not that he had made a late night of it, nor had he succumbed to the temptation to make it a boozy one, despite the attraction of ship-board prices. For the truth of it was that Mick was pacing himself. Today would be a long and painful one, with at least eight hours spent behind the wheel if he was to make Aachen by nightfall. And he was determined to do that. Through France and Belgium today and then Cologne tomorrow, and after that wherever his instruc-tions took him until he reached Switzerland and a chance of a decent life again.

The ship would dock shortly and Mick was already pacing the deck, a thick sweater worn beneath a duffelcoat to keep the chill morning breeze at bay. But it was dry and he was grateful for that. Driving was more tiring in the wet, it demanded more concentra-tion, so that his muscles cramped and his back hurt twice as much. He sniffed the air and scanned the dockside, seeing a clear, cold day and welcoming it.

He had visited Boulogne once before and his eyes began to pick out remembered landmarks amidst the rising new buildings. Not that he had much time for sight-seeing. As soon as the ship had berthed he hurried below to the transport deck, anxious that his should be the first vehicle to return to dry land. He unlocked the cab and pulled himself up, unzipping his canvas bag and arranging his travel documents on the seat next to him, then lighting a cigarette as he settled back to wait. With any luck, half an hour should see him on his way, north along the coast on the N40 prior to the long right-hand sweep which would take him past Brussels.

But as soon as he rolled down the ramp into the Customs shed, he knew it would take more than half an hour. The place was crawling with police! And there were at least twice as many Customs officials as on his last visit. Special barriers had been erected, hastily by the look of it, because men were still rolling them into position. A gendarme waved him to a halt and six men detached themselves from what looked like a battalion of officials at the top of the steps. Mick flinched as they hurried over to meet him. He sensed danger but saw no way to avoid it. His path forward was blocked by a mobile wire-mesh screen ten feet high and twice as wide. The way back led only to the ship, and was in any case blocked by the crowd of vehicles which had followed him down the ramp. Had he driven into a trap? Mary Mother of Christ – was it all over already? To be so near and . . . one of the men had opened the near side door and was talking to him in French.

"I'm sorry," Mick shook his head. "Irish – I only speak English."
"Your papers, Monsieur."

Mick handed over his passport and the little leather wallet of travelling documents which had been provided by the office at the factory.

"*Où sont les bagages?*" another voice asked from the other side, changing to English after Mick's startled protest. "Is this all of your luggage, Monsieur?" Mick nodded and the man lifted the canvas bag down from the cab. "You will please follow me to the office."

"Is – is anything wrong?" Mick stammered, cursing his nervousness and trying desperately to regain his composure. The Customs man stared at him for a long moment before answering. "Let us hope not," he said, then half turned, waiting for Mick to climb down from the cab.

Mick drew a deep breath and reached for the ignition keys. "Leave the keys where they are," the man said impatiently.

Miserably, Mick followed him to the office ten yards away. At the steps he glanced over his shoulder. Two men were searching the cab and another man was underneath the vehicle with a flashlight, while a fourth was sweeping the sides of the trailer with what looked like a lightweight vacuum cleaner.

"Sit down, please," the man indicated a chair in a partitioned cubbyhole. His mate began to unpack Mick's belongings, putting each item onto a small table. "Your name is Michael Malone?" The man glanced up from the passport long enough to register Mick's answering nod. "And you are a driver by occupation?"

Mick said yes, and then yes and no to another dozen questions which merely confirmed the details contained in the travel documents. The other man repacked the canvas holdall and placed it on the table in front of him. "You travel light, Monsieur. How long do you expect your trip to last?"

It almost caught him off guard. "I'll – I'll be away again by the end of the week."

"Back to Ireland?"

"And where else?" Mick demanded.

The man was about to reply when he was interrupted by two men from the yard, who interspersed a quick gabble of French with suspicious glances at Mick. Then all three men hurried back down the steps. More alarmed than ever, Mick stood up to watch from the open doorway. The compound was crowded with vehicles now, arranged in ranks of four, with Mick's truck, two cars and another lorry making up the front rank. The vacuum cleaner brigade were out in force and Mick's nervousness subsided fractionally when he realised that his wasn't the only vehicle being subjected to intensive examination. He took another look at the vacuum cleaners – more like metal detectors he thought, or even mine sweeps. Men clustered around his truck, one sweeping the long-handled instrument back and forth along the sides of the trailer while others crowded around a portable instrument panel. There was a good deal of excited chatter and then the three-man delegation hurried back up the steps.

"What is the nature of your cargo, Monsieur?"

"It's on the manifest," Mick said, outwardly calm but secretly alarmed. "Twelve volt batteries."

"Pardon?"

"Tractor batteries," Mick said. He reached over for his wallet of travel documents and the others crowded to peer over his shoulder. "There – see for yourselves – twelve volt batteries."

The rapid fire French dialogue which followed baffled him, and it was two or three minutes before he understood the question being put to him.

"Of course they're lead batteries," he said, thoroughly bewildered but less worried as he sensed a slackening of tension amongst the officials. "What other sort are there for Christ's sake?"

"Lead!" For a moment his questioners looked stunned, then they burst out laughing. Mick tried to follow the excited chatter, but it was too much for him. One of the men was holding one of the portable instrument panels and he tapped it excitedly, as if trying to make it work. The cubbyhole erupted into another peal of laughter, but a moment later Mick's passport was stamped and his travel documents were replaced inside the leather folder, and he was being escorted back to his cab. It was all over – he was on his way – still free – and only half an hour down on his travel schedule to Germany.

Noon – Local Maltese Time – Sunday

I sat on the edge of my bed. All in all I felt pretty good. My hands had stopped shaking and I wasn't sweating any more, and the room no longer changed shape every five minutes. "Don't try to stand up," Max said from his end of the bed.

But I wanted cigarettes from the dressingtable and might have reached them if my legs had held out.

"Knucklehead," he picked me up as if I was a rag doll with half its stuffing missing. "Listen to Uncle Max, will you."

It must have been the day they played hospital at the Health

Farm, because when I told him about the cigarettes he vetoed the idea.

"Food first," he wheeled the trolley across to the bed. "Soup, you'll enjoy it."

"What's in it – pentothal?"

"Aw Harry, don't get sore now."

"Who's sore? My skin's like a pin cushion from those damn needles, but I'm not sore."

"That's good Harry."

So was the soup. Afterwards I was allowed half a cigarette, which made my head spin, then he helped me to dress. "You've got a visitor waiting to see you."

"That's nice – Nikki Orlov's brought some grapes."

"It ain't Orlov," Max was playing Rastus again, he even rolled his eyes. "It's Suzy Katoul."

At least I was sitting on the bed. The news made my head spin faster than the cigarette, but the first thing I did was to reach for the packet again. Max poured orange juice into a tumbler and passed it to me – whisky might have been better, but he was still playing doctor, because he wouldn't hear of it. As it was, he sat there telling me to take my time while he explained it all. When he said that Ross had brought her in a few hours ago I thought he meant Ross had captured her – like an old-time sheriff. But Suzy had arrived by herself – flown into Malta and demanded to see Ross. Arrived for talks, like a summit meeting. When I said that to Max he looked startled, as if it was a strange way of putting it, but that's the way it looked to me. Especially when he said she had delivered some sort of ultimatum.

"The wires have been humming, man. Really humming. I can tell you."

"About what?"

"Reckon the Old Man wants to tell you that himself. He just sent me up to ask that you join the party."

"Real old style family retainer, aren't you Max?"

He gave me his Rastus grin again and rolled his eyes a couple of times, but underneath all the play-acting Max was nervous. He knew exactly what was going on, but was leaving the job of breaking the bad news to somebody else. And I was quite sure that it *was* bad news. I took my time finishing the orange juice, made a test flight round the bedroom, and then Max took me downstairs to meet the family.

They watched me as I came in like a jury watching a prisoner up from the cells at the Old Bailey. Nobody said a word. Max led me to the foot of the conference table and pushed a chair under me before I collapsed. I sat there for a moment taking my bearings. Suzy sat on the right, alone on that side of the table, smoking furiously and re-arranging papers in front of her in a fussy way which betrayed her nervousness. She could hardly hold her hands still, and she was twisting the cigarette round and round in her fingers like a baton-twirler rehearsing moves. Dark shadows below her eyes aged her by ten years and the ugly habit she had of chewing her bottom lip had coarsened the line of her mouth on one side. The doctor and Elizabeth stared at her from across the table, while Ross presided like a chairman of a company about to go into liquidation. It had that kind of atmosphere – not just tense but laden with gloom and shot through with fear.

"Hello Suzy." Seeing her mixed me up. I was relieved in one way – relieved to see her still in one piece and to be at hand to help her if she would let me. But the relief was tinged with heartache. Her looks were beginning to go and her nerves jangled like a doorbell. She looked ill and strained – and all I could think of was that she was my child and I had let her down.

Her eyes lashed me like a whip. "They said you were here. Negib always knew you were against us – said you'd betray us someday. It took you long enough, didn't it? To show whose side you're on."

"Suzy, I'm here to help –"

"Help them! They're the ones who need it."

I reached for her hand, but she pulled away. "Don't touch me. Stay away, you hear? I don't want your mealy-mouthed help!" She whirled on Ross, "Damn you to hell – does he *have* to be here?"

Ross seemed older and smaller than a few days ago. "I want Harry to know the threats you've been making –"

"Tell him to read the papers – they'll have headlines a foot high." Her laughter had the same hysterical ring to it as Negib's used to have and it could have been his sneer she turned on me. "The Deir Yassin Memorial wages war on Western hypocrisy. How's that Newsman? Not bad, eh? Not bad for the daughter of an Arab whore and a Jewish terrorist –"

"You're *my* daughter."

"Goddaughter! Goddaughter – that's what you used to call me. You, a man who doesn't believe in –"

"That's enough," Ross snapped angrily.

She trembled violently in a fit of agitation, watching Ross and at the same time clasping and unclasping her hands as if trying to keep control of them. Then she reached for another cigarette, but she was shaking so much that she could hardly light it. She managed eventually, but only by jamming both elbows on the table and holding her wrist with her free hand to keep the lighter still. Ross started to say something, but Suzy was twitching so badly that he lapsed into silence and just stared at her. I felt too sick to do anything to divert attention, so I just stared as well. We all did, as if hypnotized. I think the trembling spasm only lasted for a couple of minutes, but it seemed longer. Gradually she regained control of herself and after taking a few deep breaths she glared around the table: "Well? Are we going to sit here all day?"

Nobody answered immediately. The doctor scribbled a note, pushed it along the table to Ross and then asked her: "Can I get you anything?"

Her head jerked at me. "Yes – get him out of here!"

Ross looked up from the note. "Harry stays – at least for the time being." He screwed the paper into a ball and said to me: "Miss Katoul has come to us with an ultimatum."

I waited, wondering what the doctor had written and thinking Ross was being remarkably polite for somebody who usually referred to Suzy as a "screwed-up bitch".

He said: "She demands that Israel hand over certain territories to a newly-formed Palestinian –"

"Independent Arab Marxist State!" Suzy interrupted.

Ross was too tired to argue. "Broadly speaking she's claiming the whole of the West Bank and the Gaza Strip with a fifty-mile-wide interconnecting corridor –"

"It's our land!" she screamed at him. "It's no more than rightfully ours –"

"Guaranteed by the Western Powers," Ross struggled to finish. "Israel is to be compelled to co-operate by joint action from the U.S., Germany, Britain, France, Canada and Japan." The shadow of a smile which appeared on his lips never reached his eyes. "As you know there's a summit conference in Bonn this week and they've –"

"Got twenty-four hours to sort it out," Suzy gloated triumphantly.

"Otherwise," Ross finished quietly, "the Deir Yassin Memorial. will explode its nuclear device."

For an instant I felt an insane urge to laugh. All blackmail is preposterous to begin with. The crew of the first hi-jacked aeroplane probably wanted to laugh – even when they had guns poked in their faces. If something has never been done before the natural instinct is to ridicule the whole idea.

I said, "You'll never get away with it."

She jeered at me exactly as Negib would have done. "You'd better pray we do Newsman. Because if not that bomb goes off."

"Twenty-four hours," I said in a voice no louder than a whisper.

"They've had *thirty years!*" she screamed.

"But twenty-four hours is no time at all. I mean people will want –"

"It's enough time for the first step," she snapped. "A signed statement from the summit telling Israel that unless she agrees the West will break off all economic support. A televised press conference tomorrow night – it's enough time for that."

"But even supposing the summit agrees," Ross said. "That's no guarantee that Israel will –"

"Israel can't exist without American dollars!"

"They said that about Rhodesia," I said.

"Oh Christ, will you shut up!" she spat at me. "There's no bloody comparison and you know it."

I suppose I did in a way and I was trying to think of a suitable answer when Ross slid two sheets of A4 copy paper down the table. One glance was enough to recognise a press release. Suzy must have brought half a dozen copies with her, and I was reading the opening words when she said: "Copies of that will be circulated to the entire press corps in Bonn at nine o'clock in the morning. The summit will be given exactly twelve hours to endorse it."

I concentrated on the typescript. It was all there – twenty clauses of it – but only the main ones registered. Israel was given a month to formally transfer the designated territories. The Western powers were to guarantee the security of all frontiers. And Russia was to be warned off. Other clauses defined the compensation which Israel would pay to the new state, including the costs of resettling the Palestinians, and there was a lot of fine print stuff which would have needed an international lawyer to understand. An *international lawyer* like Suzy Katoul.

"This nuclear device," Ross began. "Which you claim to –"

"Don't waste time!" she stormed. "You saw what we did off Scotland. That was one kiliton, Major – the next one's ten megaton!"

"Even the I.R.A. give advance warning of an explosion."

"The I.R.A. are poets," she said enigmatically. "Anyway what could you do? Clear an entire city? Clear London of twelve million people?"

"Is it London?"

Her lips set in a line as thin as a razor blade. "No, and that's all I'm saying."

My head was spinning but I risked another cigarette. I wondered what Ross would do? Previously when I had speculated on a confrontation between them, I had imagined my sympathies being with Suzy. After all, despite everything, she was still family, she would need my help, she would be vulnerable to the terrible pressures Ross would apply. But now it was happening and she neither needed nor wanted me. And if anyone was being threatened it was Ross. The whole world had been stood on its ear.

Ross might have read my mind because he said to her, "You realise that you've placed yourself in our hands as far as interrogation is concerned?"

"People know where I am," she said defiantly.

His eyebrows rose. "But do they care? You've been thrown to the wolves, Miss Katoul. You're the one who has risked her safety, you're –"

"They said you'd try that," she cut him short. "Intimidation and torture. Like the rest of the pigs. Well go ahead, but unless I'm produced at the news conference tomorrow night –"

"Nobody said anything about torture," he said coldly.

"Neither did the Popo in Germany, but they murdered Andreas."

"Baader committed suicide."

"In Stammhein? The top security jail in Germany? Shot in the head? Shot in the *back* of the head." She erupted with sudden fury and her voice crackled with hysteria. "And Gudrun and Ulrike were hanged in Stammhein – with electrical cord. Come off it Major, just who the hell d'you think you're kidding? You're like the rest of the pigs – just like – just like –"

But she couldn't go on. Her breath came in gasps and the sudden trembling spasm which engulfed her was even more violent than the earlier one. She grabbed her handbag from the chair next to her and rummaged furiously, using both hands so that the cigarette parked in her mouth whisped smoke into her eyes and made the lashes wet with tears. Whatever she was looking for eluded her, and after spilling papers all over the place she upended the bag onto the table in front of her in final desperation. Her hands scrambled through the mess, fumbling and discarding and hunting and trembling – and all the while she made these half whimpering noises interspersed with bouts of swearing. It was awful watching her – I felt dirty, wanting to turn my eyes away yet trapped by some

212

compulsion which held me rigid in my seat. At one point the cigarette fell from her lips to roll across the table and it took three grabbed attempts of her trembling fingers to retrieve it. Nobody said anything – nobody offered to help – we just sat there entranced. Finally she found a small bottle and fumbled desperately to open it. Eventually she undid the cap and managed to spill two pills into her hands before tossing them hurriedly into her mouth.

I think Ross wanted to stop her from taking the pills but the doctor waved a hand, as if to say let her go ahead, and Ross sat down again. God knows what the pills were, but they seemed to take effect quite quickly. Within a couple of minutes her breathing became more measured and the twitching gradually subsided. She scooped everything back into her handbag, throwing it in, the pill bottle along with the rest in no particular order. Then she cast sly, furtive glances around the table, as if she had hoped that all of us had missed the entire episode.

Ross cleared his throat, but just then Smithers came in clutching a telex sheet in one hand like a rolled up newspaper. It was so long that it took Ross two or three minutes to read it. Finally he sent Smithers away to fetch Max. Then he looked at Suzy. "You're big business, lady. *Too* big for a country boy from Kansas. We're taking her into the big city for the top brass to look at."

She had quite recovered from the shaking fit by now. She looked at him without trembling and with a poisonous look on her face – a vicious expression which was some mixture of spiteful satisfaction and triumph. I think I began to hate her then. It shocked me – sickened me to realise that any man could live to hate his own daughter, but that's how I felt.

"Where are we going, Pig?" she asked.

"Bonn. We're to be there by the morning."

Startled exclamations arose around the table and all heads turned to Ross. All except mine. I was still watching Suzy and struggling with my emotions as I watched the expression on her face.

Max stood in the doorway, looking to Ross for instructions.

"Take Miss Katoul to the other room, will you Max – make her comfortable and give her whatever she needs. We'll be leaving in a few hours."

Max nodded and advanced across the room. He removed Suzy's chair and held her elbow, while she clutched her bag and walked slightly ahead of him, the triumphant sneer still on her face and her eyes forward to avoid ours.

213

Mick was beyond Calais by noon and well on his way to Dunkirk and Malo-les-Baines by half past. The N40 highway carried a fair share of heavy vehicles even on a Sunday, but the traffic was moving briskly and the skies above had lightened, so his spirits had lifted after the initial fright at Boulogne. Now he laughed whenever he thought of it. Batteries – what in God's name was so funny about lead batteries that half the Customs officials in France split their sides just at the mention of them? He puzzled on it for a while before dismissing it. Whatever it was, it was his good luck he decided. *Bon chance* for the rest of the trip.

He whistled as he drove, a thin reedy sound that was mostly drowned by the drone of the engine. And as he whistled he thought of Molly. Twenty years they had been married. Twenty years with more bleak times than bright ones, but it was a good marriage for all that. Even the blackest day had been faced without mutual reproach. They'd not grown old and crotchety the way some did, forever at each other's throats and with never a good word to say for each other. He grinned wryly. For the past few days he had resigned himself to them not growing old together at all. Until yesterday. Now there was even a chance of that!

He stopped whistling to grin about the five thousand pounds she would receive in the morning. He wondered what she'd make of it. He tried to imagine her – in the kitchen after the postman had called – opening a letter from a *bank*. That would be enough to send her into a spin, all typewritten and official. And then there would be the money itself. More money than she had seen in a lifetime. What would she do? With him there it would be predictable – she'd rush upstairs to fetch her coat and hurry round to the yard to show it to him as fast as her legs would carry her. But with him being away? He thought about it. Go to her sister's probably. And the two of them would read the letter a dozen times over and count the noughts on the cheque until they made a million pounds of it. She wouldn't cry – not Molly – not at first anyway, because she wouldn't believe it. She would know it was a mistake. The smile froze on his face. What would she do then? Not take the money – that's for sure – not if she thought there was anything wrong with it. She'd be too afraid to spend a penny in case somebody asked for it back. So what would she do?

He no longer felt like whistling, and a frown replaced his grin as he worried about it. Molly's sister would tell half the neighbourhood, that's for sure, and half the neighbourhood would tell the

214

other half, so that within a day or two the police would know. Would that matter? Big Reilly had said the plan was foolproof. But tomorrow he would reach Cologne and Reilly would notify the bank to send another cheque. And after Cologne God knows where, but it couldn't be far to the cheque for ten thousand. And then what would Molly do?

He would write to her tonight. Tonight, from Aachen. Tell her that he was all right and that she was to keep quiet about the money. But by the time she got his letter the first five thousand would have arrived! And maybe the second too. Mary Mother of Christ, what *would* she do? Like as not she'd send it right back to them, and what would happen then?

But the tall dark man at Pallas Glean had said not to contact anyone. No matter what. That was part of the bargain, to do things his way. But then, he didn't know Molly. Clever as a boxload of monkeys the man might be, but even the plans of brilliant men were upset by the whims of a woman. Christ, if only they hadn't sprung it on him the way they had – given him time to think about it – maybe explain some of Molly's little ways to them.

He puffed on a cigarette and concentrated. If she sent the money back, couldn't that just start the bank looking for Big Reilly and the tall dark man himself now? And they wouldn't like that, that's for sure. He would have to contact her. But how? They had no phone at home, so he couldn't call her. A telegram perhaps? Could he send a telegram from France to Ireland? Maybe he could, but not on a Sunday, and she would get the cheque in the morning.

A road sign showed Veurne ten kilometres ahead. Veurne in Belgium. He would cross the border soon. He checked his watch, pleased to be making such good time, but his pleasure dampened by worry about Molly. He *had* to speak to her before she got the morning mail – it was the only way. Then he could explain – put her mind at rest – let her know they would soon be together again, even if not in Ireland – provided she kept quiet about the money.

And still wrestling with that problem. Mick changed down a gear and joined the queue of traffic stretching a mile back from the Customs checkpoint on the Belgian border.

13.30 Sunday

No one said very much after Max had taken Suzy away. Smithers delivered another long telex and Ross grunted and swore his way through it. Then he signed one corner and old dog face retired,

215

looking as grim as death itself. Elizabeth was going to some trouble to avoid my eye and had been like that since I arrived. I kept having dreams about Elizabeth. Something which had happened while I was drugged. They were very nice dreams and in other circumstances I might have settled down to enjoy them, but at that moment my mind was too full of Suzy Katoul and a ten megaton bomb.

"Well," Ross said finally, "what do you make of it?"

"Take those pills away and she'll crack wide open," the doctor said.

"That's by way of being a clever twist for you, isn't it?" I said bitterly.

"Okay, Harry," Ross grunted. "We haven't time for recriminations, but if it's any help to you we're sorry as hell about what happened to you."

"Shove it."

"Been tough, huh? You don't like us *or* our set-up. So what's the alternative? So long as men exploit mixed-up kids like Suzy Katoul, there'll be people like us trying to stop them. Is that so bad?"

He was good. I especially liked the way "screwed-up bitch" had become "mixed-up kid".

"You'd have made a fortune selling soap."

"Harry, be reasonable for Chrissakes. We're on the same side in this."

"Don't bank on it."

"So, what should we do?" he challenged angrily. "Sit on our butts and let Katoul blow the world to pieces? Turn a blind eye and let half a million people fry?"

"No – no of course not, but –"

"But the way we operate offends your sensibilities, is that it?" he said scornfully. "Katoul was right about you – it's time you made up your mind whose side you're on."

I remained silent, knowing the truth of it. I was being pushed towards the most painful decision of my life. Suzy was part of it, of course, but so was Ross himself. I've spent thirty years as a liberal journalist, campaigning against the excessive powers of political police. As far as I am concerned the only difference between the K.G.B., C.I.A., S.I.S., Special Branch and all the rest of them is one of degree – they're all repressive. But so is bombing the hell out of people with a ten megaton bomb.

Ross had become adept at reading my mind because he said: "Seems to me that guys like you spend so much time uncovering Watergates, you forget you wouldn't be allowed to do that in half the countries in the world."

I smiled at the half truth. "What's this – a recruiting campaign?"

He scowled. "We're going to hit so much flak in Bonn you'll think it's a re-run of the last war. You know that, don't you?"

I stirred uneasily. Whenever Ross said "we" something bad happened. I remembered how it was my fault that Israel was going to blast nuclear bombs all over the Middle East. I closed my eyes.

"We're all tired, Harry," he said with heavy sarcasm. "But we're all dead if we don't crack this fast."

"Twenty-four hours ago," I said without opening my eyes, "I was suspect number one, remember – the man in the pale grey suit."

Elizabeth's golden voice said: "We had to be sure Harry – that's all."

"Yeah, nothing personal."

There was a long pause, but even with my eyes closed I could sense the exchange of glances. Then Ross said, "Tubby Hayes was an agent for Red China."

I opened my eyes.

He nodded. "It's true. Paul LeClerc turned over the Hayes place in Paris. Found a transmitter, code books, propaganda material, everything."

Elizabeth said, "And Tubby Hayes linked Suzy Katoul to the man in the pale grey suit."

According to a dictionary, the state of being punch-drunk is induced by successive blows to the head. That may be one way, but four days with Ross and Elizabeth can do the same job. I said, "Whatever happened to the Palestinian Marxist Front?"

"It's still there," Ross said grimly. "But Red China's behind it. That's where all the muscle's coming from. If the Summit gives in to Katoul, Red China's got itself into the Mediterranean."

I closed my eyes again. On the face of it Red China had just commenced a whirlwind romance with the West. What Nixon had started, others were finishing. You couldn't open a paper without seeing an American politician kissing a Chinese baby. I said as much to Ross.

"Oh? How many times do I tell you? Don't believe everything you read in the papers."

"Washington will be upset. They've just sold them a Coca-Cola plant."

"If that bomb explodes anywhere near this Summit, Washington loses a hell of a lot more than a bottling plant. America loses her President."

I opened one eye. "You think the bomb's in Germany?"

"Think about it. If you were going to blackmail a summit, where would you put the bomb?"

"Makes it more personal," I agreed, watching his face. If Ross could read me, then I could read him. He was leading up to something. All this *reasonableness* and "we're all on the same side" bit wasn't because he wanted to borrow a fiver. Then he came straight out with it.

"Harry, I need a favour. If my people will agree to it, will you help handle the press crowd in Bonn? Would you do that for me, Harry?"

I opened both eyes very wide. A remark like that deserves all the attention you can give to it. Something like eight hundred journalists would be camped in Bonn for the summit. And for every newsman, there would be at least one little man in a grey raincoat from the German Constitutional Protection Office, and for every grey raincoat there would be a visiting security man. Add in a few genuine spies and the local Germans would be outnumbered three to one. And in a little over twelve hours the Deir Yassin Memorial would issue a statement selling the biggest story since Nuremburg. Pandemonium would not begin to describe what was going to happen in Bonn – even before the bomb went off! Pressmen would tear the city apart checking that story. And all of that was quite apart from any personal feelings I might have on the subject. Yes, when he tried, Ross really was something special.

I smiled at him. "Sure I'll handle the press for you, old buddy. I'll organise community singing on the Friedenplatz, and when I tell them our little secret we'll all hold hands and chant the countdown together."

"Are you saying the summit will turn Katoul down?"

"For God's sake!" I said, exasperated. "There won't even be a summit. By the time we reach Bonn the politicians will have cancelled it. They'll be safely tucked up in their deep shelters somewhere with a month's supply of booze and caviar."

"You think so? Well you're damned well wrong. Everyone's there now. Sweating bricks maybe, but no-one's bolted yet."

"So they're going to give in?"

He sighed and scratched his head. "I don't know. That's the God's honest truth. This stuff's out of my league. But my guess is they'll stay put until the nine o'clock press conference. That gives us more than a day to find the bomb and –"

"The cavalry'll ride out to rescue us."

He gave me his sour look. "Okay, I'll give you another reason. If the politicians get the hell out of there, what's to stop this Deir Yassin mob from saying why?"

"Ah." There was a grain of sense in *that* – the grains politicians use to build castles in the air with.

"Makes sense, doesn't it?" Ross nodded at my expression. "So all we want is you to help calm the press."

"Ask the doctor – he'll give them a tranquilliser."

He finally lost his temper. "Listen dummy! If LeClerc's evidence stands up, someone from Washington will turn Peking into chop suey by lunchtime. You know how close that takes us to World War Three? Can you imagine the kinds of instructions going out from Bonn right now?"

I stared into his white face and tried not to imagine anything – just knowing what I knew frightened me to death.

I tried to explain. "Once that bulletin hits the streets, there's just no way you'll stop those press boys –"

"Dammit, you can try! They trust you, Harry. They know you're not one of us. If you can just get to a few of the big names and give us time. Right now there's a manhunt going on all over Europe that –"

"They don't even know what they're looking for."

He snarled with temper. "Then you damn well find out! From that little girl in the back room. Because if you don't, I swear I'll break her in half before we hit Bonn. You know what we did in Nam to people who held out on us? We hung them head first from a gunship at two hundred feet. A lot of people died that way and if you think I won't do that to her, you don't know me at all."

I winced under the blaze of his eyes. "That's murder."

"Don't make me cry. You want to know what else LeClerc found in Paris? Your little blonde doll – Monique Debray – tortured to death. So don't talk to me about murder, or I'll bust your mouth open with this tin hand of mine. Will you begin to realise what we're up against for Chrissakes? Half a million people could be murdered tomorrow and that's just for starters. And don't think you'll be nursing your lilywhite conscience when that happens, because I'll make damned sure you're right in there with the rest of us."

It was then that Suzy screamed. The thin piercing sound rose and clung to the air like a bird in flight. Then it peaked again and I was stumbling towards the door just as fast as my Indiarubber legs would carry me.

She lay across the sofa in the other room. Her dress was torn at one shoulder and her skirt was up over her knees. The wheal marks of a hand blazed on her cheek and Smithers crouched over her like a threatening animal.

"You bastard!" I reached for his shoulder, but Max grabbed me as the doctor and Ross bundled into the room after me.

Smithers swung round to face us. "She was going to give herself a shot. We fought for the syringe and –"

"Okay," Ross said. He stepped forward and picked a broken syringe from the floor. Then he turned to me. "I'll give you three hours, Harry. Then we'll do things my way."

Then they all left, Max last of all, closing and locking the door after him, and I turned to face my daughter.

19.15 Sunday

News of the destruction of the *Aileen Maloney* cast a shadow darker than a black cloud over Conlaragh. The village, still recovering from the loss of Liam Reilly and Pat Brady, went into a kind of numbed mourning. Like a family with its breadwinner lost, people closed ranks and huddled together for mutual security. A special midday mass was heard in the old grey church and the pub opposite remained closed until evening as a sign of respect. The blinds were drawn in every cottage and barely a car was seen on the streets – and those that were came from outside the area. The village, it seemed, was stunned senseless by the news.

All sorts of theories were advanced to account for the explosion. The *Aileen Maloney* had hit an old mine? Her engines had overheated and blown up? She had collided with an unknown and unnamed ship which had neither stopped, nor reported the accident? But the marine salvage experts who spent the day gathering wreckage and recovering two of the bodies discounted them all. Especially when one of the bodies found was that of Pat Brady – and even more so when police pathologists estimated that Brady had been murdered at least four days before.

Word of the "accident" was sent to the Inishmore Fishing Company's offices in Dublin and the single row of cottages owned by the company was roped off – until such time as the police finished their enquiries. But police enquiries were leading nowhere. Conlaragh had always been a close-knit community and this latest catastrophe bound it together like melted wax. Traditionally Conlaragh discouraged outsiders – and the Gardai had been outsiders for as long as folk could remember.

220

All of which was explained to Dorfman when he arrived in Dublin.

"But why keep quiet about it?"

The C.I.D. man smiled. "And there's you with an Irish grandfather. You've lived too long from these shores, Mister, or you'd not so much as ask."

But when Dorfman still frowned, the man was compelled to add some explanation. "Reilly was I.R.A. – or used to be – though he's kept clear of trouble for a few years now. But the saying goes, once a soldier always a soldier. There's no retiring from the I.R.A. – at least not with both kneecaps intact. And well the village knows it. If that boat *was* on I.R.A. business, the village will be getting a visitor – and not just from us."

"So the village is frightened?"

The man rubbed his brow as if to stimulate thought, or at least the right words. "Not frightened exactly – unless they're the ones who blew the *Aileen Maloney* sky high – and that idea's not even worth bothering with." He shook his head. "Right now they're shaken. Shocked and sickened by the whole thing. The Reilly boys were well liked in Conlaragh. They'll be sorely missed – the other men too." He declined Dorfman's offer of a cigarette. "It's numbed the village is now – but tomorrow it'll want its revenge."

"Revenge? For God's sake, what chance has a village got –"

"We want the answers as badly as you. I'm simply explaining the problem."

And Dorfman listened to explanations for another half hour before he formulated his idea. The Irish C.I.D. were far from keen on it. Three of them discussed it in his hearing and then two retired to consider their verdict. But they agreed in the end – with reservations – and they *did* lend him a car.

It was just after six when he booked into the pub at Conlaragh. After a hurried wash he whistled cheerfully on his way down to the bar, where he ordered a pint of beer. And ten minutes later he was arrested.

"Is that your car outside?" the uniformed Gardai constable asked.

Dorfman continued to examine the sporting prints above the hearth, as if he hadn't heard. But everyone else had. There were eight of them, including the landlord behind the bar, all men and all locals. Too small to have its own police station, Conlaragh was administered from Mellick seven miles away, and on ordinary days a Gardai car showed itself briefly in the High Street and was gone a minute later in a puff of exhaust. But this was far from an ordinary day and police had buzzed like flies on the waterfront since early morning.

"Excuse me," the constable raised his voice a fraction. "Is that your car?"

Dorfman turned, startled, almost spilling his beer. "What? You mean me?"

"The car outside – does it belong to you?" The policeman stood a yard away, facing Dorfman squarely, tensed up as if expecting trouble.

The door from the street opened and another policeman entered, looking about him carefully, letting his gaze dwell on every man there, as if to commit their faces to memory.

Dorfman leaned against the bar and took his time answering. "In a manner of speaking," he said.

"And what the devil's that supposed to mean?"

"It belongs to a friend of mine," Dorfman growled, a threatening note creeping into his voice.

Afterwards the locals said you could tell he was a dangerous man just by looking at him. But his voice really clinched it. Growled like a dog, they said, a tethered one.

Another policeman entered, this time from the yard at the rear. He stood with his back to the door. Both exits were blocked – and Dorfman knew it.

"Is your name Sean Sullivan?" asked the constable.

"And what the hell's it to do with you?" Dorfman snapped, and turned to the landlord. "I'll have another pint –"

"You'll not have time to drink it," the constable warned. "You're coming back to Mellick with us."

Things happened quickly then. Dorfman set his back to the bar and caught the constable with a right hook hard enough to loosen every tooth in his head. But the others must have expected it because they threw themselves into the fight like savages. A boot lashed and Dorfman was sent sprawling into the sawdust. He was up quickly to head butt the second policeman with enough force to break his nose. Then the air shrieked with whistles as more uniformed men crashed through the doors like a tidal wave.

The betting afterwards was that if there had been only three or four of them he would have seen them off – but *six* was too many for one man, even a man like this who fought like a trapped animal. He was floored in about the fifth minute and handcuffs were jammed round his wrists before he was even on one knee. And when they got him upright, he had a gash four inches long above one eye and blood poured from his nose faster than a spring tide. But at least three policemen looked every bit as bad.

They held him against the bar and rummaged through his pockets, looking for a gun some thought, but all they found was the key to his car. Then they marched him outside and sat him in the back of the Gardai car with men wedged on either side like bookends. The villagers watched from the door of the pub – watched a policeman back the visitor's car onto the road – watched other Gardai cars appear from the waterfront – watched the rest of the battle squad climb into the cars and the whole convoy set off for Mellick seven miles away. It was a day never forgotten in Conlaragh.

Not until the last car disappeared over the brow of the hill did the locals turn back to their unfinished drinks. They talked in low conspiratorial voices and threw the odd glance now and then across the counter to see what the landlord made of it all. But Shaughnessey had never hurried in his life and after making sure that every man there had a full glass, he finished his own drink and then slipped upstairs to the small back room in which the visitor had been staying.

The canvas holdall was still on the bed. It was big and long, like a cricket bag, and had been the only luggage the man had brought with him. Shaughnessey opened it carefully, listening for footsteps on the stairs, half afraid that the Gardai or the man might return to catch him at it. Shirts and underwear, a pair of socks and a cheap paperback – and beneath it all a Heckler and Koch 5.66 self-loading rifle. Shaughnessey whistled aloud at the sight of it, knowing just enough about guns to recognise a specialist's rifle when he saw one. Like a machine gun he thought – seeing the tripod and the magazine clip for automatic fire. A killer's gun – fitted with telescopic sights and with enough spare ammo in the bottom of the bag to start a small war. Just holding it excited him – to feel the sculptured wooden butt – to look down the blue metal barrel – to dare to touch the trigger inside its guard.

Afterwards he wiped it carefully with his handkerchief and returned it to the canvas bag, arranging the clothes over it in the same pattern as he had found them. Then he zipped the bag up tight and carried it up to the loft, where he hid it behind the water tank.

They watched him return to his place behind the bar. Half of them guessed where he had been, but nobody dared ask. They watched while he packed his pipe with that dark shag of his, watched the match flicker and the blue smoke curl up to the oak beams. Watched and waited. And then, when the pipe was drawing to his satisfaction, he said in words loud enough for all to hear. "Someone had better fetch Callan – tell him we've had a visitor."

And for the first time that day they felt better. A man had been sent to settle the score, and even if the Mellick Gardai had taken him, others would come in his place. And Big Reilly and the others would be justly revenged.

19.30 Sunday

I know very little about drugs. Booze and tobacco are my vices and they're bad enough. So whatever kind of hell Suzy was going through was outside my experience. The doctor and Max had taken everything, even the pills in the little glass jar, so all that sustained her were the endless cigarettes. At one stage I organised some coffee, but she wouldn't drink it. She even knocked mine halfway across the room before I could stop her.

The first hour stretched as long as a day. By the end of it I had grown immune to the insults and her vicious expressions. When you've been called four-letter words in half a dozen languages there's nothing left which jars, and repetition merely blunts the message. Mind, it wasn't all reserved for me. I got my share, but "western decadence" and "consumerism" and "Israeli imperialism" all caught some of the flak.

Whether Ross planned us to tear into each other in quite the way we did is something I never found out. But I was so afraid of him giving her the strong arm treatment that I fairly flailed her with questions. For some reason I was convinced that if I gave them the answers they wanted, I would be allowed to get her to a hospital somewhere for proper treatment. I suppose even then I clung to the hope of saving her, but it wasn't a time to analyse my confused emotions. I was being torn apart, and she was equally desperate. The cigarettes were never enough to stop the shaking fits and sometimes the spasms lasted as long as five minutes at a time. There was no talking to her then, she barely retained the power of speech let alone the power of reasoning.

By the second hour I was on the verge of panic. Nothing she said got us any closer to finding the bomb and I was convinced that if my questions failed, Ross would apply tortures as barbaric as any I could imagine. And of course I was still muzzy from my own experiences, so perhaps I wasn't thinking straight. Excuses – circumstances – self deception? All three probably, though even now I am ashamed of the part I played in what happened next.

We were into the third hour. Some of the stridency had lifted from her voice and I thought I detected a change in her attitude. The bitter outbursts and cackles of hysteria still flashed now and then, but more and more she seemed racked with a kind of whining helplessness. And halfway through the third hour she snapped.

"For Christ's sake! What are those shitheads waiting for? Are we going to Bonn, or aren't we?"

"I don't know –"

"Liar! You heard that pig. I'm too important for him. It's an insult to the Palestinians to hold me here. I demand my rights –"

"For God's sake, will you stop being such a little fool? You've got no rights. Not here. They'll kill you if you don't tell them. Can't you understand that?"

For the first time she looked frightened enough to make me wonder if I was getting through to her. "Suzy, you've got to tell them – you've *got* to!"

But before she could answer, another fit of the shakes engulfed her and she shook like a rat in a terrier's mouth. She sat all hunched up, with her rounded shoulders drawn down to her knees, while her hands fought each other to steady themselves. It was at least five minutes before she spoke and when she did she sounded pathetically close to tears. "They'll let me go in Bonn, won't they Harry?"

I sat down next to her, an arm around her shoulders. "There's a chance – if you'll answer their questions."

She shook her head, chewing her lip furiously as she fought to stifle her tears. "I can hold out till Bonn – at least I think I can – if it's soon, if we go now –"

"We might not go anywhere," I said as gently as I could.

She trembled like a leaf under my touch. "Oh Harry, be nice to me please. I'm sorry for the things I said –"

"They don't matter. But you've got to answer –"

"Please Harry," she cried desperately. "Make them give me a shot, please! They've even taken my pills for God's sake! What kind of people would do a thing like that? I'm sick – I need something –"

Her face was wet with tears and I pulled her close to me: "If only you'd tell –"

"I'll tell you Harry. I promise I'll tell you." Her eyes pleaded with me and I felt a sudden surge of hope until she said, "Get me a shot first though? Please Harry, *please*!"

Still holding her I said, "Suzy, you need a proper hospital."

"With you to look after me," she giggled, but there was no fun in

225

the sound. "Is that what you want, Harry?"

"That's right. They'll let me look after you–"

"In a hospital bed. Just you and me?"

"We'll make you better Suzy, I promise –"

Again the giggle. "You can't make me better. I'm the best. I've been trained for it. How do you like doing it best, Harry? Best of all – tell me –"

"For God's sake Suzy, tell them!"

She struggled free of my arm and tried to remove her dress, tearing the top even more and panting hopelessly as I fought to restrain her. "We could do it here, Harry. On the sofa. Wouldn't you like that? I'm good Harry, I'm the best, Abou said so –"

"Abou?" I grabbed her bare shoulders and shook her, trying to make her look at me. "Abou who?"

She twisted her head away until her hair obscured her face. "My Abou, that's who." But she swung round then and I caught the sly gleam in her eye. "A shot Harry. Make them give me a shot. I'll talk to you, I promise. I'll talk to you while I make love to you on this seat. This seat, Harry. This seat here." She was slapping the sofa with one hand, while her other arm looped across my shoulder to pull my face down to hers. "Please Harry – I'm good –"

"You're my daughter for God's sake. You're ill. If you'd only let me –"

"I'll let you do anything, Harry. Anything you like. But get me some pills – anything – anything to keep me going."

I kept trying to pin her arms to her sides, but I was still weak from the treatment. She fought me off until she was free of the dress and I could see the needle marks in her arms. "Come on, Harry. I'll give you a good time. I'm half Arab remember? Daughter of an Arab whore. Whatever my mother did for you –"

I hit her then. As hard as I could across the face. Hating myself and shouting at her. "Tell me about Abou!"

"Soon Harry, soon," she was struggling with her bra when I hit her again. "Abou hits me sometimes. I don't mind Harry. Really I don't – just get me a shot and –"

I hit her again. "Who's Abou? Where is he? Suzy, for God's sake!"

She was crying and shivering and trying to hook her thumbs into the waistband of her briefs, but I clamped her wrists tight to her sides. "Harry, I'm good – really good. Abou says so. Even better than Monique and –"

"Monique's dead." I gambled on a reaction. "Abou killed her. Abou tortured her to death."

226

She shuddered, either from shock or another convulsion, then her hands were struggling back to my neck again. "Come on Harry – on this seat – this one – I'm good –"

"Who's Abou?" I shouted, knocking her hands away and shaking her until her teeth rattled. "Tell me before they kill you!"

"Like they killed Monique?"

"Abou killed Monique. Abou killed her. Abou! Abou! Can't you understand that? Abou's a cold-blooded killer like Negib. A killer! A killer!"

I was slapping her face, back and forth, hitting her with every ounce of my draining strength, shouting furiously and watching the blood spurt from her nose and dribble from her mouth. She made no attempt to defend herself, just fell one way and then the other as I lashed into her. Something exploded inside my head, detonated by her sneers about Haleem. Suzy revolted me, frightened me, sickened me. Had I been strong enough, I would have killed her. For a moment I wanted to – the urge was there – just like when I killed Negib. But the blows had no real strength behind them, and at the moment my fingers locked around her throat Max charged in and pulled me away. Thank God that he did. I was quite out of control and there was no telling what would have happened in another few minutes.

From the open door Ross said, "The doctor will give you a shot in a minute *Miss* Katoul. Would you like that?"

Max held me in a vice-like grip, but slowly the red cloud lifted from my brain. "You bastard, Ross," I shouted at him. "She needs a proper doctor, not –"

"I asked if you'd like that Miss Katoul?" Ross said.

She had curled herself into a ball on the sofa and was whimpering like a beaten animal, but apart from that she gave no answer.

"Who's Abou?" Ross asked softly.

She summoned every last ounce of her fading energy to spit at him. "I'll never tell you. Never, never, never! Can't you understand that? You're pigs, filthy pigs, the whole stinking rotten lot of you."

I twisted in Max's grip to look at the expression on Ross's face, but there wasn't one, his features were like stone. "Who does Abou work for?" he asked slowly.

"Wouldn't you like to know," she jeered defiantly, clutching her torn dress to her body and shivering behind it.

"Abou betrayed you," Ross said. "You must see that. He knew we'd take your drugs away. Knew we'd torture you – knew we might even kill you. But he doesn't care any more. Shall I tell you why? Because he's finished with you –"

"Liar!" she screamed. "Liar – liar!"

Ross shouted back: "Just like he finished with Monique Debray and Tubby Hayes."

"Liar," she screamed again, but then her eyes widened and her mouth worked soundlessly, as if she had lost her voice. Her gaze shifted from Ross and now she was looking past him to somebody who had just entered the room. I twisted my head and watched the doctor cross the threshold, smiling his fanged smile and holding a hypodermic syringe.

The last shreds of human dignity fell away from her then. She disintegrated. She slobbered like an animal. Even the noises which came from her throat were bestial and primitive. Until that one final piercing plea for relief sprang from her lips: *"Please!"*

But the doctor stood his ground, while Ross put the question to her again. "Who is this man Abou working for Miss Katoul?"

You could see the conflict and confusion in her eyes. She stared at the syringe as if her life depended on it, while Ross fuelled her doubts with words like "betrayal" and "he's sold you out" and similar expressions. Then the most terrible thing in the world happened. An act of indescribable cruelty. Sadism. Cold-blooded and calculated to rip the last remnants of her willpower to shreds. The doctor simply emptied the contents of the syringe onto the floor.

Wide-eyed with terror, Suzy flung the dress to one side and stumbled across the room to save the precious drug, but Smithers appeared from nowhere and bundled her back to the sofa. The doctor turned on his heel and left the room.

"Who is this man Abou working for?" Ross asked relentlessly.

A long moan escaped her lips and a trickle of blood ran down her chin from where I had beaten her. A soul in torment would not begin to describe her condition. Degradation, despair, defeat – were all twisted in the pain on her face. Then the doctor returned with another syringe and her eyes came alive again with hope.

"For mercy's sake –" I began, but Max slapped a huge hand over my mouth.

"Who is Abou working for?" Ross persisted.

Suzy babbled something, but the words were meaningless, just noises, all jumbled up, incoherent and delirious. Ross asked her again.

No answer. Silence almost. Just her strangulated breathing. Then the moment of quiet was broken by the sound of the syringe once more splattering its contents over the marble floor.

When Suzy had stopped screaming, Ross said, "Start at the beginning, Miss Katoul, and tell us everything. And when we're satisfied, the doctor will stop being so careless."

I once saw a soldier die in Vietnam. He had been caught in a burst of mortar fire and should have been killed outright. But he lay in the mud suffering the most appalling agony, dying from those terrible wounds, screaming noiselessly because his vocal chords had been severed and pleading with his eyes for his own men to kill him. He begged – not for his life, but for his death – and as the doctor left the room Suzy begged in the same way.

"Who is Abou working for?"

She would have killed herself had she the means, but Smithers held her so tight in the chair that she could barely move. She said something, but the words were inaudible.

"Again," Ross said.

But even then we couldn't hear her and Ross made her repeat it.

"PEKING!" The scream which tore from her throat carried enough hatred to make the word itself obscene. Everything was in that word. It was her curse on Ross, her plea to the gods to strike him down, to make him suffer as she was suffering. And it was her demand that something, someone should punish her for her final betrayal. And it was something else. It was the signal to everyone in that room that Ross had broken Suzy Katoul.

23.30 Sunday

It was five past eleven when Dorfman returned to the pub. Shaughnessey was stacking empty bottles into crates and whistling in that toneless way people use when their mind is on something else. Half the lights were switched out and Shaughnessey was quite alone. He heaved a crate from the counter and as he straightened up he saw Dorfman – in the shadows just inside the back door.

"Is the front door locked then?" Dorfman asked quietly.

Shaughnessey nodded, sweat greasing the palms of his hands and showing in a sudden sheen on his brow.

"Are you expecting company?"

Shaughnessey shook his head.

"Cat got your tongue?" Dorfman remained in the shadows. "There's a light still on by the front door. Put it out."

Shaughnessey moved behind the bar and flicked a switch.

"That's better." Dorfman locked the back door behind him and

229

walked across to the bar. "Give me a whisky – and a cheese sandwich or something – it's hours since I've eaten."

Shaughnessey poured a double and took another for himself. He was relieved that his hand barely trembled, and he hoped that the man watching would not notice. But the man saw everything. "It's just my bag I'll be wanting – and maybe some information."

Shaughnessey removed the plastic cover to reveal two sandwiches and a sausage roll. "They're maybe a bit stale – I'll make you some fresh if you like."

"They'll do."

Looking across the bar Shaughnessey could see the marks left by the fight earlier. The gash over the eye was bad, open to the bone with swollen lips of skin like an obscene mouth, and blood was caked dry down the man's face. And his nose looked swollen enough to be broken.

The man said, "The Reilly boys were murdered. You know that, don't you?"

Shaughnessey nodded.

"Who did it?"

The man's eyes bored right through him. Killer's eyes, he thought, remembering the rifle in the bag upstairs. "God knows." He finished his drink at a single gulp.

"He ain't telling," the man growled. "But there'll be someone in Conlaragh with an idea or two, and I'll not leave till I hear them."

"There's a man wanting to see you. Shall I fetch him?"

Dorfman gave him a very hard look. "And just who the hell would that be?"

"Callan. He's the village butcher."

"It's not pork chops I'm wanting."

Shaughnessey gulped. "Callan was a friend of Big Reilly – a *special* friend."

"And?"

"He might know," Shaughnessey finished lamely. "He just might. Nobody ever knew everything – just Big Reilly himself – but Callan knew more than most. And he wants to see you."

Dorfman licked his lips, displaying a trace of blood on his teeth. "Does he know who I am?"

"We all know who you are," Shaughnessey said respectfully. "We saw what happened earlier – the Gardai."

"This Callan. Will he come alone? It's not the whole damn village I want knowing I'm here."

Shaughnessey explained about the alarm bell which rang in Callan's cold store. Big Reilly had fitted it. Shaughnessey was to ring if ever a stranger arrived asking questions.

"For Christ's sake, why didn't you say so sooner? Fetch him and be quick about it. Half the county police force are searching for me, and they'll be here any minute like as not."

Five minutes later Callan tapped on the back door. By then Shaughnessey had retrieved the canvas holdall from the attic and watched while the man checked its contents. No effort was made to conceal the gun – in fact, when Shaughnessey turned from opening the door to Callan it was pointing at both of them.

"Lock the door," Dorfman said. He cocked the rifle at Callan. "You by yourself?"

Callan nodded.

"Good, come over here and have a drink. You're to tell me everything – understand that? And be damn quick about it. It's ten minutes we've got at the most."

Callan would have liked to have asked a few questions of his own first, but was disinclined to interrogate a man who sat with a gun in his lap. Especially a man who watched every move with cut-glass eyes in a face like a battlefield. So he told what he knew. Which was just part of the story. Big Reilly never told anybody everything. Callan knew of the rifles concealed in the boathouses and knew some people had been hidden in the cottages down by the wharf. And that Steve Cassidy was to drive a lorry to Germany for them – but that was about all.

"*Was* to have driven a lorry?" Dorfman enquired.

"Did you not know? Cassidy was taken by the police – last Tuesday I think – to the Holy Cross Jail."

Dorfman swore savagely.

"And you'll not have heard the news tonight, I suppose?"

Dorfman fingered his injured face. "Do I look as though I've sat with a pint in my hand all night?"

"There's been an explosion at the Holy Cross – Cassidy's been killed."

Dorfman took him through the whole story once more, all the while throwing anxious glances at the clock above the bar. Twice he made Callan stop – sending Shaughnessey to the front door to listen – the rifle trained at the man's spine all the while. But the sounds were just night noises, nothing to worry about, and at half past eleven Dorfman left, slipping out the back way and loping quickly down to the waterfront and the borrowed Cortina.

His head ached badly and for a moment he wondered whether the bruises had been worth it. He had learned less than he had hoped – a good deal less. He coasted through the village until past the last cottage, then he wound the engine up and slipped through the gears – anxious to get back to the Gardai station at Mellick as fast as he could. This man Cassidy had been going to drive a lorry to Germany. Had been – now he was dead. Killed. Murdered perhaps? Murdered because he had talked? Or killed before he had a chance to?

Dorfman hammered the engine, rolling the car fast around the twisting bends, foot hard down on the accelerator and headlights full beam as the car straddled the road. A truck to Germany? Leaving yesterday, according to Callan. But without Cassidy, had it gone anywhere? A lorry big enough to carry a bomb. To carry a bomb all the way to Germany?

23.40 Sunday

The man known as Abou and one of his commandos had flown to Zurich the previous night. Both men had travelled economy class and had used their own passports, though neither bore the name Abou Assan.

Arriving in Zurich in the early hours of the morning had left them with time to kill, so they had dozed until dawn in the airport lounge. Numerous other transit passengers were doing the same thing, so it was not an act which invited suspicion; and at 07.00 they breakfasted in one of the airport's cafeterias until 07.45, when they parted company.

The commando had not wanted to go. By choice he would have remained even for the last leg of their desperate journey. But Abou had shaken his head and sent the man away. Nothing remained to be done which could not be accomplished by one man as easily as two. And that man was Abou himself. The responsibility was his and would remain so until the end. Besides, flexibility was more important than ever now and another man would only be something else to think about. So Abou had sent him home and promised to join him there in two days.

After which Abou had caught the morning shuttle to Bonn-Cologne, landing there at 10.50 precisely. He wore a dark business suit and a black leather coat, and again travelled on his own passport. At the airport he hired a year-old Audi from Avis, paid for the transaction in deutschmarks and arranged to deliver the car to their

Brussels office in a week's time. Then he drove to the Regent and booked in.

He had chosen the hotel carefully. Four weeks ago he had spent three days in Cologne, driving around the old city in a hired car, timing his journeys and measuring distances to the exact half-kilometre. Cologne to Aachen, Aachen to Bonn, and then back to the airport. He had been tempted to stay at the Intercontinental, or even the Excelsior Ernst on Cathedral Square. They were both large and impersonal and the anonymity appealed to him. Dressed in a suit and equipped with a briefcase he could be any one of a hundred businessmen who frequented such places. But the heavy city traffic had deterred him and finally he had settled on the Regent at Melatengurtal 15, in the western suburb of Braunsfeld. Not so grand, of course, but with two hundred beds almost as large and with such a huge garage that there was no danger of his car being blocked in the morning. And Braunsfeld gave good access to the autobahn, fifty kilometres to Aachen and even less to Bonn.

During what was left of the afternoon he rested in his room. At 18.00 hours he switched on the television for the evening news. The broadcast devoted itself to the summit conference. Familiar faces flickered across the screen as film showed the delegates arriving on the previous day. Carter from the States with a staff of two hundred. Giscard d'Estaing from France and Callaghan from Britain. Schmidt greeting the Japanese and the Canadians arriving two hours later. All were now in Bonn. Abou listened intently, alert for any hint of a change in plans. But none was given. Formal meetings would commence in the morning and the commentators speculated on the agenda. There was a lot of talk about the energy crisis and the international recession – would the dollar go down and would the deutschmark go up. And what about the Japanese yen? Abou smiled. By now Suzy would have delivered her ultimatum. The delegates would be alerted to a subject far more urgent. But that was their secret – and his.

He listened to the same news on the radio and at 19.30 took a shower. It helped pass the time and the hot water soothed him. He dressed carefully, glancing increasingly often at his watch and becoming more and more nervous. But at 20.00 hours the call came through.

"A call from Belgium," the telephonist announced.

He accepted it impatiently and waited for the voice at the other end. A man's voice, belonging to one of the three commandos who had not taken part in the raid on Holy Cross. But then how could he have, when he had followed Mick Malone's truck all the way from Pallas Glean.

"Liège," was all the man said before the line went dead. Liège! Fifty miles from the border. Malone was almost in Germany! He was making good time – good enough anyway. Provided he crossed the border tonight the Plan was safe!

Smiling with relief, Abou picked up his black leather coat and went out to dinner. There was an adequate restaurant at the Regent, of course, but he decided against it, preferring to limit his time in the hotel, especially time spent in the public rooms. He would also be inviting attention by having a meal served in his room. So he drove back into Cologne, parked on the southern side of the cathedral, and ate Swiss food at the Schweitzer Stuben.

As he ate, his thoughts wandered occasionally, to Suzy Katoul and Mick Malone and to the commandos making their ways home, but for the most part he ate contentedly, flicking through the pages of the European edition of *Time* magazine. Only once was his sense of wellbeing disturbed. He looked up and caught someone watching him. The man looked away immediately, but all the same Abou was conscious of having been thoroughly inspected. He pretended not to have noticed, but after three or four minutes he turned a page and glanced across to where the man sat. A meal had been served and the man ate stolidly, an open book propped on the table in front of him to denote that he too dined alone. He was about fifty, with the bulky frame common to prosperous middle-class Germans. Expensively dressed, Abou noticed, clothes too good for a policeman. A businessman perhaps, staying overnight with a call to make in the morning before hurrying back to his factory? With a face which reminded Abou of Khrushchev.

After his meal Abou paid his bill, collected his black leather coat and made his way to the door. Krushchev remained absorbed in his book, absentmindedly shovelling food into his mouth as if his thoughts were captured by what he read.

Outside, Abou sauntered past the floodlit cathedral to a spot thirty yards away, where he stopped to look back at the entrance to the Schweitzer Stuben. Two men came out and hurried down the road in his direction, passing him and going on around the corner. Neither was Khrushchev. A man and a woman alighted from a cab and went into the restaurant. Abou stamped his feet and blew on his fingers. Five minutes became ten and ten became twenty. And then, when there was still no sign of Khrushchev, Abou grunted his satisfaction and walked hurriedly away to the rented Audi.

He was back in his room in time to see the late night news. But the pictures and the commentaries were much as earlier – nothing had changed – there was no "news". Abou smiled. He knew differently, and as he switched his light out and prepared for sleep he wondered if Mick Malone had yet reached Aachen.

23.50 Sunday

Throughout its long history Aachen has been a spa. The classical pump room in the middle of the town even commemorates the first visitor, Candidus Caius, a Roman captain, in A.D. 150. And in the following years thousands flocked to bathe in the hottest springs in Northwest Europe. In the eighteenth century it was mostly the English, and at 11.50 on that Sunday night it was Mick Malone.

His face was grey with pain and he was close to exhaustion. Two hundred and fifty miles of highway and autobahn and the problem of crossing three borders had robbed him of more strength than he would have thought possible. The borders had been worst. The endless delays, the waiting around, tension mounting every time his luggage was searched and his papers examined – all had conspired to sap his frail strength.

Landing in France had been unnerving and crossing into Belgium had been worrying. Twice police had stopped him on the open road for a snap inspection of his papers and both times his cab had been searched. But the most terrifying part had been getting into Germany itself. The nightmare at the border had lasted two hours. Two hours during which his guts twisted with worry as he watched men take his cab apart and sweep the detectors back and forth over every inch of the vehicle. And then the now familiar discussion about his cargo of lead batteries. But worse was to come. The German officials had been adamant about breaking the lead seals on the padlocks. The cargo, it seemed, was to be examined physically. Mick had protested, not so much as to draw suspicion upon himself, but enough for the men concerned to seek a second opinion. And in the end German respect for international convention had rescued him, senior customs officials had over-ruled their more zealous subordinates. If the regulations of the Common Market Customs Union were to be breached, then no such breach would take place on German soil. And Mick had breathed a long sigh of relief, for any doubt that it was him they hunted had long since vanished from his mind.

From Aachen he was to go to the address just outside the town given to him by the tall dark man at Pallas Glean. He was to go straight there the man had said, immediately after clearing customs. But Mick needed something hot inside him to revive his strength – a bowl of soup would do, but his twisted guts demanded something. And besides food, there was the phone call which he had to make – to Molly's sister back in Cork.

He parked not far from the cathedral and, clutching his canvas bag, went in search of a meal. It was a cold night and the streets were deserted. He pulled the duffel jacket tight about his body and scurried past Charlemagne's cathedral to the corner of the Kupuziner-graben – which was where the police car pulled alongside.

Instinct rooted him to the spot as the two policemen climbed out, one moving quickly behind him while the bigger one faced him.

"Personal-Ausweiss bitte."

Mick was too tired and too weak to make a run for it and that probably saved him. But he feared the worst. "Look," he stammered, "I don't suppose there's any chance of you speaking English?"

"Your identity papers, please."

Mick recognised it as another routine inspection and sighed with relief. "Sweet Mother of Christ – what a country this is for showing your papers." He unzipped the bag and produced his travel documents. "Is there any place nearby where a man can get a meal at this time of night?"

But the policeman didn't answer. He compared the passport photograph to the man under the street lights and then flicked carefully through the travel papers. Something about the man worried him. He had looked frightened to death when they had stopped him and now he appeared to be unwell. Not fit enough to drive further tonight.

"You are staying in Aachen?"

Mick was recovering from his initial shock. He managed a tired smile. "Something warm in my belly and a good night's sleep," he nodded. "I'll not be driving further tonight, that's for sure."

"You have a hotel reservation?"

"What – and me with a bunk in my cab?" Mick shook his head.

The policeman shrugged. It seemed in order. He smiled. "Most of the restaurants are closed by now. Try one of the hotels on the Friedrich-Wilhelm Platz – you'll probably get something there." Then, seeing Mick's bewilderment, he added, "Just around the next corner – first on your left."

Mick had survived another crisis, but his nerves wouldn't stand many more. He found a coffee bar open at the first hotel he tried, and settled for soup and a piece of apple pie washed down with a cup of hot coffee. After which, feeling a good deal stronger, he went to the desk and explained that he wanted to telephone Cork in Ireland.

The clerk took the number and asked Mick to wait, showing him the telephone booth to which he would route the call once he had obtained an answer.

It was a hell of an hour to phone, Mick thought, Molly's sister would be hopping mad. He grinned wryly. But it would be worth the lash of her tongue to speak to Molly again. And it was the only way. Phone the sister tonight and tell her to get Molly to the phone in the morning when he would phone again.

But the clerk had a problem. A two hour delay on all calls to Ireland. Mick ground his teeth with disappointment. That was something he hadn't bargained for. Two hours! He was dog-tired now, if he didn't sleep soon he'd just about fall over. And he still had to find the address outside the town. But the clerk was helpful. He could book a call now for first thing in the morning. Well now, and wouldn't that be the best thing of all? But it would need to be early. Say 8 am. The clerk nodded and Mick gave him a ten deutschmark tip. It was probably too much he decided afterwards, but if it helped get him through to Molly he'd not begrudge a penny of it.

He hurried back to the lorry park and once back in the cab studied the map given to him by the man at Pallas Glean. Within ten kilometres of the town itself, the man had said. Up in the hills somewhere. Mick sighed, racked with tiredness. Go there tonight and come back again in the morning to make the phone call? Now where was the sense in that? Why not sleep here and then find this place after speaking to his sister-in-law in the morning? Sure and wasn't that the best thing to do? He'd be fresh then and have the daylight to guide him.

But the man had insisted that he go straight there. Tonight. And stay under cover until ten in the morning when someone would make contact. Mick shook his head. It made more sense to do it this way. He *had* to speak to Molly. And weren't his eyes closing even now with tiredness? Convinced at last, Mick clambered up into the bunk behind the seats and five minutes later he was sound asleep.

7

THE SEVENTH DAY

"Of war men ask the outcome, not the cause."
Seneca, Hercules Furens (1st c.), 407,

tr. Frank Justus Miller

00.40 Monday

The Mellick Gardai doctor had sewn nine stitches into the cut above Dorfman's eyebrow. After he had finished, he wrapped a blanket round Dorfman's shoulders and mixed a painkiller with a sleeping draught in a mug of tea.

Dorfman pulled a face as he swallowed it down. "Keep mixing them like that and Guinness have nothing to worry about." He wiped his mouth with the back of his hand. "Is the car ready?"

The doctor sighed. He had done all he could. If the man insisted on travelling through the night that was his business. Anyone with an ounce of sense would kip here, even if it meant sleeping in a cell, at least he'd get a proper night's rest that way. "Yes," he nodded. "The car's ready."

Dorfman thanked him and went out to meet the driver. "How long to Dublin?" he asked as he slid into the back seat.

"Three hours, if we're lucky."

"Make it two and a half and I'll buy you a beer in O'Caffety's. And be sure to wake me as soon as we're there." And with that Dorfman closed his eyes and squirmed down in the seat, trying to get comfortable and waiting for the sleeping draught to take effect.

The journey took two hours and forty minutes and they reached Holy Cross at 3.10 in the morning. The driver kept his promise about waking his passenger, but with the utmost difficulty. Dorfman finally awoke with a splitting headache, muttering and cursing Micky Finn for being an Irishman. Then he blinked out at the floodlit ruins of the detention block and limped into the main prison for his meeting with the Deputy Governor.

The interview started badly. The Deputy Governor sat bleary-eyed behind his desk, protesting in acid terms to the three C.I.D. men, who insisted that Dorfman be given every co-operation. But a horse can be taken to water and not be made to drink and the Governor was still in a truculent mood when Dorfman was shown into the office. Introductions were little more than muttered exchanges and not until they had all finished mugs of scalding hot coffee did the temperature thaw.

Dorfman listened to the details of the bombing which had killed Cassidy and another man and then began his questioning cautiously. But as his head cleared and he pushed his tiredness beyond the threshold of pain, his questions grew to a stream and the stream became a torrent.

They started with Cassidy's record. Such as it was. Nothing very solid – not much was known. Cassidy had been suspected of I.R.A. involvement – suspected of gun-running – suspected of all manner of things – but little was actually *known*.

"What happened during his interrogations?" Dorfman wanted to know. "Was Cassidy nervous?"

"Not really. He said we'd have to release him," one of the C.I.D. men answered. "Said we'd nothing to charge him with."

"And had you?"

"Not really."

"So you would have had to let him go?"

"Within a day or two probably."

"And he guessed that?"

"That's right."

"So he was pretty relaxed about the whole business?"

"Was he hell!" The C.I.D. man shook his head firmly. "Cocky enough to begin with. Said he wasn't going anywhere till Saturday, so he might as well eat our grub as his. He hadn't been charged you see, so he still had his cigarettes and things like that. But he got really stroppy on Friday."

"Why was that?"

"Because of Saturday. He was a lorry driver, long distance stuff." The detective had a sudden thought. "You did know that, didn't you?"

Dorfman had missed it in the file in front of him. His mind was still full of Conlaragh and the fishermen – men like Reilly and the others. He had assumed. Assumed Cassidy was a fisherman along with the others, but a fisherman who could drive a lorry in his part-time.

"Get back to Saturday," Dorfman said.

"Cassidy had to take a load out for the firm he worked for – that's all. But he was worried about it – you could tell that. Maybe he'd have lost his job if –"

The cut above his eyebrow throbbed so badly that Dorfman wondered if the stitches had opened. "Who employed Cassidy?"

"His job you mean?" The policeman reached for the file. "It's here somewhere – hang on a minute. Here it is – Exide Limited of Cork."

Dorfman felt a crush of disappointment. For a moment he had dared hope he had found a worthwhile lead. Callan had been so certain – "a lorry all the way to Germany". Perhaps Cassidy had planned to go sick from his job and take Reilly's truck instead? Could that be it?

"Can we get them on the phone?" he asked.

"Exide you mean?" The C.I.D. man was astonished. "At this time of night?"

"They must have a keyholder registered with the local police. Start with him and keep going until you get an answer. Get onto the bloody chairman if need be."

"An answer to what?" asked the bewildered policeman.

"If Cassidy was taking a lorry to Germany for them on Saturday." Dorfman fought off the waves of fatigue just long enough to have one more idea. "And if he was, find out who went in his place."

And with that Dorfman asked for an empty cell and went to bed.

06.00 Monday

Most people have a favourite city. Rome, Venice, San Francisco – something can happen in almost any place to give it a special touch of magic – maybe a girl, the food or the atmosphere, or even a business deal. But nobody had ever touched Bonn with magic. Whoever said it was half as big and twice as dead as the central cemetery in Chicago was being charitable. Even the Germans hate it. Come Friday evenings they flee in their thousands to the flesh-pots of Cologne or Dusseldorf, taking half the city's prostitutes with them and leaving the others to crochet a G–string or devise new ways of tempting their jaded customers. In Bonn everyone's jaded. It's in the atmosphere. Sniff the air in Kennedy Park and it *smells* of politics. Liberation Park it used to be called, and before that Adolf Hitler Park, and before that Kaiser Wilhelm Park – and if that doesn't make the point, nothing will. Bonn is dull, sterilized and neuter. But this time it promised to be different.

240

"You okay, Harry?" Ross asked.

We were in the R.A.F. Valiant which he used as a company car. Elizabeth sat opposite and the doctor and Max were towards the rear somewhere with a heavily sedated Suzy.

"I'm fine." Apart from a splitting headache. Apart from being worried sick about Suzy and the whole damn mess. Apart from being convinced we would all be dead by the end of the day.

He had been forward with the pilot and air crew, accepting a coded radio message from a man called Twomey.

"Any news?" I asked.

He shook his head. The location of the bomb was still unknown.

"What happens in Bonn?" I asked.

"You've a suite registered at the Steigenberger-Hof. Booked last night."

I was impressed. Steigenberger-Hof was class all year round, but you had to be a Foreign Secretary to get a *suite* there during a summit conference. Whoever was pulling the strings was yanking them pretty hard. Bonn's not as short on hotels as it used to be, but when the circus is in town people camp out at Bad Godesberg or Konigswinter, or even as far away as Cologne.

"*I've* got a suite?" My surprise was obvious. "You turning me loose?"

He bared his teeth in a smile. "Elizabeth will be with you – just to make sure you don't run away."

"Perhaps we'll elope."

His look said the idea was preposterous. "You'll find a copy of the hotel's register in your room. The guests are fifty-fifty, politicos and newsmen, but the newsmen are the heavyweights. You know most of them – talk to them at breakfast and find out all you can."

"Like if their morning wheaties came wrapped in a Deir Yassin Press Release?"

"You got the idea."

"And if they were?"

"Play it down – dismiss it – some crank or a hoax – you know the patter."

I was tired of telling him that "the patter" wouldn't make a scrap of difference, so instead I said: "Suppose whoever publishes the bulletin calls a press conference?"

He smiled grimly. "That will never happen. Every hotel within twenty miles of the Bundestag is under surveillance. All mail is being screened. All messages are being monitored. Telephones are being tapped wholesale and we've got a man in every bar and lobby

241

in town. With luck we'll make an intercept before anyone gets within a mile of a newsman."

"All the hot breath on their necks will upset the press."

"At a summit they expect it." He kept the fixed smile firmly in place. "Harry, I'll tell you – Bonn's sewn up. If someone as much as sneezes he'll be in the infirmary before he can reach for a tissue."

I hoped he was right, but I had a nasty suspicion that all the breezy confidence was as much to reassure himself as to convince me. I sighed and closed my eyes, only to be confronted with the nightmare scenes of Suzy's interrogation. It had lasted hours. Most of the time she was incoherent and delirious, but Ross had extracted a lot of information from her, even if every answer she gave had to be repeated four or five times for us to understand. Altogether Ross had collected quite a story. Such as the man, Abou Assam, being an agent for Red China and having run Tubby Hayes for at least two years. And if *that* had already been suggested by LeClerc's discoveries in Paris, then other parts of her story were a revelation. For instance, Abou Assam himself would be distributing the press release in Bonn. For instance, Assam had promised Suzy that Ross would be compelled to release her for the nine o'clock press conference. But the biggest for instance of all was confirmation that they really did have a bomb! When Ross heard of the Irish connection his face mottled, and when he learned that the bomb was being transported from Ireland he swore non-stop for about five minutes. But after that Suzy's information was all a bit vague. She neither knew the type of vehicle being used, nor its registration – she neither knew who was accompanying it, nor its route – and most important of all, she neither knew its destination in Germany, nor what was the ultimate plan. During the telling of her story she had collapsed three times, and after the fourth they mercifully sedated her and were keeping her that way until we reached Bonn. By then it had been almost midnight and Ross had spent the next hour sending signals – but it seemed there was still no trace of the bomb.

"The doctor took some blood samples from that girl of yours," Ross said.

"And?"

"She was hyped up to the eyeballs when she reached us."

"He needed a blood test to find that out?" I gave him the look I normally reserve for gullible old ladies.

"Just to confirm it. But you see what it means, don't you?" He was going to tell me anyway. "It means whoever sent her knew she would crack."

242

The thought ran wild in my mind for a moment until I made a guess at it. "So they're not worried about what she told you?" I still couldn't say "us", even though I had been there when it happened.

"Wrong. They wanted us to know."

Even if that was right I could see no sense in it, but the world Ross lived in had taught him to expect sugar in a salt-cellar. "And that helps?"

"Twomey has a theory about it," Ross said, looking at Elizabeth.

Whoever Twomey was, he must have been triple A classified because they made no effort to enlighten me. After a while Elizabeth said: "I can guess."

Ross looked at her and waited. Then she said, "He's saying it's not Red China at all."

"You got it," Ross said.

I shook my head in bewilderment. "But what about LeClerc's evidence? You said it was so damn solid –"

"Perhaps we were meant to find it." Elizabeth's eyes watched me so carefully I might still have been number one suspect in her book. "Sooner or later."

"Is that what you really think?"

"Twomey does," Ross said, still looking at Elizabeth.

After a moment's pause Elizabeth asked, "And what do the China watchers say?"

"Same as Twomey," Ross said. "They're amazed."

"Like the Yanks at Pearl Harbor," I said helpfully.

Ross scowled. "No. Nothing like the Yanks at Pearl Harbor. There's a deception in this which runs a million times deeper. Even the opening move was a blind. I never told you, but that hi-jacked container was a dummy. There never was any plutonium in that shipment. Yet they demonstrate a one kiliton capability?" He shook his head furiously. "Twomey's right – we've been fed phoney information from the word go. Vampire Katoul turns out to be a pin-cushion. The P.L.O. have never heard of the Deir Yassin Memorial. And we're being fed planted evidence that Red China's running the show."

I struggled to keep up, but if Elizabeth was having the same difficulty she showed no sign of it. Her face was expressionless.

Ross rubbed the side of his jaw with his tin hand hard enough to get shrapnel in his chin. "It's the old magician's trick," he growled. "Everyone watches the left hand and the right rips your balls off."

"Suzy must believe the Palestinian end of the deal," I ventured.

He bit a cigar, picking the end from his teeth with gloved fingers.

243

"She'll believe anything to get that heap of sand back. She'll even believe smoking is good for her. A hundred cigarettes a day for Chrissakes! I bet she has a fall of soot each month instead of a –"

"What else did Twomey say?" Elizabeth asked pointedly.

Ross puffed the cigar. "Says Dorfman's late in reporting back. Says my people are saying 'Yanks go Home' to the President every five minutes. Says the French are wetting themselves, the Japs are ready to fall on their ceremonial swords and the Germans have worked out how to rebuild Bonn in forty-eight hours."

"And the politicians?" she asked.

"Screaming bloody murder, but still sitting tight."

"What about the search?"

"From midnight last night every vehicle coming out of Ireland is being stripped down to its back axle. All cargoes are being opened, whether Customs sealed or not. All phone calls to and from Ireland are being tapped. The German Army is in police back-up positions and every border crossing is swarming with men." He paused for breath. "Christ, wherever this bomb is, they *must* find it soon!"

I looked at my watch. 06.30. *Soon* would have to be within two and a half hours to stop that press conference from ripping the town apart in panic.

07.35 Monday

The knock at the front door had awoken Molly. Heavy-eyed with sleep, she shuffled down the narrow stairs in her faded blue housecoat, opened the door by the narrowest crack and blinked out in the morning light.

"Registered letter, Mrs Malone." It was the Connery's boy, all grown-up in a postman's uniform. She could remember him running the streets with his backside hanging out of his trousers. Trust him to make a mistake.

"It'll not be for me," she said and went to close the door.

"Mrs Molly L. Malone," he said. "And it's your address."

Not many people knew about the *L*. L for Lillian. Horrible English name. Why her mother had chosen to saddle her with an English name was something she had never fathomed. But her mother was long since dead and her father had been too drunk most of the time to know her first name, let alone her second. She reached for the envelope and inspected it as if it might bite her.

"You'll have to sign for it," Connery's boy thrust a book towards

244

her, held open with an elastic band and a chewed stub of pencil. "Sign there, please."

She didn't want to. It couldn't be her letter. Why should she sign for something not hers? But the address was right and she was Molly L. Malone, wasn't she? Frowning furiously she wrote her name along the line he indicated and got rid of him.

In the kitchen she put the kettle on and sat at the table to stare at the envelope. A crest was printed on the flap with the words "Bank of Ireland" underneath in blue print. She turned it over and studied her name and address at the front. All typewritten and official. It seemed funny to think of somebody she didn't know sitting at a typewriter to type her name. She wished Mick was here. Mick would know what to do. Perhaps she would leave opening it until Mick got back? She brightened at the thought. That would be best, they could open it together.

She took a cup of tea up to the boy and went to her room to get dressed. Her sister, Kathleen, would be round early to take her into Cork to get the week's shopping. Not that they would need much – she and the boy would be eating at Kathleen's at the weekend, so there were only a few days to bother about – and now it had come to it she wished she hadn't promised Kathleen that she would go. But she had and she couldn't get out of it.

"What's the letter about, Mum?" the boy asked over breakfast. He picked it up and read the Bank of Ireland inscription on the back.

"None of your concern, whatever it is."

"Aren't you going to open it?"

"It can keep till your Dad gets back."

"But if it's addressed to you?" He caught the warning look in her eye and contented himself with some final advice. "I just thought it might be urgent, that's all."

She took it away and put it on the mantelshelf. When he had finished eating she helped get his school things together and watched him leave the house. Urgent! How could it be urgent? When it had to be a mistake in the first place. She washed the breakfast things and tidied the kitchen in preparation for Kathleen's visit, thinking all the while about the Dublin postmark on the letter and that whoever had sent it knew her middle name. Or at least her initial. Perhaps she should tell Kathleen about it? Half of her wanted to, but the other half said Mick wouldn't like it. Mick thought Kathleen an old tittle-tattle, forever gossiping about other people's affairs. Well, *everyone* did that didn't they? Even if perhaps Kathleen did more than most. She'd need to think about it – there was an hour yet, more even before Kathleen arrived. No need to rush a decision she might regret later.

But Kathleen arrived much earlier than expected. Anyone could see they were sisters. Kathleen was two years older and had never been as pretty, but she shared the family nose and the fair hair whisped white like the fur of a marmalade cat. She was out of breath and her coat was lopsided where she had buttoned it wrong in her hurry. The headscarf thrown over her head had worked loose and lay rumpled around her collar, and her face was red from the exertion of walking quickly.

"Whatever's the matter?" Molly, still recovering from the shock of the letter, was ill equipped for further emergencies.

"You'll spend the day guessing and never get it." Kathleen unbuttoned her coat, her face alive with the satisfaction of someone about to impart a secret. "But haven't I just had the strangest phone call of all my life."

"Phone call?"

"Long distance." Kathleen nodded smugly, sitting at the kitchen table, folding her hands and quivering with undisguised pleasure.

Dublin, Molly thought. I've had a letter and she's had a phone call.

"From Germany."

Molly sat down quickly, her hand clutching her throat, fear all over her face. "Mick!"

"And who else would it be? And him as clear as being in the next room."

"What's happened?" Oh Mary Mother of Christ – how do I get to Germany? Me, who's never been past Dublin in my life and there only once. He should never have gone. Bonus or no bonus. He's not strong enough these days. The factory should have known –

"He's *all right*, Molly – he's all right."

Molly bit her thumb and tried to believe her. Once Mick was back she'd never let him away again. Never, never!

"He's phoning again," Kathleen said excitedly. "This afternoon, he said. Molly, he wants to talk to you – urgently. You're not to worry yourself though. There's nothing wrong and it's good news he's got. Molly, he sounds so excited!"

Molly unwound enough to put the kettle on. Mick phoning all the way from Germany? To talk urgently. Her eyes strayed to the mantelpiece and the letter still unopened.

"What can it be about d'you think?" Kathleen said.

246

It had to be the letter, Molly thought. Didn't the boy guess right after all? An urgent letter from a Bank in Dublin – addressed to her? She walked over to the mantelpiece and took it down, turning it over and over in her hands while she thought about it. She could tell Mick about it when he phoned. But wouldn't he want to know the insides of it? Not just the envelope. The kettle shrilled behind her and she put the envelope on the table, while she made the tea.

"Phone calls and a registered letter?" Kathleen said, eyeing the envelope. She picked it up and read the inscription on the flap. "From a *bank*! You're mighty important all of a sudden Molly Malone, that's for sure. And aren't you going to open this then?"

Molly poured the tea and then opened the letter, while Kathleen twitched with excitement at the other side of the table. It took Molly a long time to read such a short letter. There were only six lines above the signature after all. The Manager himself had written about an endowment policy which had matured in her name. For five thousand pounds! And he had pleasure in enclosing the cheque for said amount. Molly looked at it with wondering eyes – five thousand pounds and her without as much as a bank account!

"It's bad news, Molly," said Kathleen. "I can tell by your face."

"It's no news," Molly's voice trembled. "It's some kind of mistake."

But there was her name on the envelope – and again on the cheque itself. Could there be another Mrs Malone? Another Mrs Molly L. Malone? Without another word she passed the letter across the table for her sister to read.

09.30 Monday

We were installed in the Steigenberger-Hof by 07.30. Three white Porsche police cars collected us from the airport at Arne and blazed down the rain-washed autobahn with more flashing lights than a Christmas tree. On the outskirts of the city the convoy slowed down – and split up – one car taking Suzy and the doctor to the clinic Ross had told me about. We followed the lead car along the Am Bunderekantserplatz and round the corner to a side entrance.

Suite 120. Mr and *Mrs* Harry Brand. Arriving at the service entrance took some of the gilt off the gingerbread, but at least I offered to carry Elizabeth over the threshold. The sour look she gave me changed to nervous confusion when Ross intercepted our glances.

LeClerc was waiting for us with two German security men who greeted Ross like visiting royalty. They explained how to make a call on the direct line telephones which they had just installed, promised Ross that the suite had been screened for electronic plumbing, and then they left.

"Any news from Archie?" Ross asked LeClerc, and I realised my last sight of Dorfman was when he was being pulled aboard the helicopter back at the Health Farm.

"Half an hour ago," LeClerc said. "He's still in Ireland. He thinks he's got a trace on the vehicle used to transport the bomb."

"Jesus," Ross whispered, "so tell me."

"Truck load of batteries. Left Ireland on Saturday for Cologne and –"

"Batteries! You mean auto batteries?" Ross sat down in the nearest chair. "Batteries! Oh Jesus! *Lead*. They'll have run past every geiger counter between here and –" He punched the side of his jaw. "Shit! Does Twomey know?"

LeClerc nodded. "He's running a trace on the vehicle now – description, plates, the lot. Within half an hour every cop in Europe will be looking for it."

"I'd better get over there." Ross could have meant Ireland for all the explanation he gave. Halfway to the door he waved at the newly installed telephones. "Check in when you can – immediately if anything breaks." He looked at me. "We're counting on you, Harry. Sell those guys the hoax story. Keep them off my back for a few hours and I'll pin a medal on you."

"Posthumously of course," I countered.

Ross swore over his shoulder and collided with LeClerc in the doorway. Max trod on their heels and they left.

Elizabeth took her overnight case to the bathroom to replace the colour which strain and lack of sleep had drained from her face. When she came back she was wearing a cream crushproof suit and an uncreased expression. "I packed a clean shirt for you, Harry. If you wash and change, you might persuade yourself you've had a restful night."

I did as I was told and when I returned she was looking out of the window. It was growing light outside, but only just. The Rhine looked as wide as the valley of death and twice as evil. The thick carpet deadened my footfalls, and when I touched her elbow she jumped a mile. It made me feel better in a way. To know that for all her apparent cool, she was as wound up and frightened as I was.

I commandeered a table for twelve in the breakfast room, explaining to the waiter that others would be joining us. At least I hoped they would. Reporters are not renowned early risers, and when he

248

told me about the Reuter's party the night before I guessed this morning would be no exception. So Elizabeth and I sipped good coffee and waited for something to happen. We both tried to make conversation, but gave up after a while and sat in silence. I remembered dinner at the Baracuda a few nights earlier and thought how different it was. We had been tense and worried then, but somehow we had raised enough spirit to flirt with each other and make a game of it. Now so much had happened to us that we could have been two different people. I suppose she was right. Time had run out.

At about 09.30 the first one wandered in. He stood in the door, sniffing like a bloodhound and blinking at the morning light which flooded in from the window. I waved him across to the table and introduced Elizabeth. She was like an actress, five minutes earlier she had been shaking with nerves, but once he appeared the curtain went up and within a few moments he was eating out of her hand.

During the next ten minutes some of the other boys drifted in, all in search of black coffee and hang-over cures, so that gradually our table became the kind of gathering point Ross must have hoped it would be. One thing became clear fairly quickly. None of them had receive an unusual press hand-out. Neither Elizabeth nor I needed to ask. Something like the Deir Yassin story would have had them pawing the ground with excitement, but instead most of the talk was of the difficulty of getting through to their offices overseas. Direct telephone dialling had broken down for some reason and all overseas calls were being routed via the international operators with consequential delays. The boys were furious.

Back in our suite Elizabeth was jubilant. "They've intercepted it. Don't you see that Harry? They've probably got this Abou Assam locked up somewhere already – and this truck from Ireland."

But LeClerc disillusioned her as soon as she reported on the direct line telephone. As far as they could tell nobody had even tried to circulate a press release. No attempt had been made to contact even one journalist, let alone the entire press corps. And the worst news of all was that the truck from Ireland had still not been located, though its route had been traced. It had crossed into Aachen last night. If there was a bomb, it could now safely be assumed to be in Germany.

Ross came on the line afterwards and summoned us to Police Headquarters.

"And Harry?" Elizabeth asked.

"Certainly and Harry!" Ross's reply could be heard a yard away from the telephone. "Do you think I want him left there with an army of newsmen without you keeping an eye on him?"

A plainclothes man picked us up in the lobby, and we were there within ten minutes. Ross was in conference with what seemed a United Nations of policemen. About twenty of them, mostly German, but with the top security man from each of the delegations holding a nervous watching brief.

Ross was doing his best to reassure them. "We know the truck. We know the driver. We know the route taken into Germany," he hammered away, ticking the fingers of his right hand. "Dammit, the truck was even sighted in Aachen in the early hours of this morning. We expect to locate it any minute now. Any minute! There's no need for panic – repeat, no need for panic."

Nobody contradicted him, but nobody passed a vote of confidence either. The mood of the meeting was decidedly uneasy.

Ross tried again. "We're monitoring all outgoing and incoming telephone calls. We've mounted road blocks on all likely routes. Bonn itself is sealed off I tell you. Every known member of the Red Brigade has been pulled in for questioning. Now for Chrissakes – will you guys relax! I tell you there's nothing to worry about."

When they filed out Ross mopped his brow and removed his jacket so that Elizabeth could massage his shoulders. Then LeClerc arrived, on his way from one meeting to another.

"Well?" Ross demanded.

"Twomey's still with the diplomats. None of them believe it's China," LeClerc said helplessly. "Not one of them."

"What do our people in Peking say?"

"Ross, it's 01.00 hours in Peking!"

"What are you – a talking clock? What kind of answer's that?"

"They've asked for another hour," LeClerc protested. "But first off they're incredulous." He made his way back to the door. "I'm on my way to Matthews now – I'll see you in about half an hour."

Ross turned to me. "Harry, you sure none of those newsmen has a sniff of this?"

"Ask Elizabeth," I shook my head. "They don't know a damn thing."

He sighed heavily. Lack of sleep had painted black circles beneath his eyes, and his face had a pinched nervous look to it. "You know what I think? That press release story was another blind. A sop to keep Katoul happy while she was in the game."

"And now she's out of it?" My mouth went dry.

"I don't know," he shook his head. "But if you take Katoul's threats out, you remove the blackmail theory. And if it's not blackmail, what the hell are you left with?"

I looked at him blankly, half understanding what he was driving at but hoping against hope that I had got it wrong.

"It's an act of war," he said softly. "A direct attempt to destroy the leaders of the Western World. There aren't going to be any demands. There isn't going to be any negotiation, because none will be offered. All we're going to get – if we don't find that truck fast – is a very, very loud bang."

And it was as if we were listening for it, because it went very, very quiet in that room.

The man known as Abou had awakened early. He reached for the travelling clock and snapped it shut before it buzzed. Then he lay back on the bed, catching his breath in his excitement as he realised that the day had arrived at last. Today he would begin the long journey home. Home! After being away for so long. Home to the old country to join his people in time of war.

He dressed in the clothes which he had brought with him. Suede shoes, casual slacks and a knitted shirt under a loose-fitting blazer. Holiday clothes. Quite different from the business suit worn yesterday.

At 09.10 he paid his bill in the lobby. He wore the long black leather coat and hoisted his suitcase easily, as if it was only partially full. Then he collected the rented car from the garage and began the journey to the autobahn, listening to the car radio as he drove. The news programme was still full of the summit conference and still there was no hint of a change in arrangements. The first formal session would open at 10.30 this morning in Bonn. The commentators continued to speculate on the plight of the dollar and the power of the yen, and were all convinced that today's agenda would be dominated by economic affairs. Abou smiled, he knew otherwise.

It took half an hour to reach the autobahn, including the time taken to stop to pack the leather coat into the case and withdraw the fawn lightweight raincoat he would wear in its place; and once on the autobahn he drove in the direction of Aachen, driving carefully and well within the speed regulation.

The hills on either side of the road were heavily wooded with trees so thick and numerous that there was barely room to swing an axe between them. These days it was the most popular camping area in Germany. In the summer the wilderness of the Eifel soaked up campers and hunters and holidaymakers by the thousand. But it

251

had been different once. In the last war it had been a bloody battle-ground. The first place where Americans had fought Germans on German soil. The densely packed trees had delayed the American tank attack and they had suffered heavy losses until their artillery had pounded the Germans into retreat. Abou smiled at the irony – it was appropriate that Aachen, once the scene of American victory, should play its part in an American defeat.

He passed the turn-off for Eschwiler and waited for the sign to Stolberg to appear on his left. Then he drove through the little town and out again, the road climbing through hillsides still dense with trees. He drove steadily, always alert for a prowling patrol car. Here they could be either State Police or Border Police with Federal authority. Both were to be avoided. Twice a traffic helicopter dipped low above the treetops to flutter briefly across the cut in the forest made by the road. He glanced nervously upwards as he thought of Malone. It was very unlikely that the search had yet concentrated on the Exide truck, but even if it had it wouldn't matter a damn – so long as Malone had followed instructions. And Abou never doubted that Malone would obey orders to the letter. After all, when you offer a man his life he is unlikely to betray you. Besides, the commando who had followed the truck to the German frontier would have reported any cause for alarm.

The road continued to climb, past a deserted picnic area no more than a fire break in the forest, and then running on for another mile before reaching the secondary road on the right hand side. After checking his mirror Abou bumped quickly down the rutted lane. It was exactly ten o'clock.

He had rented the chalet a month before. It was a primitive place, but the lack of comfort had not disturbed him. He had no intention of living there. The chalet's appeal lay in its remoteness, high in the hills above Aachen, well away from habitation and screened by trees. And with a disproportionately large garage – big enough to house a lorry.

He drove round the back, switched off the engine and listened. Neither sign nor sound of life. The big garage doors in front of him remained closed. For a second he panicked. Surely Malone had arrived last night? But the doors were still padlocked – he could see that from here. He opened the car doors and stepped out.

"*Cead mile failte,*" a voice said softly.

Abou swung around, his hand instinctively reaching for his shoulder holster.

"I wondered if you'd come yourself," Mick Malone stepped out of the bushes.

Abou's relief mingled with suspicion. "What was that other thing you said?"

"A hundred thousand welcomes," Mick bowed. "In Irish, of course."

"Is the truck inside?" Abou jerked his head towards the garage.

"Where else?" Still smiling, Mick took the padlock key from his pocket.

"Open up then. We've work to do and barely the time to do it."

While Mick unlocked the doors, Abou scrutinised his face. "You got here all right then, last night?"

Mick had arrived little more than an hour before, but that was his secret. Something told him that the tall dark man would not have understood his anxiety to contact Molly. Nor would he have approved.

"Just before midnight," Mick lied, using the excuse of opening the doors to avoid the man's eye. "I parked in the garage and slept in the cab."

Reassured, Abou followed him into the gloom of the building and closed the doors behind them. He flicked a light switch and looked at the sealed padlocks above the lorry's tailboard. Then he took a wrench from the wall and started work. Five minutes later the locks were broken.

"It's an offence to open Customs seals," Mick said cheerfully. "But I daresay you know that." He was anxious to see inside the truck now and more curious than ever about the cargo which had brought the police forces of three countries to a state of nervous exhaustion. But when the doors swung back all that was revealed was a stack of batteries, all roped securely into position.

"Is that all?" Mick said in bewilderment. "All this trouble to –"

"Give me a hand up," the man said, already clambering aboard the truck. "We'll have to move them one at a time. Start stacking them over there." He indicated the far wall and lifted a battery down to Mick who grunted and did as he was told.

Altogether they removed one hundred and eighty batteries – two entire stacks – and Mick was groaning with fatigue when they finished an hour later. But then he saw his real cargo.

"Sweet Mother of Christ! What is it then – a Trojan horse?" He shook his head, looking at the sleek radiator of a Mercedes ambulance. "Do I get to ride in that all the way to that clinic of yours?"

Abou wiped the sweat from his forehead. His blazer and shoulder holster had long since been discarded, and he rubbed his aching back. He turned to look at the ambulance. It was the low modern kind, with two blue lamps mounted on the roof above the front seats. The walls of the truck either side of it were still lined with batteries and the floor and ceiling of the truck were clad with lead sheets.

He remembered Mick's question. "Only for part of the way. Loosen the ropes at that end – we'll have to unload one wall of batteries before I can open the door to get into the ambulance."

And so the backbreaking work continued. When they had finished, another ninety batteries were stacked on the garage floor.

"Lower the tailboard," Abou ordered, climbing behind the wheel of the Mercedes.

Five minutes later the ambulance had been safely unloaded. Mick walked around it carefully, noting the German number plates and the inscription painted on the sides. "What's that mean?" he asked.

"Ravensburg private nursing home," Abou translated.

"Is that the place where I'm going to have this operation?"

Abou shook his head. "Ravensburg's in Germany," he smiled. "But it's close to the Swiss border." He paused to collect his shoulder holster and jacket before turning towards the doors. "Come on into the house. We've just time for a wash before we leave."

12.25 Monday

"Mum!"

Molly heard the boy's shout above everything. Above Kathleen's silly chatter and the background music of the radio, above the turmoil of her own thoughts and the muted traffic noise from the street outside.

"Mum!" There was fear in his voice, some kind of warning, mixed with a desperate need to reach her. Her slippered feet knocked the cat's milk flying as she rushed to the door.

"Whatever –"

He flew into her arms. "Mum, there's Gardai all round the house. They tried to stop me –"

"Mrs Malone?" A uniformed policeman followed the boy into the kitchen.

Molly tightened her grip on the boy and bristled up at the man, her head barely reaching his shoulders. "And what's bothering you? Frightening the boy half to death and –"

But the policeman never stopped to listen. He brushed past her to the hall where he opened the front door before running upstairs. Another policeman followed quickly through the open back door, looked hard at Kathleen and went through into the hall.

Despite everything, despite her shouts of abuse and despite Kathleen's meeker protests, the search went ahead. Every piece of furniture in the house was moved, upstairs and down. Drawers were emptied, cupboards ransacked, cushions prodded and mattresses examined. Even the loose floorboards in the kitchen were lifted – although nothing was hidden there, nor had been for eight long years.

"You've no *right!*" Molly followed them from room to room. "You've no right at all. Frightening quiet-living folk half to death. Is it a warrant you've got, because I've seen no sight of one. You come in here –"

"Mrs Malone?" the man said quietly from behind.

She whirled round to face him. He was dressed in a suit and an open shirt, and something had happened to his face, as if he had been in an accident. "My name's Dorfman."

"Your name's a black-hearted devil!" she told him angrily, waving a hand about her. "If this is any of your doing –"

"There's nothing here, sir," one of the policemen said.

"Very well. Please put everything back to Mrs Malone's satisfaction."

"Satisfaction!" Molly's face was crimson. "That's a fine kind of word to be using when you've –"

"Mrs Malone, I'm *sorry*," said the man with the bruised face. He stood smiling at her – him as big as a house and twice as ugly. "The policemen will tidy up and leave everything as it was – and then they will go."

"And so I should think," she wiped her dry hands in her apron and glared up at him. "That's how you got that face is it? Barging in on people and throwing your weight around." She caught sight of one of the policemen rearranging bits and pieces on the dresser. "And leave that alone – the whole house will need a good clean, but not from the likes of you."

The man looked to Dorfman for instructions. Dorfman nodded and the man departed, others with him, a car door slammed outside and an engine started as Molly walked to the kitchen door. The temper which had sparked her courage was cooling now, and she looked at Dorfman with apprehensive eyes. There was more to come, she sensed that and it frightened her.

255

He twisted his bruised face into another grin. "Do you think we could have a cup of tea and a bit of a chat?"

Kathleen snorted. "Some nerve! Who are you anyway? You're not from these parts. Gardai, are you?"

"Sort of," he admitted, still looking at Molly.

"There's only one sort," Kathleen said acidly.

Molly stood at the table, watching Dorfman's face and wondering what he wanted. Instinct told her he was trouble. He was another like Big Reilly. Whenever men like that appeared, it was always bad news they brought. She tried to keep her voice from trembling. "You're making the place untidy there. You'd better sit down. You'll not be gone without saying what's on your mind – I can see that from your face."

Dorfman sat by the fire and exchanged uneasy glances with the boy and the other woman.

"We're sisters," Kathleen announced, as if explaining why she was there. She sat on a hardbacked chair at the table, watching him carefully in case he walked off with the coal scuttle.

"Hello," Dorfman said without getting up. The boy worried him. There was no telling what might come up in the next half hour, but none of it was gossip for the playground.

Molly set cups into saucers and poured the tea, her hand trembling and her mouth set in a straight line across her white face. "Michael," she nodded at a cup and the boy carried it carefully across to Dorfman.

As gently as he knew how Dorfman said, "You're away back to school are you?"

"Not now." The boy returned to stand by his mother as she sat at the table. He rested one hand lightly on her shoulder, while the other made a small fist at his side. About twelve, Dorfman guessed, not much older, frightened to death and trying hard not to show it. "I'll stay with my Mum," the boy said, a slight tremor in his voice. He cleared his throat. "It's what my Dad would want."

Dorfman accepted the inevitable with the best grace possible. "Good lad." He twisted his bruised lips into a smile. "That's what any dad would want."

Molly reached up and patted the boy's hand, catching his eye with an encouraging glance of her own, while the sister's nod was barely perceptible. Then all three turned to look back at Dorfman.

The tea was too hot to drink. He put it carefully on the floor by his feet. He wondered how to begin. A good interrogator never specifies charges, nor reveals the extent of his knowledge. A good interrogator would break this little party up and talk to them one at a time. But they were frightened enough already, and he wanted them on his side. He wanted them to co-operate willingly – not hold back.

"Mrs Malone – I want to talk to you about Liam Reilly," he began quietly. "You know him of course?"

"I met him," Molly replied cautiously.

"A likeable man," Dorfman's eyes twinkled. "Nobody I've met will have a word said against him. You'll be the same, I'll be bound?"

"I like him well enough."

Dorfman nodded. "Did you ever meet that friend of his? Pat – Pat Brady?"

Molly fidgeted, biting her thumbnail, wondering where this was all leading. They were I.R.A. – Big Reilly's men – she knew that well enough and knew what Mick would say if he heard she'd been gossiping to the Gardai. So she said nothing.

Dorfman sighed. "Mrs Malone, I'm trying to help. I'm sorry you were upset by a car load of policemen. Having them trample over one's house is enough to frighten anyone. That wasn't my idea." He attempted another smile. "And I promise you one thing – there's nothing you can say about Liam or Pat, or even Big Reilly himself, that will get them into trouble."

Kathleen didn't trust him. "Then why ask about them?"

"Ask?" He seemed surprised. "It's more discussing we were surely? I just said how popular they are – Liam, Pat and Big Reilly." He paused, but if to gain a reaction he must have been disappointed. Nobody said a word, not a head as much as shook in agreement. He began to reconsider his views on splitting them up. Even now it was not too late. "Did you hear the news last night?" he asked, his tone still conversational. "There was an explosion at the Holy Cross."

"And what's that to do with the likes of us?" Molly asked with a show of determination.

Dorfman shrugged. "It's just that a man was killed. Someone you might have known. Steve Cassidy. He worked with your husband at the factory round the corner."

"Oh my God!" Molly gnawed at her clenched fist. She had heard something, but she had not taken any notice. There were always bits and pieces about explosions – especially in the north. But someone who had worked with Mick! She remembered meeting Cassidy once, a slim young man with thin yellow hair, but she had not known him – not the way Mick must have done.

"An accident," Kathleen said. "According to the news I heard."

Dorfman nodded. "A tragic one," he said, then his voice hardened as he asked, "Mrs Malone, where is your husband?"

"Mick?" Her fear was obvious. "And what's it to do with you?"

"Where is he, Mrs Malone?"

"He's working away from home. Overseas. He's not even in Ireland."

"I'm glad," Dorfman said.

Molly bit her tongue to stop herself asking why. Her misgivings grew by the second. There was something threatening about this man. Yet he sipped his tea and watched her over the rim of his cup, as calm and casual as one of Mick's mates dropped in for a bit of a chat. And he was trying to be helpful, she sensed that. But his eyes missed nothing. She glanced at the letter on the table, now back in its envelope, stained by a splash of tea over the word "Bank". Carefully she slid her cup over it and looked up to find him still watching her.

"Do you know why I'm glad, Mrs Malone?"

She was too frightened to answer. Her last reserves of temper and courage ebbed away as if sucked dry by the staring eyes in the bruised face.

"Because a lot of people have been killed in the last few days," he said. "Liam Reilly for one."

"Oh no! Liam killed?"

"And Pat Brady. And Big Reilly himself, along with eight fishermen."

"Sweet Mother of God! What are you saying?" She couldn't believe him. It was a lie – a terrible lie. Hadn't Big Reilly sat in that very chair no more than a week ago?

"All murdered," the man went on relentlessly, a hard edge to his voice. "And Steve Cassidy's death wasn't accidental – whatever they said on the radio. Cassidy was murdered, Mrs Malone."

Why was she shaking? She was on the verge of tears and for no real reason. Mick wasn't amongst them. Mick was safe. Mick was in Germany. She shook her head. "I don't understand. Why are you here? What's this to do –"

"Where's your husband, Mrs Malone?" the man pursued her relentlessly.

"Away – he's away in Germany – for the factory –"

"Are you sure? Can you prove it?"

"Prove?" she struggled to understand. "Prove? But why? Mick's done nothing. I don't understand," she turned to Kathleen for support.

"Mick's in danger," the man said quickly. "We're trying to contact him. The factory is helping –"

"Danger?" It was the only word she heard. "But how? Why? I tell you Mick's done nothing. He's not a well man –"

"We're trying to help," the man said insistently. "If you know anything –"

"Know? What should I know?" Molly was beside herself with worry. "I tell you he's done nothing wrong. I know that."

"I do too, Mrs Malone." Dorfman was on the point of believing her, but he had to be sure, so he gambled. "But the men who killed Reilly and the others will – will hurt Mick if they reach him before we do –"

"Oh merciful God!" Molly gripped the boy in her terror.

"So if you know anything –"

Kathleen jumped up. "For pity's sake you're frightening her half to death. Can't you see that? And the boy too."

"I'm sorry but I must contact Mick Malone." Dorfman brushed past her and placed his hands on Molly's shoulders. "It's a matter of life and death."

Molly's eyes blurred with tears as she stared at the letter on the table. It had all started with that! That and the phone call. "He phoned," she wept, pushing Dorfman away. "He telephoned this morning."

"What time? When? From Germany?" Dorfman hammered her with questions.

Suddenly the boy screamed. "Leave her alone. You bully! Leave her alone." Tiny fists pumped into Dorfman's face. "Leave my Mum alone."

He grabbed the boy and held the trembling body at arm's length.

Kathleen said, "He phoned my place. Early – and he's phoning back this afternoon."

"What time?"

"We don't know what time! Sometime this afternoon. We were going to my place after giving the boy his dinner –"

Dorfman felt a surge of relief – and pity, as he looked at Molly sobbing and the boy's white frightened face. "Remember what you said earlier?" he asked the boy, softening his voice so as not to frighten him. "About doing what your dad would want? Remember that? Well, he'd want you to do this. I promise. We're all on his side.

259

All of us. You, me, your Mum and your Aunt here. We're all on his side, aren't we?"

The boy stopped struggling and turned bewildered eyes to his mother's tear-stained face and then back to the man who held him.

"I promise," Dorfman said earnestly.

Even Kathleen was weakening. "I hope your soul burns in hell, Mister, if you're not telling the truth."

"Of course it's the truth," Dorfman said urgently. "Now come on, help your sister get ready. We're all going to police headquarters."

"But the phone call!" Molly protested.

"We'll have it transferred. Don't worry. Now hurry up, we haven't a minute to spare."

Mick was enjoying himself. He swerved out onto the fast lane and sent the ambulance thundering down the autobahn, lights flashing and sirens blaring. Other vehicles edged out of his path, and Mick chuckled with excitement. Now wasn't this the only way to travel? And didn't the tall dark man think of just about everything?

Just drive, the man had said, drive like the devil himself was chasing you – all the way to Bonn. There'll be road blocks and goodness knows what else – but just drive. Nobody ever stops an ambulance. And if anyone did, he was simply to say "Orders of Major Ross." That's all – like a password – the tall dark man had smiled as he said it – that's all, but it would be enough.

At Bonn he was to park near the railway station, lock the ambulance up and go to the Königshof hotel in Adenaurallee. There he was to wait in the lobby and the "courier" from Switzerland would collect him within an hour.

"Then Bonn is my final destination?" Mick had asked eagerly.

The tall dark man had taken his meaning at once. "Don't worry. Reilly will cash both policies today."

The tall dark man had left shortly afterwards, driving back down the rutted track in the crimson red Audi. But he had given Mick some very definite instructions. He was to wait one hour exactly. Then he was to set off like a bat out of hell. And the man had shown him another thing. The switch he was to set when he left the ambulance. It was mounted next to the radio on the dashboard. "Switch it on when you leave, lock up and just walk away."

"It's not a bomb, is it?" Mick had asked in sudden alarm. He had fallen out with the Movement about that. He didn't hold with it. Fighting soldiers and armed police was one thing – indiscriminate bombing another – and he'd not be a party to that.

"It's an electronic homing device," the man had pointed to the aerial. "Someone will be collecting the vehicle tonight. In the dark. That switch operates a signal our people will tune into. It will save them time in tracing the ambulance, that's all. That's why it's not too important where you park it. The nearer the station the better, but anywhere in the city centre will do."

Mick looked at the switch and chuckled. God, there was never another man like this one. Electronic homing devices! Whoever heard the like. But then wasn't that the man all over? Didn't he think of just about everything?

The road was blocked ahead. Just like the man said it would be. Near Duren – and sure enough there was a signpost. Mick slowed down to sixty miles an hour as the traffic ahead of him bunched up like the webs in a concertina. All three lanes in front were blocked. "Keep going" the man had said. "Whatever you do, keep going." But how the devil did a man do that when every lane there was blocked with traffic? Mick eased his foot from the accelerator until his speed fell to forty. He was fast approaching the tail end of traffic now and would have to decide quickly. His headlamps blazed full beam and the blue lights on the roof revolved like spinning tops. Then he swung the wheel and mounted the central divider. Cars flashed past on the other side of the autobahn and the ambulance bucked wildly as he drove with two wheels still on the road surface and two on the divider itself. He added the blare of his horn to the scream of the sirens and pushed his foot hard down on the floor. Forty crept back up to fifty and fifty became fifty-five.

He could see the road block now – maybe a mile ahead. Soldiers too! A whole truck full of soldiers. Mary Mother of God, armed bloody soldiers. He held his speed, swerving inwards to avoid a truck with its tailboard too near the divider. Half a mile to go. The soldiers had seen him. They were moving the truck. Moving out of his way or turning to block his path? Sweet Jesus Christ – *will you get out of the way*! Ahead of him the truck straddled the divider, facing away from him so that he could see the troops in the back. He hammered his hand down on the horn. Two hundred yards to go. The truck lurched – and pulled clear. Praise be to God! And there was a man waving him through. Half a dozen men waving him through. As if he was a jockey riding the Derby winner and they were gamblers with fortunes to come. Sixty yards. The traffic ahead had been cleared from the outside lane and he bumped all four wheels back down on the road surface. Then he blazed through the gap at sixty miles an hour.

Thirty miles to Bonn. Past the turn off to Cologne. And him still going flat out. Fast enough to be there well within the hour – road blocks or no road blocks.

Marlene Vesper was nineteen. She was a pretty girl who spoke three languages in addition to her native German; French fluently, Italian passably and English with a strong American accent. Normally she enjoyed her work as a telephonist on Bonn's International Exchange. The pay was good and the working conditions suited her, and the occasional spell of overtime did not unduly interfere with her love life. But today was different. Today was very definitely different.

For some reason all direct dialling to overseas countries had been suspended from seven o'clock this morning. The consequence of which was that all such calls were re-routed via the exchange, and the delay and inconvenience this was causing telephone users meant that Marlene had suffered more abuse in the last few hours than in the whole of her previous experience.

What she did not know, at least until later, was that the restriction on overseas calls related not just to Bonn, but to the whole of the Federal Republic. Not that knowing would have helped. Her customers would still have given her trouble about the delays – especially the delays to the Republic of Ireland.

When Marlene had arrived that morning she had been amazed to see the number of others reporting for duty. Normally the crew she worked with comprised twenty girls and two supervisors. But this morning more than twice that number had arrived, men as well as girls, all of whom had received phone calls and telegrams telling them to report for extra duty as a matter of urgency. And the surprises had not ended there.

A grim faced supervisor had led them not into the exchange itself, but to a conference room normally reserved for instruction courses, and when the telephonists had seated themselves a man had hurried in to speak to them. His complexion was a dull grey colour and his eyes were red-rimmed, as if he had slept badly, or not at all. And he was a policeman he said, although he wore no uniform.

All overseas calls were to be monitored. Bugged, tapped, listened-in to, however they liked to describe it. The telephonists were to accept and process calls but the "common circuit" switch was to be left open at all times to enable the supervisors to dip in and out of conversations without clicking the line. And today the "supervisors" were in fact a squad of policemen already at work in the exchange.

The grey-faced man had fended off their questions with a mumbled apology for the inconvenience. Then he had concluded by stressing that the entire exercise was of supreme importance and was to be conducted in total secrecy. And with that the mystified telephonists had filed into the exchange to relieve their colleagues who had worked the earlier shift.

Marlene glanced at the big clock at the end of the room. Three minutes to two. She breathed a long sigh of relief. At two o'clock she would have an hour's break. What a blessed relief! An hour in the cafeteria and the rest room – an hour away from bad tempers and the sometimes shocking language of her customers.

"London is on the line now caller," she said into her mouthpiece. "Please go ahead, and I apologise for the inconvenience this delay has caused you."

Getting out of Germany was a lot easier than getting into it that day. But the man known as Abou had always thought it would be. Of course, he had been delayed at the Aachen border post, but only for about twenty minutes, whereas judging by the length of the queues on the Belgian side, those travelling the other way would be delayed for hours.

His watch showed two o'clock. Malone would have left for Bonn by now. But the journey from Aachen to Bonn would take at least an hour and a half, more perhaps if he had trouble with the road blocks. Whereas Abou only had another five minutes driving to reach the private airfield from which he would fly to Zurich. Zurich – and then the long journey home.

The bomb would explode before he reached home. It would explode as soon as Malone touched that switch. Or the minute someone tried to force the locked doors at the back of the ambulance. Which was why Abou hurried. Liège, in Belgium, was little more than forty miles from Bonn as the crow flies. But the commandos who had followed Malone to the German border last night had driven directly to the airstrip and would be in the Lear jet by now, with the engines warmed up, awaiting Abou's arrival. And they would have landed in Zurich by the time the bomb went off.

He swung off the main highway towards Boullion, where the air strip was located. The countryside was still wooded, but more thinly than on the German side of the border, and he caught a glimpse of the grey waters of the Meuse through the trees.

Behind him, in the stream of cars flowing down the highway from the border, a Mercedes indicated that it too was taking the road to Boullion. Glancing in his mirror, Abou watched the car dislodge itself from the line of traffic to follow him. He felt no alarm, even though the Mercedes seemed to be keeping pace with him.

It was a quiet country road, narrow in places, but not so narrow that the following car could not overtake if it wished. Abou drove steadily, his gaze alert for a signpost to the airstrip.

His thoughts turned to home in the hills above Taipei. In two days' time he would be back there with his father. They would walk through woods not unlike these, up towards Taichung from where they could look out across the Formosa Straights to the mainland of China. Communist China. He remembered walking in the woods years ago. An American general had been their guest that day, and they had led him to the crest which looks out towards China.

"That's it, eh?" the general had said. "The vastness of China. It's big all right. But not big enough. You people have got nothing to worry about. So long as America's your ally, you're as safe here as the folks back home. And that's a promise."

Abou grunted with disgust. Some promise. Tell that to Nixon. Tell it to the peanut farmer now in the White House. Tell it to all the other Americans who were planning to sell Taiwan out to Red China. A thirty-year-old alliance was going to be discarded like an old boot. American troops stationed on Taiwan would be withdrawn, leaving the island virtually defenceless against the might of the mainland. Then there would be a bloodbath of a purge as the communists stripped the ruling families of their power. Killing millions as they had done in Tibet and elsewhere.

Abou swore. The Plan might not save the lives of millions of his countrymen, but it would change the course of history. If the Americans suspected that the bomb in Germany was an act of communist Peking's treachery, then recognition of China was finished. And if it meant a Third World War, would it really make all that difference when American betrayal would force Taiwan into war in any case? War was no worse if the whole world was fighting.

He was so engrossed in his thoughts that he drove mechanically. He slowed down as he approached the lane to the air-strip. And it was then that the Mercedes decided to overtake. It drew alongside with a sudden rush, its horn blaring and headlights flashing. Abou looked through the side window, surprise and irritation all over his face. Then he saw the man who looked like Khrushchev. The man who had been in the restaurant in Cologne. Who had followed him here? Abou was gripped with sudden terror. With split second timing he rammed his foot down to increase speed. But a split second was too long. The rear window of the other car was rolled down and the automatic rifle was already blazing fire. The big shells shattered the glass and tore half of Abou's head away before he even had a chance to turn.

The Audi bucked wildly as it hit the verge, bucked and skidded onto the grass and into the trees, crashing to a halt within twenty yards. The Mercedes turned and the marksman shifted his position to take sight on the petrol tank. A burst of fire, the whump of ignited gas, the explosion of flames, and the Audi was ablaze like a funeral pyre.

Orlov nodded but that was all. His face was expressionless. A twenty-six year old blonde K.G.B. agent had been avenged. And as the Mercedes drove quickly back to the main highway Orlov's hooded eyes closed in sleep.

Some time later Mick reached the outskirts of Bonn. He had been lucky. Three road blocks had barred the route into the city, but all three had waved him on when they had seen the flashing blue lights of the ambulance. But now, driving through the suburbs, he could not maintain the same speed as on the autobahn, and the risk of being stopped and questioned was greater. So he drove carefully, slipped into the flow of traffic and headed towards the centre of the city.

Thoughts of Molly still bothered him. Molly would be sitting in Kathleen's kitchen by now, waiting for his telephone call. Nervous and worried probably, dry-washing her hands and watching the clock. He *had* to speak to her. But the tall dark man had said to park the ambulance and go to the Königshof hotel and wait. For an hour. But what if the delay on calls to Ireland was more than an hour? Would he have a chance to telephone later? Probably not – not once someone had made contact. And not without disclosing that he was breaking the rules.

Then Mick had his idea. Why not phone first? Or at least book the call. Then if there was a delay he could drive to the railway station, park the ambulance and keep his rendezvous at the Königshof.

There was another road block ahead. His stomach turned over at the sight of so many policemen. Traffic was grinding to a halt all around him and he touched the brakes to avoid bumping the car in front.

"Just say Major Ross," Mick said aloud, comforting himself. Like a password. But in *English*? Him, driving a German ambulance in a German city and answering questions from a German policeman. Now wouldn't someone just ask themselves why?

The car in front stopped and Mick made up his mind. With sirens screaming and blue lights flashing he pulled across to the wrong side of the road and put his foot down hard. The police block was a hundred yards ahead. Less – sixty, fifty yards. Startled faces turned in his direction. Oncoming traffic swerved violently to avoid him. Thirty yards to the block. A policeman holding up one hand. Mick ignored him. Twenty yards. Shouts and other policemen blocked his path. Ten yards. The men threw themselves to one side and Mick hauled on the wheel to regain the right side of the road. One glance in his mirror revealed angry faces staring after him. But no attempt was made to give chase.

He took the first right-hand turn, drove for about a hundred metres and took another right just before a major intersection. The traffic about him appeared normal and no great attention was being paid to him. He cut the blare of the sirens and killed the lamps as he reduced speed to match the traffic flow. And then he saw the Königshof Hotel.

"Phone now," he told himself, looking for a parking space. "Phone now and afterwards ask directions to the railway station."

Ahead of him a white Volvo pulled away from a parking space and Mick swerved sharply. A driver behind stuck his head out of his window and swore loudly, but Mick just grinned. He was as good as there. Twenty thousand in the bank and him on his way to Switzerland. But there was Molly to speak to first.

The red telephone rang in the little room at Cork Gardai Headquarters which Dorfman had designated his communications centre. Six other telephones cluttered the table and a mass of loose cable snaked across the floor. Dorfman grabbed the phone and answered yes and no a dozen times.

"Okay, one last thing," Ross bellowed in his ear. "That number you gave us. Cork, seven-six-*five*-zero, right?"

Dorfman knew it off by heart. He no longer needed to look at the paper in front of him. "Right."

"We've had it two hours and nothing so far," Ross sounded

frantic. "I know I checked before, but –"

"That number's right!" Dorfman said, watching Kathleen take another ball of wool from her shopping bag to finish her knitting. Next to her Molly Malone sat perfectly still, but with a face as white as a ghost.

"Okay," Ross, said, "over and out."

Dorfman sighed, replaced the telephone and lit another cigarette. He glanced sideways and grinned at the boy next to him. The earphones on Michael Malone's head were at least three sizes too large and looked like giant earmuffs. But it was the expression on the boy's face which pleased Dorfman. Total concentration. At least for a while the boy had forgotten his own role in the terrible drama being played out in Germany. Now he was absorbed by the radio messages being transmitted from the station to its patrol cars.

"Another cup of tea, Mrs Malone?" he asked.

"What? Oh – if you like, I don't know –"

"Good idea." Kathleen put her knitting back into the shopping bag and looked across to Dorfman. "Will I get you one as well?"

Dorfman was already swimming in tea, but the fetching and drinking of it helped to pass the time and kept the women occupied. So he smiled and said yes, please, to another cup.

When Marlene Vesper returned to the exchange after her one hour break another development had occurred. The grey-faced policeman explained it to them in the conference room. They were searching for one number. A number in Cork in Ireland. If any telephonist was asked for the number, she would key all supervisors in immediately and keep talking. Under no circumstances was she to let the caller off the line.

"Promise you're about to put him through – ask him to hold on – chat him up – engage his attention – but under no circumstances are you to let him off the line," the grey-faced man said. "Do you all understand that?"

The girls had nodded and filed back into the exchange, swapping curious glances and nervous giggles of speculation.

Marlene took her seat and settled down for the afternoon's work. Glancing up she caught sight of policemen hanging large cardboard placards from the ceiling. Six placards, angled in every direction, so that every telephonist there could see the number written on them.

"Cork, seven-six-five-zero."

Ross chainsmoked cigarettes. A chewed cigar lay discarded in the ashtray. Numerous half empty cups of coffee littered the desk and the wastebins were full of used cardboard cups. Behind him, an illuminated panel showed a street plan of Greater Bonn and the location of all road blocks. On the other side of the room six radio operators maintained contact with fifty prowl cars and at right angles to them, another bank of operators talked in low voices to the men on the road blocks.

LeClerc paced the room like a caged animal and Elizabeth sat so close to me that I could feel nervous tension running through her body like an electric current.

A German technician had just finished explaining that a direct link had been installed at the International Switchboard, so that if anyone called the Cork number the conversation would be relayed to the loudspeaker mounted next to the illuminated wall chart.

Downstairs, squads of armed men were already sitting in Porsche police cars awaiting the word to go to any part of the city.

And so we sat and waited.

Marlene Vesper had just connected the Bonn office of Lufthansa to Copenhagen when the call came through. She felt herself go cold, and it was as much as she could do to keep her voice steady. Her eyes flicked upwards to focus on the big sheets of cardboard.

"Would you repeat the number please, caller," she said in her clearest voice.

"Cork – in Ireland, seven-six-five-zero."

"There is a delay on all calls –" she began automatically and then froze in horror as she remembered the grey-faced policeman. She touched the "alarm" button in front of her and knew that all of the police supervisors had keyed into the conversation. Collecting herself she said quickly: "But if you could hold on a moment, I'll try to route you via London."

"Would you do that?" the voice said and she could hear the relief. "It's very urgent."

"What number are you calling from please, sir?"

"This is – er, hang on a minute – this is one-seven-two-nine."

"Thank you caller. My colleague is trying London now. Please hold on."

Ross barked. "One-seven-two-nine. Where's that, for God's sake?"

The German policeman at the end of the desk was already searching his list.

Over the loudspeaker we heard the girl say, "We're through to London caller. If you'll just hold on they will try Cork for us."

"Good girl," an Irishman's voice said. "It's *very* urgent."

"We'll do everything to help – please hold on now."

The policeman looked up from his list. "He's calling from the Königshof Hotel. It's a public call box in the lobby."

Ross knocked his chair over and ran to the door. "How far away is that?"

The policeman caught up with him, and Max already had the door open. "Not far – we'll be there within ten minutes."

In Cork the red telephone on Dorfman's desk never had a chance to ring a second time. His face whitened as he listened, then he replaced the receiver.

"They'll put him through in about four minutes time'," he looked at Molly. "Now don't forget Mrs Malone – act naturally."

Molly trembled like a leaf and clutched the boy tight to her shaking body. She was racked with doubts. Mick had never been a great one for the Gardai, and here she was sitting in the Gardai station itself and about to pretend that she was at Kathleen's place all the time. It was deceitful, that's what it was. Please God make Mick understand, or he'll never forgive me.

Dorfman looked at Kathleen. "When the phone rings you're to answer it, understand? The way you normally do. Then say you'll fetch Molly and put the phone down." He switched his gaze. "And a moment later I want you to pick it up Mrs Malone."

Molly's mouth was as dry as a bone. The boy squeezed her arm and shared his courage with her while Kathleen reached across to hold her hand.

Dorfman wiped his battered face with a handkerchief and watched the clock.

In the exchange Marlene was improvising like mad. Written signals were being placed in front of her by the policemen who crowded around her seat at the switchboard. She was trying to keep calm and read them at the same time.

"Hello caller, I'm sorry but lines from London to Cork are engaged, but my colleague is onto Liverpool and we think we can get through from there."

"Good girl," the man encouraged. "Keep trying."

Another note was held in front of her eyes. Her mind raced and the words tumbled from her lips. "We're through to Liverpool caller, and they expect to have a line free within a minute or two."

"You're doing a *grand* job – a grand job!"

Marlene hesitated. "You – you did say this was an emergency? We're really not supposed to do this and if my supervisor –"

"It *is* an emergency," the voice was adamant. "Almost a matter of life and death, you could say."

"Oh, that's all right then. I mean we're supposed to do all we can to help in emergencies," Marlene said. And then she dried up.

It was warm in the telephone booth and Mick's cigarette had made the atmosphere stuffy. He blinked his eyes against the smoke and peered out into the lobby.

"Are you still there?" he asked.

There was no reply. He pounded the receiver rest. "Hello operator? Hello – Mary Mother of Christ, don't leave me now. Hello operator."

"Sorry caller. Lines from Liverpool are busy too. But we're through to Dublin and expect to connect you shortly."

He breathed a long sigh of relief. "You're doing fine," he encouraged, congratulating himself on finding such a helpful girl. Most wouldn't have bothered. A two-hour delay would be a two-hour delay, and that would be an end to it. But at least this girl was trying.

"Connecting you now," the girl said suddenly.

His heart leapt. "Thanks operator – thanks very much indeed – you've been a great help."

"My pleasure," she said, and then went off the line.

Mick listened to the ringing tone. Once, twice, three times. Come on Kathleen, *come on*!

Then Molly's sister said "Seven-six-five-o. Hello."

"Hello," Mick shouted into the telephone. "Kathleen, it's me – Mick. Did you get hold of Molly for me?"

"Hello Mick. Molly's right here. And Michael. Both waiting to say hello. Hold on, I'll get them for you."

The boy? Mick frowned. And shouldn't the boy be away to school?

"Hello, Mick?" said Molly.

His eyes blurred at the sound of her voice and all of his carefully rehearsed words went out of his head.

Molly clutched the telephone to her ear. "Hello Mick – are you there?"

"Sure now – and who else would be calling you from Germany?"

"Oh thank God! Mick I've been that worried. I had a letter – did you know that? Is that what you're calling about? Mick, you're all right, aren't you?"

"Molly, I'm fine. Look, I'm going away for a bit. Maybe a month or two. I'm not sure yet. But you're not to worry –"

"Going away?" Molly repeated, wide-eyed as she watched Dorfman listening on the extension.

"Now everything's going to be fine," Mick said quickly. "Molly, there's more money on the way to you and –"

But Molly was no longer listening. She had borne the shocks of the morning as best she could, but this was one shock too many. *Mick going away?* The money from the bank? The Gardai? The man with the bruised face? Suddenly the flood gates opened and she burst into tears. Mick was saying something – an operation – the best doctors in the world – keep quiet about the money. But it was no good, she could restrain herself no longer.

"Mick, listen," she cried, ignoring the warning in Dorfman's eyes. "Mick, we're with the Gardai. They came to the house – searched it – Mick, Big Reilly's been killed – and they say the same men are after you! Mick – for pity's sake – I'm worried sick about you – Mick, can you hear me?"

Mick was looking through the glass door of the booth into the hotel lobby. Half a dozen men had just burst through the front doors and were fanning out in all directions. A man with a black glove on one hand had started to run towards the telephone booths. Molly's words exploded like a bomb. BIG REILLY KILLED. The man with the glove was only twelve yards away. THE SAME MEN ARE AFTER YOU!

"Molly, I've got to go – there's more money on its way – I love you and the boy – Moll, I've got to go!" The man with the black glove was running directly towards him. Mick left the receiver hanging, opened the door and ran for his life.

"Stop!" Ross roared as Mick came out of the booth and started to run diagonally across the lobby. He tried to cut him off, but furniture blocked his path. Then he collided with a man with a suitcase and lost his balance.

"Halt!" shouted one of the G.X.9 squad, already dropping to one knee, his revolver clear of its holster, his left hand coming up to steady his right as he took aim. "Halt!"

But Mick ran on, running for his life, easily avoiding the hall porter's outstretched arms as he made for the door.

The crack of a bullet whined over his left shoulder, but then he was at the door and through it.

Molly screamed into the telephone: "Mick, for God's sake, what's happening?"

Dorfman had already reached for the blue phone, but the red one was still cupped to his ear. He heard Ross shout and a split second later heard the flat crack of revolver fire. He heard it, and they all heard it.

"Dad!" the boy screamed. "Are you *all right?*"

But Mick never heard him. He was ten yards from the hotel entrance and running hard for the ambulance. His back laid pain across his body like a cloak and he was gasping for breath. Twice he collided with people and the second time he fell to his knees. Only thought of Molly and the boy drove him on. If anything happened to *him*, what would happen to *them*? Had Reilly sent the policies to the bank? Had the bank sent Molly her money? Dammit, it was her money, her money!

He ran across the road, bent double with pain, his hand searching his jacket pocket for his keys.

"Stop that man!" someone shouted, and over his shoulder he saw the man with the black glove less than thirty yards behind.

He flung himself at the ambulance door, fumbling with the lock, opening it, swinging the door wide. And then the first bullet hit him, smashing him sideways, turning him away from the ambulance and spinning him around to face his pursuers. A second bullet blew half his head away and a third broke his rib cage. Mick Malone was dead, before he even reached the ground.

Monday evening – Bonn

We were back in the suite in the Steigenberger-Hof. Elizabeth was pouring drinks at the sideboard as Ross gazed moodily out of the window. Max sat near the door, playing patience with a pack of cards provided with the compliments of the management, and

272

LeClerc filed his nails at the other end of my sofa.

"It would have gone off, you know," Ross said over his shoulder. "All Malone had to do was to set the trigger device."

"Ten megatons?" LeClerc asked.

"Ten megatons," Ross nodded and turned back to the room. He walked across to an armchair and flopped into it gratefully. He looked dog-tired, but then all of us were coming apart at the seams.

I had pieced together most of the story by now. Suzy's role in the affair was more easily understood. How she had been used, how she had been made to believe that she could restore to the Palestinians that land which they believed had been stolen by the Jews. How she had believed that the bomb would have been used only as a threat. It made me feel better somehow, until I wondered what might have happened if her threats had not been acceded to.

A television set flickered in the corner of the room with news of the summit. Apparently most of the first day had been devoted to a discussion of economic affairs. There was a lot of talk about the weakness of the dollar and the strength of the deutschmark. And outside the three hundred thousand Germans who lived in Greater Bonn went about their business as if nothing had happened.

A buzzer sounded faintly, and Max picked up a walkie-talkie from the chair next to him. "We have a visitor," he said after listening for a moment. He looked at Ross. "You want me to stop him?"

But someone knocked on the door before Ross could answer, and when Max opened it Orlov stood there. He beamed a greeting across at Elizabeth and presented her with a dozen roses.

"Elizabeth, darling!" He cupped her bottom in his hands in traditional greeting and when he sat down he even had a smile for me. "So Harry Brand, still playing the Big Game?"

"Still digging holes for other people, Nikki?"

"It gets harder every day," he chuckled. "Sometimes there's not even time to bury them."

Ross eyed him keenly. "Like a man who died in a car in Belgium?"

Orlov seemed surprised. "You heard about that? A shocking incident. Someone was telling me about it –"

"Monique Debray was one of your girls, wasn't she?" Ross asked.

It was the only time I ever saw Orlov look sad. Then he said, "But *not* the man in the pale grey suit."

"I never thought he was," Ross said wearily. "But it might have helped to have had a word with him before his unfortunate accident."

Orlov nodded soberly. "His real name was Wu Teh. He was

Chinese. His father was a distinguished soldier against the Japanese. By the end of the last war he was one of Chiang Kai-Shek's generals and afterwards his family was one of the most important in Formosa." He smiled. "Or Taiwan as you Americans prefer to call it."

Ross nodded and rubbed his jaw with his tin hand. But he never said anything, so I was left in the dark as to whether Orlov's information was news to him or not.

Elizabeth set light to a glass of zambuca and sat on the arm of Orlov's chair, while the Russian watched me with speculative eyes. Then he nodded at the television, still faintly audible in the corner as the commentator wound up on the summit.

"The show must go on, eh? Men never tire of playing it. I suppose it's because it's the most fascinating game in the world, don't you think so Harry?"

I shook my head. "Also the most dangerous one."

He pulled a face. "Only for the pawns."

January 1st, 1979

At today's historic Press Conference devoted to the new diplomatic relationship between the United States and China, President Carter announced that the U.S./Taiwan defence treaty would be terminated by the end of this year.

Source – Reuter's Service – Washington

March 31st, 1979

The United Kingdom withdrew the last of her troops from Malta today after maintaining a military presence on the Island for the last one hundred and eight years.

Source– Reuter's Service – Valletta

April 26th, 1979

The U.S. Defence Command headed by Rear Admiral James Linder lowered the U.S. flag yesterday afternoon, signifying the end of twenty-eight years of military presence.

Source – Reuter's Service – Taipei, Taiwan

A millionaire by the time he was thirty according to the British national press, Ian St. James retired from business in 1977 to become a full-time writer, an occupation which he considers "the last refuge of the individual." Mr. St. James is now living, writing, and pursuing his individuality in Ireland. *The Balfour Conspiracy* is his second novel.